GEOFF HILL is the author o...
Motorcycle Journeys, The R...
Alaska on a Motorbike, Oz: Around Australia on a Motorbike and
Anyway, Where Was I? Geoff Hill's Alternative A to Z of the World.
He has either won or been shortlisted for a UK Travel Writer of
the Year award nine times and is a former Irish, European and
World Travel Writer of the Year. He has written about travel and
motorbikes for the *Sunday Times, Irish Times, Daily Telegraph,
Sunday Telegraph, Metro, Independent on Sunday* and *Motorcycle
News.*

Praise for *Way to Go*

'Shift your arse, Kerouac, Geoff Hill's on the road –
faster, funnier and still alive.'

COLIN BATEMAN

'Brilliant.'

Mensa Magazine (and they should know)

Praise for *The Road to Gobblers Knob*

'The most inspiring and laugh-out-loud funny travelogue of
the last fifty years. The yearning of an unmitigated
adventurer leaps off every line.'

GARBHAN DOWNEY, *Verbal Magazine*

'A brilliant, very funny travel book. It's enthralling, amusing,
and an absolute must - 100%.'

Biker Magazine

'The clash of the reality of biking and the romance of the journey is what I enjoyed most and Hill's style, honed over years entertaining and surprising readers, suited it perfectly. This is a great yarn.'
GARY QUINN, *The Irish Times*

Praise for *Anyway, Where Was I?*

'Geoff Hill is a comic genius. I laughed until I cried, my nose bled and I lost control of my bowels. I may well have to kill him when I meet him.'
PATRICK TAYLOR, author of *New York Times* bestseller *An Irish Country Doctor*

'Incredibly funny. I loved it. I was laughing out loud on trains in a thoroughly embarrassing fashion and going to sleep with a smile on my face after the completely anarchic tales of killer dormice, Xavier Furtwangler and how not to get eaten by bears.'
MELISSA SHALES, Chairman, British Guild of Travel Writers

Praise for *Oz: Around Australia on a Triumph*

'More trees should die to support this book. It makes Ewan and Charley look like George and Mildred.'
COLIN BATEMAN

IN CLANCY'S BOOTS

BOOTS

THE GREATEST EVER ROUND-THE-WORLD MOTORBIKE ADVENTURE

GEOFF HILL

·THE·
BLACK
·STAFF·
PRESS

ACKNOWLEDGEMENTS

The publisher and author are grateful to Dr Gregory W. Frazier
for permission to use the words of Carl Stearns Clancy as
published in the 2010 publication *Motorcycle Adventurer*.
(ISBN 978-1-45022-141-2 [sc]; ISBN 978-1-45022-140-5 [ebk])

Back cover photograph of Carl Stearns Clancy
provided by Dr Gregory W. Frazier

First published in 2013 by
Blackstaff Press
4D Weavers Court, Linfield Road
Belfast, BT12 5GH
with the assistance of
The Arts Council of Northern Ireland

Typeset by CJWT Solutions, St Helens

Printed in Berwick-upon-Tweed by Martins the Printers

A CIP catalogue record for this book is available from the
British Library

ISBN 978-0-85640-913-4

www.blackstaffpress.com

To Cate; to Carl Stearns Clancy
and Dr Gregory Frazier, adventurers both;
and to my friend Kevin Ash.

'The longest, most difficult, and most perilous motorcycle journey ever attempted.'

The Bicycling World and Motorcycle Review

Prologue

'One must die sometime, and to die with one's boots
on is very noble.'
Carl Stearns Clancy, riding through Spain at night in 1913

I t is a dark and stormy night, and although the rain is attacking
the study window with bitter vengeance, inside all is calm and
still.

The cat is sleeping on a rug in front of the fire, his paws curling
now and then with dreams of kittenhood, and I sit at the ancient
oak roll-top desk that my parents bought for me to revise for my
A-levels.

Downstairs, my wife is cooking dinner, and everything is
normal … except for the pair of hundred-year-old boots that sit
by my desk, causing my heart to lift and flutter every time I look
at them.

Although there is no indication of who made them, whoever
did made them well, because they have worn but sturdy leather
soles, strong high-laced uppers and the deep, nutty lustre that
comes from good materials and a lifetime of care. But even
more remarkable than their condition is the fact that they had
more adventure in their first year than most of us will have in a
lifetime.

You see, these are the boots of Carl Stearns Clancy, a man I
had never even heard of until in February 2011 I got an email
from a Dublin biker called Feargal O'Neill. This is what it said:

Dear Geoff,

Firstly may I say a huge thank you for your motorcycle travel writings. I have thoroughly enjoyed them. However, the main reason I write is to let you know about a big event which will happen in October 2012 and hopefully entice you to attend.

The 23rd of that month will be the centenary of the start of the very first round-the-world trip by motorcycle, and the really amazing thing is that the man who did it, an American writer for the advertising industry called Carl Stearns Clancy, started in Dublin because his father had been born in Ireland.

After his travelling partner Walter Storey dropped out in Paris, Clancy completed the journey alone, sending back articles and photographs for publication in the US magazine *The Bicycling World and Motorcycle Review*. These, unfortunately, faded into the background and might eventually have become lost forever were it not for the work of multiple round-the-world rider and author Dr Gregory Frazier who in 2010 published *Motorcycle Adventurer*, a book about Clancy's journey.

It is a really remarkable story which epitomises the spirit of adventure which has carried countless round-the-world travellers on their journeys ever since. However, I think it is a real shame that Clancy is not better known, when you think that he accomplished this feat before the outbreak of the First World War, and six years before Alcock and Brown crossed the Atlantic.

With the centenary looming, myself and some other motorcyclists are going to recreate the Irish leg of the journey, setting out from Dublin on the day of the centenary and going on to Mullingar and Donegal and back through the North via the Giant's Causeway to Belfast. Clancy and Storey got the ferry from there to

Glasgow before travelling down through England and on to France.

I feel that there is a duty on us modern-day motorcyclists to do our bit to honour the memory of this great pioneer of our sport, and I really hope that you might be able to come to Dublin for the big send-off and maybe even do some of the trip in Ireland. Would you be interested?

Naturally, I wrote back immediately and said yes, opened up the browser and did some googling (as we writers call research these days) and found that Clancy and Storey had indeed set out from Dublin in 1912 to 'girdle the globe', as one witty sub in the *Bicycling World and Motorcycle Review* had put it.

Why did they do it? Because, as Clancy said, 'We are ordinary businessmen who are supersaturated with work and who have decided to invest a year's time in something else other than the everlasting chase for the almighty dollar.'

Why from Dublin? Because Clancy's father had been born in Ireland and, as Clancy said, 'So little is known by motoring America about the attractions of the land of many of its forefathers – Old Erin – that we decided to place it first upon our list of globe-girdling explorations.'

And why motorbikes? Because, again in Clancy's words, 'Old Mother Earth has already been circled by almost everything at one time or other. Sailing craft, steamships, railway trains, bicycles, pedestrians and motorcars have all had their turn. Nothing remains but the airship, the submarine and the motorcycle – and now we are going to give the motorcycle a chance.'

Clancy knew, of course, that it would be the longest, most difficult, and most perilous journey ever attempted on motorcycle since there were few surfaced roads, let alone maps by which to find them. Motorcycles were not built for endurance travelling, tyres were basic and repair shops were almost non-existent.

His friends, who obviously suffered badly from common

sense, variously told him it was insane and impossible which, of course, made him all the more determined to do it.

The motorcycles Clancy and Storey chose were Henderson Fours from the Detroit company set up the previous year by brothers William G. and Tom W. Henderson. Will had the ideas and enthusiasm for motorcycling, Tom had the better financial acumen, and their machines rapidly became the weapon of choice for sports riders and police motorcyclists, who loved them because they were larger and faster than any other bikes on the road. The model introduced in January 1912 boasted a trademark long wheelbase and inline four 934cc engine pumping out 7bhp, a folding hand-crank starter handle and a price tag of $325 (about five months wages at the time).

All of which made them a bit of a challenge for the inexperienced Storey, who was rammed by a tram on the first day in Dublin, badly damaging the bike and leaving him shaken. He struggled on through miserable weather in October and November, but in Paris gave up and returned home.

Clancy soldiered on alone, an astonishingly brave decision for a twenty-two-year-old armed with only a tweed jacket and two mottos for the unknown dangers ahead: 'Never believe what you hear', and 'Take nothing for granted'.

Pressing on, he rode south to Spain and across North Africa, then had his planned route across India scuppered when he discovered no petrol would be available. Undeterred, he shipped his motorcycle to Ceylon, where he toured for a week or so, and then shipped again to Penang. Once there he discovered there was no road to Singapore, so it was back on to a boat for Hong Kong, Shanghai and Japan.

Landing in San Francisco, he rode to Portland, Oregon in what was ironically the most difficult part of the ride, and then across the northern part of the United States to return to New York. His journey lasted ten months and he rode over 18,000 miles.

All the while Clancy worked to pay for some of the $4,000 cost of the trip by keeping a diary with a large fountain pen, typing it up on a portable typewriter and sending it back to The *Bicycling World and Motorcycle Review* with photographs for publication.

Almost a century later those articles and pictures, which had lain gathering dust in the archives, were tracked down by Doctor Gregory Frazier, who had spent sixteen years researching Clancy and compiling his words and pictures into the book *Motorcycle Adventurer* – a real labour of love from an author who had ridden around the world five times himself.

I ordered a copy, and as I read through the pages and marvelled not only at the courage of Clancy in tackling such an adventure, but at his witty and precise descriptions of the route, I began to think how wonderful it would be to recreate that journey on its centenary, to see how everything he saw and experienced had changed in a hundred years.

So I could blame any number of people for what happened next. I could blame Feargal for emailing me in the first place, or Dr Frazier for writing *Motorcycle Adventurer*, without which retracing the journey would have been impossible.

I could blame Gary Walker for coming up to me at the launch of my previous book, *Oz: Around Australia on a Triumph*, and casually saying, 'Here, if you're ever planning another one, keep me in mind.'

Gary was a former actor and ace road racer turned theatre school owner and rigger, whose memorable experiences so far had included being chatted up by Lena Zavarone, minding Julie Christie, being kissed by Donald Sutherland, having lunch with Bobby Davro when he was supporting The Krankies, and riding his motorbike sideways along a dry stone wall at 140mph, although not all on the same weekend. He obviously felt none of this had been exciting enough, and had turned to me in desperation, the poor sod.

I could blame Sam Geddis, the MD of Adelaide Insurance Services, who had sponsored the Oz trip.

Funny enough, when I'd gone to see him about that, he'd started by saying that sponsorship was a complete waste of time, but five minutes later was filled with so much enthusiasm that he and his wife Gloria came out and rode the first three weeks of the trip with us. So I wasn't too surprised when I phoned him this time and his initial response was, 'Geoff, it sounds brilliant, but there's a recession on and I can't be seen to be throwing money around, and …'

Five minutes later, of course, he was saying, 'You know, this is too good a story to miss, and a centenary only comes once. Count me in.'

I could also blame Tony Jakeman of BMW for providing two R1200GS Adventures, and his successor Lee Nicholls for helping with getting the bikes shipped.

I could blame Cate, since not every wife would put up with her husband buggering off for three months every few years.

Or I could blame Carl Stearns Clancy, whose boots sit beside my desk.

When Clancy died in Virginia in 1971, his housekeeper had given the boots to Liam O'Connor, the teenage son of Clancy's neighbours. Liam, now a professor at the University of Western Australia, had kept the boots all these years and, when I tracked him down through Dr Frazier, had agreed to loan them to me. The plan was that they would recreate their journey of a hundred years ago and then be passed on to a museum, along with several of Clancy's other possessions, such as his original notebooks and Irish and French driving licences.

At lunchtime today, the postman had knocked the door and handed me a parcel from Australia with Liam's name on the outside.

I'd felt a real shiver of excitement as I carried it to the kitchen and carefully opened it, and I'm not ashamed to say that I came close to shedding a manly tear as I unwrapped and held at last the boots that Carl Stearns Clancy wore all those years ago, when he was a young man full of hopes and dreams and an ambition to see the world.

I'd say his feet were a size nine, but his heart was of a size that cannot be measured. And, although he is no longer with us, as long as there are men and women who look at the horizon, wonder what is beyond it, and then climb on a motorbike to go and find out, his memory will live on.

I look at the boots now, their nutty gleam reflecting the dappled firelight even after a hundred years, and then down at my own brogues, and feel in that moment a beautiful sense of empathy with a man who knew what it was to care for a good pair of boots or shoes, with a bit of saddle soap and a bit of spit and polish.

So I could blame Liam, or even the boots. But ultimately, I can only blame myself for not staying at home and leading a normal life. Sorry about that. I did try it once, but it didn't agree with me.

Chapter One

A short history of Ireland

8000 BC
Mesolithic hunter-gatherers arrive on the Larne ferry.

5th century
St Patrick invents Christianity and drives snakes out of Ireland, checking regularly in the rear-view mirror that they're all right in the back.

8th century
Vikings arrive and wreak havoc, starting a trend continued by the Normans and English.

1534 on
English and Scottish settlers arrive on the Larne boat, roll up their sleeves and start making money, in between describing locals as feckless, drunken romantics.
Locals, well used to it, order another pint then write a song about it.

1652
Cromwell voted off Irish *X-Factor*.

1690

William of Orange, backed by Catholic Pope, defeats King James II at the Battle of the Boyne and is hailed as Protestant hero, creating logic which is basis of all future Northern Ireland politics.

1922

Ireland divided into North (for dour Protestants) and South (for guilt-ridden Catholics, and priests who it turns out should be guilt-ridden, but aren't).

1969 on

Troubles break out in North. Protestants blame Catholics, and vice versa, starting a thirty-year-process known as whataboutery, in which to understand Northern Ireland politics is to miss the point (See 1690 for details.).

1990s

Southerners discover money and try to get rich by selling the entire country to each other and a million Polish waiters, giving birth to the Celtic Tiger.

2008

Polish waiters go home. Celtic Tiger found dead in a half-finished housing estate in Mullingar.

Carl Stearns Clancy and Walter Rendell Storey arrived in Dublin on 18 October 1912, all set to conquer the world on their Hendersons. Except for one small but significant detail – Storey had never ridden a motorbike in his life. A fact which even the normally imperturbable Clancy admitted people might find a little queer.

Undeterred by such a hurdle, they did what any men in their

right minds would do: saw the sights and went shopping.

They visited the Bank of Ireland in College Green which, until the passing of the Act of Union in 1801, had once housed the Irish Parliament; admired the Book of Kells in Trinity; bought woollen underclothes and waterproof shoes and gloves; and at City Hall registered their machines and secured UK licences for 10 shillings each. Clancy's verdict on Dublin at the end of the day: 'nearly everything at least 50 years behind the times'.

The next day Richard McCready, editor of *The Irish Cyclist* and inventor of bicycle polo, gave them road maps and helped them plot a route from Dublin to the northwest. Then, filling their petrol tanks to the brim for a shilling and seven pence, they set off for Phoenix Park so that Clancy could teach Storey to ride. It was, according to Clancy, a relatively successful lesson, 'By dark, he had mastered his steed completely, but we were compelled to leave our machines in a nearby house till morning, having no carbide in our lamps.'

The next morning, they affixed to the Hendersons two around-the-world pennants made by a pair of charming Irish girls who had befriended them on the transatlantic crossing, mended their clothes and adopted them as brothers, and set off at last on their grand adventure.

Only to be stopped before they got to the end of the street by a policeman – 'a beautiful specimen of a gigantic, almost wax "Bobby"' – who insisted they get number plates for their front mudguards.

Getting those made and painted with their registrations – RI 2016 and 7 – took all day, and the next morning they set off again.

'Dublin had not finished with us, however,' reported Clancy, 'for before we had gone a block, one of those two-storey, bobtail tramcars which are universal in Great Britain, coming from behind another, ran smash into Mr Storey, demolished his rear wheel, threw him to the pavement, ripped off the starting-crank casting, bent the handlebars and front fork badly – but allowed Storey to escape with a sorely bruised thigh.'

What Clancy described as 'an eager crowd of loafers' then helped carry the wreck to a repair shop and refused to disperse until paid double for their efforts.

Storey's bike would take some days to repair and so, with Clancy riding, Storey astride the petrol tank and 75lb of baggage on the back, they finally made a 'third and triumphal start' on roads made slippery with rain at noon on Wednesday, 23 October.

One hundred years later to the day, it was raining again as Gary Walker, Khal Harris from BMW and I stood waiting for the Clancy cavalcade to arrive at Joe Duffy's, the BMW dealer on the north of the city which Feargal had chosen as the starting point after the Phoenix Park authorities asked him for a €6.5 million Public Liability Insurance Indemnity (which he couldn't quite lay his hands on), then told him that in any case they couldn't have the innocence of their leafy glades sullied by commercial razzmatazz.

Indeed, they would have had a fit, I thought as I looked behind me to where Adelaide MD Sam Geddis, Nichola Pearce, the dynamic Rhodesian-born farmer's daughter who was his head of marketing, her trusty sidekick Stevie and paddock girl Shauna, in a lycra catsuit, were admiring the Adelaide marquee and giant inflatable arch.

At nine, the party began, like a reunion of old friends we had never met. There was Feargal, pulling in on his own GS Adventure, as friendly and convivial in person as he had been on phone and emails. There were the bikers who had signed up with him to recreate the Irish leg of Clancy's journey – at least sixty of them roaring up, in spite of the rain, on everything from a spotless 1959 BMW to state-of-the-art machines.

And there, at last, was Paddy Guerin, the owner of the only

Henderson in Ireland, who had risen at dawn with his wife Rena and driven up with it from Cork despite having been stricken by a streaming cold.

I don't know about Gary, but my heart stood still as Paddy swung open the back doors of the trailer and we saw for the first time a machine of the sort that Clancy had ridden a century before.

Paddy, a former stainless steel engineer specialising in giant milk vats, and a collector of exotic machines, including a Morgan and a Brough Superior of the sort favoured by Lawrence of Arabia, had bought the Henderson four years before from a man in Bristol who had acquired it from Australia.

Making several of the parts himself, he then spent six months turning it from hundreds of bits in a box into the immaculate creation which stood before us, its deep blue paint and gold and red Henderson logo contrasting perfectly with the tan solo saddle.

'He spent ages trying to decide what colour to paint it, then saw this van that was the perfect shade of blue, and chased it to find out from the driver what colour it was,' said Rena.

'The sad thing is, she's right. Would you lads like a go?' said Paddy with remarkable generosity, considering that the bike was worth at least £30,000 and he'd never met us before.

'Tell you what,' I said, 'I'll leave that to Gary, since he's a proper biker, and he looks the part.'

Indeed he did, thanks to an inspired idea by Khal for Gary to dress as Clancy for the trip in a three-piece tweed suit, flat cap and Clancy's boots, which he'd just tried on for the first time. 'They may fit me, but I'll never fill them,' he said modestly as he climbed aboard.

With the replica around-the-world pennant draped from the handlebars – which Feargal had had embroidered, not by two charming Irish girls but by an equally charming, although not as good-looking bloke called Trevor McDevitte – the effect was uncanny as Paddy talked Gary through the arcane process of starting the Henderson, with a squirt of petrol here and a drip of oil there.

Paddy cranked the starter and, after a deep, sonorous cough like history clearing its throat, the engine settled into the rhythm of all the years between then and now as Gary rode it around the block several times for the benefit of cameramen and photographers – Clancy's boots planted firmly on the footboards of a Henderson for the first time in a century.

'Superb. And with the man's boots on as well. What a fantastic experience,' he grinned as he pulled in and we stood listening to the big inline four ticking over.

To Clancy and Storey, that sound must have resonated just as much as it did for Gary and me, as we climbed on our GS Adventures and pressed a button to bring them coughing into life; a sound that grew like rolling thunder as the dozens of bikers around us climbed aboard and started their own engines.

We rode north, my head giddy with nervous euphoria that the great adventure had actually begun, and full of wonder at how Clancy must have felt as he wobbled along the same road at 20mph with 75lb of luggage on the back and Storey on the front, his feet balanced on a rod pushed through the axle.

I wondered, too, what would have changed and what stayed the same in the century since.

They had spotted their first whitewashed thatched cottage on the outskirts of Dublin, but today, the only ones still like that had been long since abandoned, their modern replacements sporting pebbledash, plastic windows and satellite dishes.

The Georgian houses and grey chapels had stayed the same, but the big houses which would then have been the last symbols of Anglo-Irish Edwardian hauteur, just about to be torn to shreds by the First World War and the Irish Civil War, had either been converted into hotels or conference centres or had lain empty since being torched after partition in 1922, their gate lodges guarding only overgrown gardens and the wind and rain whispering through grand rooms which had once hosted glittering social evenings.

My own grandfather Edward had been a butler in one of these, and at that moment, I thought of my father telling me how, when the great and the good rolled up the drive in their carriages for a grand ball, all the children of workers on the estate would climb the great oak tree on the lawn and gaze in through the windows at a world that was denied to them.

And then it struck me: there were two things that had not changed a bit. One was the same urge that drove Clancy, me, Gary and all the bikers around us: the unstoppable desire to get on a motorbike and ride off with the sense of infinite possibility we had as children but lose as adults, and in the process forge the sword of our destiny in the crucible of adventure.

Or, since we were mostly blokes, maybe we were just victims of the bugger-off gene, which compels men to bugger off now and again. Resistance is futile.

And the other thing that had not changed, of course, was Clancy's boots, which were nestled in one of my panniers along with an around-the-world pennant which I would give to Dr Gregory Frazier in San Francisco some months hence.

Riding through a damp Irish morning, California seemed like another world, but slowly, the mizzle (which is just rain that can't make up its mind whether to be rain or drizzle) slowly cleared, and the sun began to peek around the clouds then fling them back to bathe the trees all around in autumn glory.

Wobbling north on this same road, their way blocked by numerous herds of cattle and flocks of sheep, Clancy had covered an impressive 88 miles by the time they rolled into Newtownbutler as darkness fell at 5.30 p.m.. There, as they rode up the main street past the thatched town hall, they spotted the yellow and black 'Cyclists' Rest' spoked-wheel sign above the door of the Temperance Inn, and inside found shelter for the Henderson and bed and breakfast for 6s 6d, or $1.56.

It had, without a doubt, been a grand first day.

Today the Inn was boarded up and its door weathered by the wind and rain, but the hefty cast-iron knocker which Clancy would have used to gain admission was still there. I was giving it a hearty knock, just for old time's sake, when a local man came wandering by.

'Och aye, it was still a hotel up to the Fifties or thereabouts, then Harry Sewell the postman and his wife lived there,' he said in answer to my question.

'And what was his wife's name?' I said.

'She would have been Mrs Sewell,' he said, and wandered on.

After a hearty breakfast the next morning, Clancy spent an hour hunting in vain for petrol, then gave up and bought a pint of paraffin, which got them to, what he describes as, 'Lisnaskal', but the only Lisnaskal that Google throws up are his book and a fascinating Danish pharmaceutical site, so I fear he meant Lisnaskea.

There, they filled up with Pratt's Motor Spirit, named after Charles Pratt, one of the founders of the Standard Oil Company of New Jersey, and rebranded as Esso, from the SO of Standard Oil, in 1935. In the British Isles of Clancy's day, it was sold in two-gallon tins from small shops and hotels, so heaven knows what he would have made of the shiny plastic and neon petrol stations of today, or the prices of almost 11 dollars for the same gallon.

Their tank brimming with finest Pratt's, they forged on, maintaining an average of 20mph in spite of wet and slippery roads, cattle and sheep on their way to market, suicidal hens, ducks and turkeys, apparently deaf pilots of donkey carts who twice forced them to swerve and tumble into the ditch, and by the habit of locals shouting 'Straight ahead!' when asked for directions at a fork in the road.

Still, at least the kindly officers of the Royal Irish Constabulary they met in every town were good sports, never questioning their speed and taking pains to give them accurate directions.

They might not have been quite as sporting had they realised that Clancy and Storey had two pistols tucked in their belts under those tweed jackets, for since the third Home Rule Bill had been given royal assent in September 1912, rumours were rife that civil war was imminent, and the globe-girdlers had not come unprepared.

'After backing out of several violent Home Rule discussions, we decided to be prepared for the worst so, before entering Ulster, we got out our Savage automatics and, to practice, banged away at a tree on the lonely roadside beside the beautiful Lough Erne.'

When the tree showed no signs of either retaliating or starting a Home Rule discussion, they remounted and rode into Donegal.

Sadly, in spite of me sending Gary out to check the estimated one million trees in Fermanagh for the one which had been the innocent victim of their target practice, he failed utterly, so in the golden light of late afternoon, we started up and followed their tracks for a glorious run through the russet forests and steely lakes of Fermanagh to the cliffs of Slieve League.

We could not have asked for a better finale to the first day of Clancy's boots on their second journey around the world, and you could see why Clancy had loved Donegal: it was like Middle Earth, with white cottages nestled in the nooks and crannies of its hills and dales, their aromatic turf smoke rising into the limpid air.

Parking their machine in the yard of a hut where a fisherman lived with his wife and five children in a single room containing only a plate rack and a bed, Clancy and Storey were led by the eldest boy up to the cliffs. Although he was clothed in rags and had never been to the nearest town, ten miles away, he was well versed in Irish history, and could also tell them the height of Niagara Falls.

At last we stood just where the two men had stood a hundred years before, as the sun sank in a blaze of glory and a half moon rose to take its place. Speechless with wonder at the sublime grandeur of the scene, then equally speechless with regret that they had forgotten their camera to record it, Clancy and Storey had stood here and gazed west as we did, possibly thinking that somewhere out there was a New York they would not see for almost a year, then turned and made their way back down to the Henderson.

Keen to see if their young guide's global knowledge had been passed down the generations, when we stopped at the next petrol station, I said to the teenager behind the counter: 'Listen, my mate and I are trying to solve an argument. You wouldn't happen to know the height of Niagara Falls, would you?'

'Not a bother,' he said, tapping the Google app on his iPhone.

I climbed back on the BMW, filled with admiration for how Clancy had ridden the Henderson on these steep and winding Donegal roads with luggage on the back and Storey on the front; and wondered what he would have made of the sure-footed but nimble GS, never mind our armoured Gore-tex suits and state-of-the art flip-up helmets.

Although the Henderson engine was the fastest and most advanced motorcycle in the world, with a top speed of around 70mph, the 934cc engine made just 7bhp and the bike had only one gear and no front brakes. In comparison, our machines made 110bhp from only a slightly bigger engine, never mind having traction control, ABS, heated grips, fog lamps, everything from average speed and mpg to the time of high tide in Hong Kong on the dash, and what I imagine would have been most astonishing to him, an electronic suspension system you could toggle on the move between Normal, Comfort and Sport, and within those modes set it for every riding load from 'Victoria Beckham on Diet' to 'Two Fat Ladies with Kitchen Sink'.

No, on second thoughts, what would have astonished him most was the fact that to fill the tanks of both Hendersons back in Dublin had cost him a shilling and sevenpence, but to do the same with the Beemers worked out at about 92 quid.

By now it was the time of day which in Ireland is called day dapple: when the shadows lengthen towards twilight and it becomes impossible to tell a man from a bush. After which everyone goes to the bar, and it becomes impossible to separate a man from a Bush.

'Here, Feargal, how does it feel now that it's all come together?' I said as we climbed off outside the Abbey Hotel in Donegal town and watched the Clancy cavalcade roll into town behind us.

'In a word, fantastic. Even better, it's your round,' he said, leading the way to the bar.

'I really liked that GS from the word go,' said Gary as we cradled pints of Guinness, making up for Clancy's single failure in Ireland in not having a pint of its most fabulous product, apart possibly from Black Bush and charming girls. 'Bags of torque, nice gnarly engine, great presence on the road.'

'Aye, me too. And don't think I didn't see you pulling that wheelie away from the petrol station. What did you think of my slow in, slow out cornering technique?'

'I was really impressed by the even slower bit in the middle. I might pick up a few hints from you on this trip.' He paused, and took a sip. 'But I doubt it.'

Bastard. I hated him already, and it was only day one.

The next morning, as the Clancy cavalcade saddled up and rode out of town, we passed, with sweet irony, the Forget Me Not flower shop on the way to the 'queer little town' of Ballybofey, today a slightly down-at-heel spot littered with scraps of dead

Celtic Tiger in the shape of charity shops offering 20c a kilo for clothes and 10c for books and magazines.

We crossed the border at Lifford, leaving behind a Donegal which had impressed Clancy deeply as being 'wildly beautiful' and 'the most Irish part of all Ireland'.

'The older people speak Gaelic, live in tiny stone huts perched in the barren, heather-covered, wind-swept valleys, and represent the extreme in poverty. Here a donkey is an unheard-of luxury, and even hens are very scarce. Every family raises one pig a year, which is sold to pay the rent – never eaten,' he mused as they rode north through Prehen – which I'd always thought should really be called Egg – and into Londonderry, where they stopped to cash a Thos. Cook & Son travellers' cheque.

They would hardly have recognised the city today. All the great shirt factories which employed the town's entire female population had gone, killed by cheap Oriental fabrics after the war, leaving the city rife with discontent and resentment at Unionist supremacy. This flared into the Civil Rights movement of the late Sixties and the birth of the three decades of mayhem which people in Northern Ireland politely refer to as The Troubles.

Today, the city was born again: the day before we arrived, *Lonely Planet* had intriguingly named it the fourth best city in the world to visit after San Francisco, Amsterdam and Hyderabad, and in 2013 – as UK City of Culture – it would host, among various other events, the Turner Prize, safe in the knowledge that if a pile of bricks won this time, the locals wouldn't start throwing them at the police.

A cool breeze brought autumn leaves tumbling down like gold coins from a gunmetal sky as we pulled up en masse to the Giants' Causeway, the 37,000 black hexagonal columns first publicised in 1693 by the Royal Society as one of the great wonders of the natural world.

The fairy story goes that these were created by a huge subterranean explosion 60 million years ago, but locals know the cold scientific truth – that they're the remnants of a causeway built by a Scottish giant so he could come over and fight local giant Finn McCool. Thinking quickly, Finn's wife had tucked Finn up in a cot, and the Scottish giant thought: 'If that's the size of Finn's baby, I'm out of here,' and fled home, tearing up the causeway as he went.

To his credit, Clancy managed to be the only person in the world to visit the Causeway and not mention the dour verdicts of Dr Samuel Johnson who famously said it was 'worth seeing, but not worth going to see,' and William Thackeray, who muttered, 'I came 150 miles to see *that*?'

With the wind and rain howling around and the afternoon sky growing dark, Clancy and Storey had the Causeway to themselves and, although he thought it sadly commercialised after being greeted with a fence and a sixpence entry fee, after the two men had wandered around, they agreed that it was a 'remarkable freak of nature', even if not quite as wonderful as the surrounding cliffs.

He would not have been impressed, I fear, by today's £8.50 entrance fee to the new visitors' centre, or by the plump chap who came hurrying over to tell us that we couldn't park on the pavement in front of the gate because we were blocking wheelchairs which weren't there and denying access to a farmer who wasn't there either.

Naturally, we all then parked in the disabled spaces and limped away just to really piss him off, and it worked. Working up a fine head of steam, he stomped off threatening to call traffic branch to have us all towed away.

While we waited patiently for them to arrest us, I was signing a copy of one of my books, *Way to Go*, for a man called Ged when he spotted a friend of his, Aidan.

'Aidan, you've grown your hair – and put on weight – since

I saw you last,' said Ged, prodding Aidan's paunch by way of punctuation.

'Aye, I married a woman who can cook and I'm fading away to a small mountain. My ambition's to end up like a fat Willie Nelson,' said Aidan, then saw the book and turned to me. 'I enjoyed your bit in that about how straight the roads were in Texas, for I rode them myself. I was so bored that if I'd met a man selling corners, I'd have bought a whole bag of them.'

Traffic branch having failed to appear, we decamped to the Causeway Hotel for soup, then followed Clancy's route along the Antrim coast, famous even then as one of the great roads of Europe.

Not that the weather was allowing him to appreciate it: after only 15 miles, with the storm soaking them to the skin and nearly blowing them over several times, and with Clancy getting constant electric shocks from the Henderson through his sodden gloves, they returned to Ballycastle and took refuge in the Antrim Arms.

Today the iconic hotel, which has been owned by the same family for over two hundred years, was closed and shuttered for the season. As I rang the bell, more in hope than expectation, I was tapped on the shoulder and turned to find a local man with hair like a small explosion in a mattress factory and what Clancy would have called typical Irish breath.

'Don't stay in Ballycastle. It's crap. Ride back to Ballintoy and you'll get a nice room with a shower and a bath for 15 quid,' he muttered, then set sail for the pub across the road.

Clancy and Storey had enjoyed their stay though, and woke to find that the storm had spent its fury in the night. But as they rode the 65 miles along the coast to Belfast the next morning, they were still drenched with spray, buffeted by wind and stung by rain, and when they got to Belfast at lunchtime, Clancy's ears were frozen and aching.

Still, since on my first adventure – riding an Enfield back to the UK with Paddy Minne – we had arrived in Delhi on the hottest day of the year, with the mercury hitting 46°C and even the locals dying of the heat, we were all just maintaining a proud Irish tradition of applying Murphy's Law to the letter.

Leaving Storey in Belfast, the tireless Clancy took the afternoon train back to Dublin to collect the repaired Henderson, pay the £3 bill and next day ride it back the five and a half hours to take the night boat to Glasgow.

Remarkably, although on the way out of Belfast Harbour they passed the RMS *Olympic* – *Titanic*'s sister ship which was docked at Harland & Wolff for winter repairs – Clancy doesn't mention the *Titanic* disaster which had taken place earlier that year. Unless he wasn't aware, like many then and since, that the ship had been built in Belfast.

In any case, they left Ireland feeling good about the place. 'Ireland is so quaint,' Clancy reported, 'so different from Scotland, England and America, so blessed with charming, picturesque hillsides of the most entrancing colours, and inhabited by the most fascinating people, that we urge every motorist to visit it – and especially Donegal.'

As for us, we stood on those same docks thinking how much the scene had changed in a hundred years. The clatter and clang of Harland & Wolff, once the world's biggest shipyard, employing forty thousand people in a city which, at the time, also boasted the world's biggest linen mills, rope works and tobacco factories, had long gone, replaced by the quiet hum and click of laptops.

The yard now employs a mere four hundred people, and in place of the once-vast slipways is the new Titanic Quarter. Designed by Chicago architect Eric Kuhne, this city within a city (complete with homes, shops, hotels, university and technology parks) is centred around the glittering metal edifice of Titanic Belfast, the £97 million building designed by Kuhne to emulate both the bows of ships and the star which is the emblem of the White Star Line. Locals, who when asked about the *Titanic* invariably say: 'Well, she was all right when she left us', have already christened it 'The Iceberg'.

As the setting sun danced and died on The Iceberg's shards, we watched the ghosts of Clancy and Storey sail east on the night boat to Glasgow, then we rode to Adelaide HQ for tea, buns and farewells.

The plan was for us to spend our winter months in Belfast – just as Clancy and Storey spent their winter months in Paris – and resume our journey in the spring.

I could not help thinking, as I rode home that night, that we had got the worse deal, but Paris would still be there in the spring, and in the meantime, we'd always have Belfast.

Or we'd possibly always *be* in Belfast. We were due to leave there on Sunday 24 March 2013 on the morning ferry to Cairnryan but we woke on the Friday to 2 feet of snow outside and several baffled robins in the garden saying 'WTF?', as robins do.

Still, we made it to down to Adelaide HQ for the grand press conference and official send-off, even though the TV crews and photographers who turned up were only there because of the free tea and buns.

'Make sure you have plenty of disasters to make the book interesting. In fact, I've arranged several along the way to help you out,' said Patsy Horton, the MD of my publishers, as we tucked into some rather nice chocolate digestives before Sam Geddis could polish them off.

In fact, it looked like she'd arranged several before we even started: despite being due a month before, we still did not have our bikes and so hadn't had a chance to run them in – I was assured that they were finally due to arrive on a truck from England the next morning – or kit them out with our panniers, top boxes, tank bags and satnavs (all of which had been tucked away by Jim Hill at BMW Belfast).

Back home, I started printing out the schedule, only for the printer to run out of ink. Sighing deeply for what I suspected would not be the last time over the next three months, I got into the car and headed across town to the cartridge shop.

Only for the car to break down with a banjaxed flywheel. Just before I realised I'd left my mobile at home. Still, never mind. There was a phone box across the road.

Hauling out my AA card, I then realised that I'd forgotten my glasses, and couldn't read the number on it. Thank heavens, then, for the nice girl in the Starbucks across the road, who let me use her phone to call home and get Cate to alert the AA.

I finally got home that evening, just in time for Gary to call and say that he was snowed in so badly that he couldn't even get down the road in a Land Rover, had no power, and he and his wife Janet were cooking supper for their kids on a single gas ring.

'Gary, why you have to live halfway up a mountain rather than in a nice sensible town house is beyond me, but do you want the good news?' I said.

'Tell me.'

'The Raj is still delivering in spite of the weather, so we're just going to phone out for a curry.'

I won't even repeat what he said, in case you're a sensitive sort.

The next morning, Jim Hill phoned from the BMW dealership to say it was so snowed in that he had to park half a mile away and couldn't get the gate open. He drove home, got a pair of wellies and a spade, and dug his way in to get the bike gear, and I got a taxi up to help him carry it to his car.

Just as Nigel McFarland phoned from the shipping depot in Belfast to say that the truck bringing the bikes was still in Scotland, stuck in an 18-mile tailback to get to the ferry at

Cairnryan, and wouldn't be in Belfast until at least Sunday.

Somewhere, in a dictionary far away, the expression 'a perfect storm' permitted itself a smug smile at its elevation from the ranks of cliché.

I called Stena to put our sailings back a day, Jim and I brought all the kit back to our house, and I started packing things into a tank bag for a motorbike that wasn't there.

At six, Nigel rang. 'Good news. The bikes are on the boat. They'll be here late tonight, so you can pick them up at nine in the morning from the depot. I was supposed to be playing golf, but I think it might be off,' he said.

I looked out at a scene from *White Christmas*, and suspected he might be right.

'Not unless you've got luminous balls, chum,' I said, hanging up and calling my dear old dad, who'd just turned eighty-seven, to say farewell before we finally set off.

'Here, son, this Gary Walker you're setting off with – is he any relation to Graham Walker the racer?' he said. 'He was the editor of *Motor Cycling*, and when I was having a bit of bother getting insurance for my 1926 flat tank BSA, I wrote to him and he got me sorted with the RAC. Decent spud. His son was Murray Walker, the commentator.'

'Funny enough, we're calling in with the RAC on Thursday, so I'll check your BSA insurance is up to date, Dad,' I said.

'Grand job, son. Have a good trip, and hope you get nice weather.'

The next morning, everything started going disturbingly smoothly. Gary called around with his mate Mark Cheah so we could all drive down and collect the bikes, and at the entrance to the docks we found several hardy bikers who had braved the cold to turn up and wish us a warm farewell.

And then, five minutes later, we were climbing on the machines which would be our trusty companions for the next three months.

They looked perfect. Especially the button for the heated grips – I'd been so busy giving Gary the booklet from that week's *MCN* called 'Face Your Fear and Ride Like a Pro' that I'd left my gloves sitting on the hall table.

Back at the house, Gary and Mark soon had the panniers and top box on, and half an hour later Jim Hill, who by now had earned a DSM and Bar in service above and beyond the call of duty, arrived at the same time as his former employee Billy McCutcheon, who had just called around to wish us well, but ended up helping Jim fit the satnavs and check the pannier locks.

'There we go,' said Jim, stepping back to admire his handiwork. 'Where there's a Hill, there's a way.'

'Jim, you're twice as witty as I think I am. Which probably makes me a half-wit. Fancy writing the book and I'll just stay at home?' I said, as the rumble of an approaching GS signalled the arrival of Peter Murtagh, the Foreign Editor of the *Irish Times*, who'd joined us for part of the Irish leg and who was coming with us as far as Alicante where he would celebrate his birthday.

He is as witty and urbane as you'd expect a foreign editor of the *Irish Times* to be, and by the time we went to bed that night, after a fabulous dinner rustled up by Cate, we had found the answers to every problem in the world.

Sadly, we had drunk so much wine that by the time we woke up the next morning, we had forgotten the questions.

Chapter Two

A short history of Scotland

1286 on

English King Edward I's claim to Scotland disputed by William
Wallace and Robert the Bruce. Wallace ten-year campaign ends
slightly badly with him hung, drawn and quartered, but Bruce,
inspired by spider in cave designing world's first inspirational
website, beats English at Bannockburn in 1314, only for
English to return the favour by beating the Scots at the Battle of
Flodden in 1513.

15th century

Scots invent golf to work up a thirst for Scotch, and Scotch as
something to look forward to after golf.

16th century

With priests responsible for 40 per cent of illegitimate births,
Scots welcome Reformation until it turns them all into
Presbyterians. Fun, games and smiling in public places is
banned.

1746

Battle of Culloden, after which tartan, guns and bagpipes
banned. Now, having nothing to do except go to church,

Scots turn to perfecting whisky and building ships and mills, turning the country into industrial powerhouse until Thirties depression puts paid to all that.

1971
North Sea oil discovered, leading to clamour for devolution which eventually succeeds in 1999 with election of first Scottish parliament whose first act is to spend country's entire budget on new parliament building, leaving it broke again. Scots sigh, open a bottle of single malt and watch *Braveheart* to see what really happened.

How did I feel the next morning, as the moment which I had both longed for and dreaded became real? The moment when I said goodbye to my mum and brother Trevor, then hugged Cate, tears in our eyes, and rode off down the avenue as, in the rear view mirror, her waving figure became smaller and smaller, and then disappeared.

Fear and sadness, that's what, since here I was again buggering off for three months to leave her rattling around our big Victorian house with only our neurotic cat, Chunks, for company.

Oh, and if you're wondering about the name, it was after his phenomenal nuts.

'I suppose you'll be calling him Chunkless now,' was the dry comment of the vet when we went to get him de-chunked.

In the same way that Clancy and Storey had set off with two which became one, we were setting off with three which would become two: me, Gary and Peter, who had with him a glorious set of Clancy era maps of the UK so we could follow the route exactly.

'Shame we're not gay,' I said as we settled into our seats on the Stena crossing to Cairnryan. 'We could have had loads of fun for the next three months.'

'Give it a month,' said Gary. 'Those long, lonely nights in the desert with only me and a camel to choose from …'

'I'll take the camel,' I said. 'Fancy some of Clancy's nuts?'

Yes, just as we had left with Clancy's boots safely tucked into the panniers, we had his nuts safely tucked into our pockets. Well, not his exactly, but the roasted variety produced by Aldi and called Clancy's Nuts for no reason I could fathom other than the whim of a Friday afternoon marketing meeting.

Several bags of them had been sent for our sustenance by Mary Dinan, an Irish author, and her mad mum Josephine, who after a previous ride from Chile to Alaska had knitted me a pair of dongles because she was worried about me losing mine on future adventures.

I was beginning to see a theme developing.

As Belfast faded into the distance for the last time, I sank into my seat, turned my gaze at last towards the Scottish shore and, after all the hullabaloo and crowds of the Dublin to Belfast leg and a grand send-off at Adelaide HQ, felt for the first time that the trip was actually beginning. Two years of planning had gone into this particular adventure and, as always, had driven me so mad with the complexity of the logistics that I swore I would never do this again. But then I had realised I was mad to start with, and that I always said the same thing.

Having said that, there had been times, even in the last weeks, when it seemed as if the whole thing would be scrapped.

Take shipping the bikes, for example. I'd thought, in my innocence, that blagging this would be a doddle, but after nine months of contacting every shipping company in the known universe to try to get them to ship the bikes from Rome to Sri Lanka, there to Kuala Lumpur, from Shanghai to Japan, Japan to Los Angeles and New York back to the UK, I had still got nowhere. Can't think why, apart from the fact that it was the middle of a recession and my demands were going to cost them several squillion pounds.

In the end, the only solution which was financially possible was to use the Beemers for the European and African legs, rent or borrow bikes locally in the Far East, then pick up the Beemers in Los Angeles for the USA section.

It was hardly ideal, but then again, the only riding Clancy had done in the Far East was Ceylon and Japan, and our aim was to follow his journey as faithfully as possible.

Even so, the best deal I could get from James Cargo the bike shipping specialists was that they would waive their profit, which still left me with three grand to find, until BMW and my mate Geoff McConville the Belfast optician came up with the dosh with a month to go.

Which only left a couple of minor details to sort out. Like the fact that no one in the *Mirror* was answering my emails to confirm that they'd take a weekly spread from the trip. You know, the weekly spread that the whole sponsorship deal with Adelaide hung on.

They finally said yes five days before departure, after causing me countless sleepless nights thinking I was going to be jilted at the altar, like a Miss Havisham of biking.

All in all, planning this trip, as with all the previous big ones, had included days on end of waking up to face apparently impossible logistical problems which somehow, eventually, got worked out.

So here is a message for the couple of whingers on Amazon who complained that previous trips were a paid holiday. You try organising one, then get back to me.

In the middle of all this emotional sturm und drang, and with work sporadic and the baby lambs of my own income being torn to shreds every month by the savage wolves of bills, my good mate Kevin Ash, bike correspondent of the *Daily Telegraph*, was killed on a bike launch we'd both been attending in South Africa.

On the first day we'd had lunch together, chatting and

laughing as we always did, and twenty minutes later I was first on the scene to find him lying in the road, already gone. The image haunts me still.

Still, at least I was alive to feel haunted, I thought as we trundled off the boat and rode north towards Glasgow, where Clancy had declared the people as being 'very individual' and the accent of the 'red-nosed, bare-kneed women' who gathered around them at every stop 'almost unintelligible', as they rolled their 'r's and generally sounded like Harry Lauder.

Storey was still too nervous to ride through the heavy city traffic, so Clancy give him a lift to the city limits then went back for his Henderson. By that time it was almost dark, and before long they were lost in the gathering gloom, made almost infernal by the lurid glare of countless iron foundries, and were forced to stop for the night in the unprepossessing Black Bull in 'the dreary town of Stonehouse'.

Still, at least it only cost them $1.15 each for a hearty supper, a big feather bed and breakfast the next morning, during which a clergyman, as Clancy puts it, 'told us that, although he had been a weekly visitor at The Black Bull for several years, we were the first guests he had met; the bar being the inn's principal mainstay and pure whisky its principal staple'.

Naturally, things that good could never last. Today, Stonehouse doesn't even mention a merit in the *Rough Guide*. The Black Bull closed for years then reopened in 2010 in spite of the police complaining that it encouraged booze-fuelled antisocial behaviour. An enlightening review in the online *Big Red Directory* had this to say about the pub: 'Food: Unknown, Menu: None uploaded yet, Plays music: Unknown, Wifi: Unknown, Disabled access: Unknown, Beer garden: Unknown, Real ales: Unknown, Credit cards: Unknown, TV screens: Unknown.'

Our satnav, entering into the Clancy spirit, took us over the most antiquated roads possible, and after a long haul over the frozen moors with the temperature hovering above zero, and just as I was beginning to suspect that Stonehouse didn't actually exist, as we finally rolled into town around teatime, chilled to the marrow in spite of our state of the art gear.

Only to find that The Black Bull, a peeling monochrome pile on a windy corner, had finally been closed because of the inability of its customers to pop in for a small glass of sherry without finishing the bottle then breaking it over their neighbour's head. It was now being turned into flats by a man called Adam from Poland, but since his English was as bad as our Polish, it was to an old dear passing by who had offered to take our photograph that we revealed the thrilling part The Black Bull had played in history.

'Get away with you,' she said, and pottered off, although thankfully not before recommending a local hotel, The Shawlands, into which we gratefully staggered half an hour later. It had warmth, food and beer, and would do very nicely for all of those reasons.

Warmed, fed and watered, we fell gratefully into bed. Gary and I took turns at keeping each other awake by snoring in shifts, and we rose at seven and were on the road at eight, heading for the balmy south. Before long, the temperature on the dash had climbed to a positively sub-tropical three degrees.

It is, I thought, remarkable how simple the pleasures of motorcycling are. The snow or the rain falls, and you're sad. The sun comes out, and you're happy. You crash and nearly kill yourself, and you're sad. You realise you're lucky to be alive, and you're happy again.

As were Clancy and Storey, for with an equally early start, they made a record 133 miles that day, proceeding speedily along splendid roads past assorted bleak moors, ravines, waterfalls and assorted picturesque shepherds with story book crooks minding their enormous flocks, and stopping briefly in Gretna Green.

One hundred years later we followed in their footsteps, riding into the village through flurries of snow. Yes, there was the KFC at which Clancy and Storey would presumably have stopped for a bargain bucket, and where we would have followed suit but for the fact that a local café was doing a special offer on Ecclefechan tarts which was too good to miss.

'Excuse me,' I said to the cheery girl behind the counter, 'is there a cash machine around here?'

'Aye, it's in the toilets,' she said cheerily. Of course it was. Where else would it be?

Suitably solvent, I emerged to find a statue called 'Girl Awakening' by John Tonks, of a sweet and naked nymph resting on a rock. She looked freezing, poor girl, but at least the visible signs of that gave me somewhere to hang my helmet and gloves.

Nearby, continuing a tradition of nudity entirely at odds with Scottish Calvinism, was a statue of an equally unclothed boy and girl having a snog on the green. Still, at least they'd found a way to keep warm, I thought as I wandered into the Wee Big Shop to find quaint local artefacts such as the Instakilt, a combined beach towel and kilt.

An Instakilt was, sadly, not quite what we were after. What we were looking for was The Old Blacksmith's Shop, the infamous wedding chapel that Clancy had dismissed as ugly in spite of 'its many memories of elopements and the exciting chases of ardent lovers by heartless English parents'.

Gretna, the first village in Scotland on the old coaching route from London to Edinburgh, became a mecca of elopement after Lord Hardwicke's 1754 Marriage Act stopped minors marrying without the permission of their parents. In Scotland, though, the Act didn't apply, so boys could marry at fourteen and girls at twelve and, as long as there were two witnesses, almost anybody could conduct the ceremony.

Gretna Hall Blacksmith's Shop, built in 1710, and The Old Blacksmith's Shop, built around 1712, became the focal tourist points for the trade, and their blacksmiths became known as 'anvil priests'. Many a couple would rush through the door of the blacksmith's shop, breathless in their haste to be wed. Flinging down his hammer and tongs, the anvil priest would do the deed at speed, lest an angry father was right behind them; and if he was, the priest would push the couple into his bed and tell the fuming father that he was too late, for the marriage had already been consummated.

For several years after 1754, the blacksmiths continued their trade, fitting in weddings when couples arrived, but before long they were making so much money at the new job that they laid down their tools, leaving a queue of increasingly frustrated horses standing outside tapping their hooves.

Joseph Paisley – an impressive character who, from 1753 to 1814, concluded his ceremonies by straightening a cold horseshoe with his bare hands – was so successful that before long he was earning £900 a year, most of which he then spent on drink, ballooning to 25 stone and becoming increasingly unreliable. Told after a joint ceremony that he'd married the wrong couple, he said: 'Ach well, just sort yourselves out.' Still, he lived on to be over eighty, and was still conducting ceremonies from his deathbed.

And not only were the priests characters, but so were the people they married; like Lord Erskine in 1818, one of three Lord Chancellors to be wed there. After fathering eight children with his first wife, at the age of sixty-six he ran off with Sarah Buck, who had been his housekeeper and mistress long enough to produce several more illegitimate ones. Just to be on the safe side, he had turned up for the wedding dressed flamboyantly as the mother of the bride, only casting off his bonnet and cloak when the priest turned up.

As we looked around The Old Blacksmith's Shop we were greeted by the most poignant sight of all: a wall of letters written to the popular priest Richard Rennison who from 1926 to 1940 had performed a staggering 5,147 ceremonies. In a 1938 article in the *Daily Express* he had spoken of the hundreds of letters he got from lonely bachelors begging for his help in finding a wife and in reply to the piece, one girl had written

Dear Mr Rennison,

I thought I would write to you to see if you could find me a husband. I belong to the North, and am 26 years old, quite good looking, kind-hearted and sporty. I am a domestic servant. I enclose my latest photo, taken dressed as I was for a play. Trusting I will get a reply.

PS: Please do not put this in the paper, as my parents would be very angry.

Another said

I am a lonely young woman, and I thought you might be able to settle my problem by also settling that of one of the young men. I am 23 years old, tall, quite good looking, good temper, and would like to marry a man in a good position and a year or two older than myself.

Another twenty-three-year-old wrote

I belong to the North, so I feel very lonely. I come of respectable people, and am in service.

The answer to all their problems was possibly to be found in another letter from a chap with the right attitude to life, and possibly everything, who wrote

Dear Sir,

No doubt you had a letter from me on Monday or Tuesday concerning this lonely man business. I am extremely sorry I forgot to enclose my photograph. The instrument which you see in it is a ukulele, but I also play the Hawaiian Guitar, as I have already told you.

Well, I don't think you should have much difficulty in doing what I am asking of you, because all young girls love music. Also on my list are cycling, swimming and walking, and I have appeared on many stages with my instruments.

Hoping to hear from you in the near future.

James Davidson

Richard Rennison, it seems, was the internet dating site of his day, and a diplomat, judge and jury to boot, for in the middle of these lonely cries from the heart is a telegram saying simply

TO RENNISON THE PRIEST, GRETNA GREEN. MARRIAGE CEREMONY MUST NOT BE PERFORMED. GROOM KNOWN EX-CONVICT. BRIDE'S MOTHER IN STATE OF COLLAPSE.

Gretna Green remains one of the world's most popular wedding destinations, hosting over four thousand ceremonies a year, or one of every six Scottish weddings. So as we left the village – after treating ourselves to another helping of Ecclefechan tarts – we made sure to keep a careful lookout for 'Warning: Bride and Groom Crossing' road signs, before speeding south, crossing the border into England with a small but noticeable bump.

Chapter Three

A short history of England

Christmas Day 1066
William the Conqueror crowned as King and invents England, previously a Roman Anglo-Saxon suburb of Denmark, leading to a thousand years of meritocratic rule by icons such as Richard I (buggered off on the Crusades), Edward II (useless), Henry VI (mad), Henry VIII (ask his wives) and George III (even more mad).

1837–1901
Victoria reigns over an empire on which the sun never sets.

20th century
After two world wars, empire reduced to Wales and the Falklands.

1979–1997
Everyone claims to hate Maggie Thatcher, but vote her in three times.

1997–2007
The Blair years. Everyone loves Tony. Until Iraq.

2012

The Olympics, and torrential rain. Entire country delirious, although mostly underwater.

By lunchtime that day, Clancy and Storey were clattering through Carlisle, and that afternoon they crested the brow of a hill to have their breaths taken away by the Lake District in all its autumn glory. 'Wild skylines of fantastically jagged summits faded mysteriously into the distance, partially hidden by a golden haze, which rested on the air and transformed the whole district into fairyland,' wrote an entranced Clancy.

With not a soul in sight, they coasted down the hill to Windermere bathed in a smug glow for arriving in the off-season so that their dreams were 'not shattered by the foolish cries of summer tourists', as Clancy put it, sounding exactly like a gap year student today giving himself a little pat on the back for being a traveller rather than a tourist.

The only pats on the back we got, sadly, were the ones we gave ourselves in a vain bid to stay warm, and the only thing we saw through the blizzard was a Japanese couple in brightly matching windcheaters on a refreshing lakeside stroll, their faces frozen into expressions of polite disappointment.

Exchanging bows with them (although to be honest it was unclear whether they were bowing back or just leaning into the gusts) we sped on, shivering gently, to Northwich in Cheshire, where after their record-breaking 133-mile day, Clancy and Storey stayed at the Crown and Anchor Hotel, an establishment with a somewhat up and down history due to subsidence.

Indeed, that was the reason Clancy went there, after reading that the local salt mine had undermined the town to the extent that, as he put it, 'large lakes had been known to disappear in one night, and many a burgher had woken in the morning to find his second storey bedroom window level with the street.'

He was exaggerating, but not much: the most notorious length of High Street for subsidence was outside the Crown and Anchor where he and Storey stayed. After parts of the street had collapsed several times, it was raised by three feet in 1890 and both the Crown and Anchor and the Bee-Hive Inn across the street were taken down and rebuilt.

The builders slotted the last brick in place, stood back with a sigh of satisfaction, then over the years watched in horror as the road ignored them and continued to subside anyway.

Cinders were regularly dumped in to level it, and the summer before Clancy and Storey arrived, the entire street was dug up for new sewers, water mains, gas and electricity. Between 1920 and 1924 the entire length of the street was raised again, and in 1924 the Crown and Anchor rebuilt for the second time.

Ten years later, Lawrence of Arabia checked in under the pseudonym Aircraftsman Shaw and spent three weeks there with Flight-Lieutenants Norrington and Beaufort-Greenwood overseeing the completion of the 296-ton Royal Air Force Auxiliary *Aquarius* at the nearby Yarwood's shipyard.

They should have known better: coming from a town known for sinking, the *Aquarius* inevitably followed suit in February 1942 off Singapore after it fell to the Japanese.

As for 33 High Street, the address of the Crown and Anchor, it continued the town's shifting tradition, with the satnav giving two separate postcodes for it. Following both of them to be on the safe side, we found the street pedestrianised, and walked down it between half-timbered houses which would have been familiar to Clancy and Storey, as would the Bee-Hive Inn, which opened in 1885, and Hilton's of Northwich, established in 1848 and, according to its windows, Diamond Merchants of Repute and Purveyors of High Class Jewellery and Watch Repairs.

If they were relying on me for business, though, they were out of luck, for I was wearing my lucky expedition watch, a

Casio digital quartz job I'd bought in 1998 to take on the Delhi to Belfast ride rather than risk losing my good watch, and which was still going on the original battery fifteen years later.

Sadly, the Crown and Anchor had not fared as well – it had closed in 1960 and was now Madison's Bar and Restaurant, the forthcoming attractions of which included the Playboy Bunny Party on Friday, with free bunny ears and a prize for the best costume.

'I can just see Clancy and Storey rolling up the street on their Hendersons and saying: "Playboy Bunny Party? That'll do us!",' said Peter, whose hands had gone a funny shade of blue thanks to the cold.

Given that my nose was now a similar colour, we decided that it was time to find somewhere warm to stay the night, and after riding around for a bit, we found the Blue Barrel, a pub with rooms and a sign outside advertising a Psychic Evening.

Funny, I'd had a feeling we were going to stay there.

That night, we went out for an Indian in a restaurant down the street which was named with commendable accuracy, The Indian. Inside, as we tucked into several dozen courses, each more delicious than the last, we chatted to the charming young waiter, Sulhag. He had been born in London, moved to Birmingham and then Manchester, and had made several lengthy trips to his parents' native Bangladesh, resulting in such cultural confusion that he had bought a house in Wales and none of his friends in any of the above places could understand his accent.

'Going around the world, eh?' he said when he heard of our plans. 'Throw away the satnavs and get lost. The journey's the thing, chaps!'

Thus enlightened in mind and heavier in body, we pottered back to the Blue Barrel to find that the Psychic Evening had been cancelled due to unforeseen circumstances.

As we were ordering three pints of bitter from the bar due to an equally unforeseen thirst, a striking brunette called Hayley swayed up from the back snug, looked at me and announced, 'Here, you're gorgeous. Will you marry me?'

She was obviously as short-sighted as she was striking, but luckily, just as Gary and Peter were preparing to get back on the bikes and return to Gretna Green to arrange the nuptials, it transpired that she had a seven-year-old son and a boyfriend called Basher.

Having called off the wedding, we then fell into conversation with a roofer called Ken who had ridden his GS all the way to northern Russia. 'Don't go there,' he said. 'The buggers shot at us. Like another pint?'

When Clancy woke the next day in the Crown and Anchor, he decided he wanted to see down one of the town mines, and after securing official permission, he and Storey climbed into an iron bucket and were lowered 250ft to a vast cavern, where they followed a flickering miner's taper to the point where a blast 50ft away left them covered in salt crystals, gasping for breath and glad to be hauled back up 'into sunshine and God's free air'.

Sadly, today health and safety has put an end to casual mine tours, a fact we discovered as we pulled up outside nearby Winsford, Britain's oldest working mine which lies 600ft under the Cheshire countryside: 'Unfortunately,' the notice outside the mine read, 'due to the Health and Safety Regulations that govern working mines, members of the public are unable to visit Winsford Rock Salt Mine.'

Dusting off the last of the salt, Clancy and Storey rode on to Chester, through a landscape of trim patchwork fields, toy lakes and tidy horses so idyllic that Clancy thought they had discovered Mother Goose land.

Finding the old Roman walled town of Chester so quaint and picturesque that they were surprised not to be charged admission, they wandered in a daze through a town laden with history, photographed the heavy rings to which Roman and Venetian ships had been moored, sat at the window where Charles I witnessed his army's defeat at the hands of Cromwell's Roundheads, and stood solemnly in the vaulted crypt where De Quincey wrote *Confessions of an English Opium-Eater*.

As I read Clancy's account of Chester, I was concerned that he was in severe danger of coming down with Stendhal's syndrome, named after the writer who was so overwhelmed by the beauty of his first visit to Italy that he had to be revived regularly by copious draughts of the local brandy.

Still, we had to take our helmets off to Clancy for letting his boyish enthusiasm remain untarnished by the cynicism of the editor-in-chief of *The Bicycling World and Motorcycle Review* who advised him before he left, 'Europe has been done to death – slide over it'.

You can almost see the green eyeshade, the cigar smoke, the striped shirt straining at a paunch and the sleeve bands behind those words, I thought as we rode between the frozen fields the next morning to stand in the exact spot where Clancy had stood a century before when he took a photograph looking up St Werburgh Street towards Chester Cathedral.

It hadn't changed in all that time, apart from the large Chrysler parked on the double yellow lines. And the double yellow lines, come to that. Still, at least Clancy would have been pleased that it was an American car.

As Gary was setting up his camera to replicate Clancy's photograph, a young man came wandering down the street clutching a coffee and stopped to admire the bikes and their burden of baggage. 'You're not just out for the day on those, then,' he said, then turned out to be a biker and IT technician called Oliver Stirling, and the first person we had met on the trip who had actually heard of Clancy. 'Read about him in a motorbike magazine. What a fabulous thing to do,' he said, heading off to work as another biker came over.

Bikers are always doing this, which makes travelling by motorcycling such a sociable experience. You don't really find Toyota Corolla drivers wandering over to other Corolla drivers and swapping thrilling tales of another day on the M25.

This time, it was Tony Charnock, a metallurgist who'd travelled all over the world, biked over half of it, married a Mongolian woman, owned houses in Ulan Bator, Thailand and Goa, and had not once but three times done the Mongol Rally, the car rally in which ancient bangers are driven to Mongolia for charity.

'First time was a Rover 2000, and second time was a Daihatsu Fourtrak that only got as far as Leningrad,' he said.

We shook his hand and piled into a café for breakfast and to escape the snow which had been falling almost constantly since the previous day, watching perfect flakes creating a fairy tale chiaroscuro as they drifted down past the black and white mock Tudor facades and Victorian gargoyles of a town which was built with no expense spared by rich Londoners who came here because of the balmy microclimate.

So much for global warming, I thought, as we dusted the snow off the bikes and retraced Clancy and Storey's steps back to Northwich.

They covered the seventeen miles in a cracking thirty minutes, taking great pleasure in the fact that they hadn't seen a single speed trap in Great Britain. Sadly, thanks to rush hour traffic and several blind farmers with no rear view mirrors on their tractors, we took much the same time. Though I did take great pleasure in the fact that Gary saved me from three points on my licence by honking as I was accelerating briskly past a speed camera.

They were even more thrilled when they pulled up outside the Crown and Anchor to find that it hadn't sunk and, after spending another night there, Clancy and Storey rode south next morning, trundling through the dull Black Country with coal mines all around, and amusing themselves by noting the queer names of hotels and pubs such as The Hen and Chicken, The Lad in the Lane, The Ring o' the Bells, The Blue Boar, The Swan with Two Necks, The Malt Shovel, The Dog and Duck, The Six Ashes and The Bricklayer's Arms in the hamlet of Hogpits Bottom, most of which, they would be pleased to hear, are still in existence.

Already, they were becoming so toughened by the outdoor life that they were quite happy riding for hours in the rain, stopping only to get directions from their maps or from the endlessly courteous AA or RAC guides on bicycles. They were now also so unfazed by the prospect of getting lost – having done it so frequently in the large cities – that one of them would often find himself waiting for the other who had already gone on ahead.

Indeed, I knew the feeling: riding Enfields back from India with Paddy Minne, I had once completely missed the fact that he had pulled into the bushes in Turkey to answer a call of nature, sped past him in the rain, and spent the rest of the day trying to catch someone who wasn't there.

In Birmingham, the home of the vestigial British motorcycle business, Clancy and Storey saw many small, belt-driven single-cylinder machines with sidecars, which in spite of two or three-speed gearboxes weren't a patch on their mighty Hendersons. In fact when the two men stopped at Aston Hall – the Jacobean-style mansion which was used by Washington Irving as the model for Bracebridge Hall in *The Sketch Book of Geoffrey Crayon* – their bikes drew a large crowd of admirers who marvelled at the mighty engines and the fat Goodyear tyres.

The construction of Aston Hall started in April 1618 and took almost twenty years to complete. When 1631 came around, and the house was still not finished, the owner Sir Thomas Holte finally got fed up waiting and moved in in a despairing attempt to get the builders to get a move on.

They finally did, finishing it in April 1635, only for it to be badly damaged in an attack by Parliamentary troops in 1643 – you can still see the hole in the staircase where a cannonball went through a window, an open door and into the banister.

It stayed in the Holte family until 1817, when it was sold to James Watt Jr, the son of industrial pioneer James Watt. In 1858 it was sold to a private company for use as a public park and museum, but after financial difficulties it was bought by the Birmingham Corporation in 1864, becoming the first historic country house to pass into municipal ownership.

Clancy was certainly impressed with the building, realising as he wandered around how useless books and photographs were at capturing the magnificent atmosphere of such a place.

Today, I take nothing away from its magnificence when I say that the most satisfying part of our visit was holding our hands under the hot air machine in the toilets and groaning gently as the circulation returned.

Sadly, the person in charge of picking a charming and friendly hostelry for lunch (which may well have been me) then managed to ride past the splendid Aston Villa football stadium and select the worst Irish pub in the world – a cavernous hall occupied by a gloomy Mexican and an inexplicably cheery Jamaican watching the horse racing on a giant screen.

We dined on ham and cheese rolls washed down with instant coffee, and as we were leaving, I asked the Mexican man where he was from.

'Oaxaca, senor,' he said.

'A beautiful city. Why are you here?'

'I am not sure,' he said gloomily, ordering another pint.

Outside, the takeaway across the road promised an even more international selection of delights than the customers of the pub: Caribbean, Indian, Chinese, Italian, Balti and chicken of no obvious origin.

Clancy and Storey, favoured with slightly less bracing weather, polished off the bar of milk chocolate which by then had become their customary lunch, and rode 16 miles south to the ruins of Kenilworth Castle – the once ornate palace best known as the home of Robert Dudley, the great love of Queen Elizabeth I, who built it in 1575 to impress her.

Sadly, the same person who had been in charge of finding our lunch venue was now in charge of navigation, and managed to miss not one but two turnings, sending us several miles up the motorway in the wrong direction. As a result of which it was quite some time before we pulled up outside Kenilworth, confirmed through the falling snow that it was still in ruins, and rode the four miles to Warwick Castle.

The winter before beginning their trip, Clancy and Storey had attended a lecture in Brooklyn by Lady Warwick, who had jokingly invited the entire audience to come and stay if they were ever in England. In the same spirit, they took her at her word, but finding her out of town when they arrived at Warwick Castle, climbed back on the Hendersons and motored on.

They don't know what they missed, for when we called in forthcoming attractions included The Firing of the Mighty Trebuchet, the Sword in the Stone Show, the Flight of the Eagles birds of prey display, The Raising of the Portcullis Show, the How to be a Mediaeval Knight Show, The Ghosts of Warwick Castle haunted tour of the dungeons, and last but not least, Take Siege, in which the castle grounds would be transformed into a siege encampment, culminating in a magnificent mediaeval battle.

'Re-enactors will spend four days eating, sleeping and living the conditions of a real battle,' said the pamphlet, although it failed to spell out whether being shot, trebucheted, attacked by eagles, stabbed by the portcullis or lightly boiled in siege oil was included in the price.

Given the sort of day it was turning into, I think I would have gone for that last option, for when we arrived at Warwick Castle

Gary had somehow managed to back into my bike (which had been parked on a slight slope) causing it to roll off the side stand and collapse elegantly against a very expensive Volvo. As we hauled the bike upright, I could not help but notice the large dent we had left which was highlighted beautifully by the car's metallic silver paint.

Sighing deeply, again, I was just writing out a note to leave under the windscreen when the owner, a charming blonde called Amanda Hobbs, returned from the castle with her two children. 'Flipping expensive in there,' she said. 'Sixty-nine quid for a family ticket, and even more for the attractions inside,' making me think that just sticking the admission fee on the door would have been a much more effective way of repelling besiegers in the old days than all that boiling oil nonsense – 'How much? Right lads, back to France/Yorkshire/Scotland/Jerusalem.'

We exchanged insurance details, and I rode off glumly, feeling slightly sick and nervous the way you always do after an accident, no matter how minor.

Still, I suppose the bike was only honouring the spirit of Clancy who, on his way from Warwick Castle to Oxford, fell badly after swerving to avoid a car overtaking a team of horses.

Nevertheless, he and Storey covered 70 miles that day, and arrived in Oxford at 5.30 p.m., an hour after dark. For seven shillings – and an extra four for a hearty dinner of pork chops – they secured beds for the night at the Roebuck Hotel, which stood on the site of the Roebuck Inn. Built in 1610 and named after the arms of Jesus College, by 1740 it had become a large coaching inn on the London to Gloucester run. In 1850 it was rebuilt as the Roebuck Hotel to rival the Star on the opposite side of Cornmarket.

The next morning, after a good night's sleep, they secured a guide, went to visit Magdalen College and came face to face with the future King Edward VIII, 'a rosy, undeveloped boy of 18' who had just arrived there to study Classics, and who they wouldn't have noticed but for the excited antics of their guide.

Edward, for his part, lasted only two years at Oxford before dropping out and joining the Army, and no one knows what became of him after that.

In 1912, students went from lecture to lecture 'on bicycles by the hundred and motorcycles by the score', their black capes cut to denote their rank. When we visited, the only difference was that their capes were white with snow

Since I was in sombre mood after the events of the day, and since the Roebuck is no more – having been taken over by Woolworths in 1924 and since demolished and turned into a branch of Boots – we rode on, and found ourselves somewhere down the motorway in a branch of Ibis, which was about as charismatic as a branch of Boots, but at least had beds. We dined royally on McDonalds and a bottle of wine from Marks & Spencer, went to bed, and flung back the curtains the next morning to reveal the glorious sight of blue skies, sunshine and not a snowflake to be seen.

At the stroke of nine, we were pulling up outside the Ace Café, which Clancy didn't visit for the simple reason that it only opened in 1938 to accommodate traffic on the new North Circular Road.

Because the café was open twenty-four hours a day, it started to attract motorcyclists. It became popular with the Ton-Up Boys (and girls) in the 1950s, then the Rockers in the 1960s, and many bands and motorcycle enthusiast groups such as the 59 Club formed there.

It closed in 1969 following the decline in motorcycling as a leisure activity, and the building became a tyre sales and fitting shop. But after the success of the Rocker Reunion movement in the 1980s and discussions with its founder and original 59 Club member, Len Paterson, the first Ace Café Reunion was organised in 1994 by Mark Wilsmore. The café reopened in 1997 and was completely refurbished in 2001.

It was, you'll be glad to hear, exactly as it should have been: down one end were three Triumphs, a Royal Enfield, a BSA and a Brough Superior – the machine favoured by Lawrence of Arabia (up to the point where he met his death on one) and the first one I had ever seen in the flesh. Down the other end was a jukebox on which Mick Jagger was complaining, yet again, that he couldn't get no satisfaction; and in the middle, a bunch of grizzled chaps with faraway looks in their eyes were sitting at scrubbed wooden tables, tucking into bacon butties washed down with mugs of tea.

Under the circumstances, it seemed impolite not to join them, then buy an Ace Café sticker as a memento (as well as a Castrol sticker because it reminded me of the metal sign that once turned in the wind outside my dad's motorcycle garage). Once we were all suitably stickered up, we mounted the bikes and rode to London.

When Clancy and Storey arrived in the city, they found their intended hotel, the New Strand Palace Hotel, packed due to an automobile show at Olympia, so instead booked into a nearby commercial hotel.

The next morning they braved the traffic to ride to the Robertson Motor Company, the Henderson dealer in Great Portland Street, where the bikes were placed in the show window as a temporary exhibition, conveniently saving the two men the cost of garage charges.

Robertson Motors is long gone, but Clancy could still walk into the Royal Automobile Club building, where he and Storey spent the next few days happily planning their route east, and find it just as magnificent today as it was then.

Clancy had joined the RAC associate organisation, the Auto-Cycle Union of England, before leaving the States, and had called into the RAC at 89 Pall Mall, which had only been built the year before, to enlist the help of the RAC's resident experts in getting maps, GB number plates and international passes; though they only received these after having their riding skills approved by an RAC examiner in the street outside.

Clancy was deeply impressed by the magnificent building and interior, and he had every right to be, for it is still a soaring hymn to tasteful opulence, from the richly carpeted reception room in which someone had carelessly parked a Bentley Continental, through the marble neoclassical swimming pool, saunas, steam room and gym, to the St James's Room in which we were expected for a press conference – an appropriate venue, since it was named after the saint whose bones had inspired centuries of pilgrims to set off on their own adventures to Santiago de Compostela.

In deep armchairs all around, the descendants of the same chaps who had sat in the same chairs when Clancy was here were busily unscrewing their fountain pens, just as their grandfathers had, to write letters of withering erudition to the *Daily Telegraph* about the state of the nation's roads, 'Sir, as I was driving my Bentley down from the country this morning …'

'You know, Geoff, you've made me very happy, then very sad,' said Michael Bedingfield, the club's splendidly affable head of sales and marketing.

'Oh? Why's that?'

'Well, you said in the *Sunday Times* that the KTM Duke was the best 125 in the world, so I went out and bought it. Then a few weeks ago you said the 200 was even better.'

'Whoops. Sorry about that,' I muttered shamefacedly, tucking into another sandwich filled with salmon which had been smoked to the club's own secret formula, and trotting outside to have, by my estimation, three and a half billion photographs taken.

What felt like hours later, as Gary and I were wearily leaning against the club portals for what the photographer promised would be the very last shot, a tall, elegant man and his equally tall, elegant wife walked up.

'Sorry to bother you, but are you Geoff Hill, Bob's son?' he said.

He turned out to be Mike Young – the son of William Young, my dad's cousin, and his wife Stevanna – who had just happened to be wandering down Pall Mall with his wife Melanie, and had recognised me from newspaper photographs.

It was a rather astonishing piece of serendipity, since the last time I had seen him he'd been about seven and he, his sister, and their parents had come down to Termon, the big house in Tyrone where my grandfather Edward worked as the butler.

They had arrived in a magnificent Rover P6, and William had given me and my sisters a pound note each; an impossible sum which, for most of my grandfather's life, had been his weekly wage.

At last, all the photos were done, and we climbed back on the bikes and left the RAC, as Clancy and Storey had after getting all their documents in order, the only difference being that I doubt either pulled a wheelie, as Gary did. Honestly, he's such a hooligan. Just don't tell BMW what he did to their brand new bike.

After getting all that sorted out, Clancy and Storey went sightseeing, which gave the usually optimistic Clancy a chance to brilliantly dismiss Buckingham Palace as ugly, the Horse Guards as amusing, the Parliamentary debate of the Home Rule Bill as a roughhouse, and the Lord Mayor's Parade as burlesque.

'London did not appeal to us, not because of its grimy old-fashionedness, but because of the cold-blooded life of the simple, self-contained English people, so different from the "push" of New York and the vigorous vivacity of the Parisian,' he wrote, then had a bad attack of hubris as London got its revenge – the slimy streets making him fall and break the Henderson's starting crank housing so that it had to be carted to Fenchurch Street Station and loaded onto the Tilbury train for the boat to Rotterdam.

At least they were moving, I thought as we crawled south to the friendly BMW dealers at Redhill – where everyone was called Darren to keep things simple – to get the bikes serviced. The average speed of traffic in the capital today is 8mph, exactly the same as it was a century ago.

When Clancy and Storey finally made it aboard the night boat, their circumstances improved only a little, as they were greeted by a lukewarm meal and a stiff bill of $13 to get them and their machines from London to Rotterdam.

'Next time we will cross from Harwich to The Hook,' harrumphed Clancy as the continent, and the next chapter of the grand adventure, hove into sight through the rain.

He was quite right, for our crossing on that route could not have been more different: we boarded the shiny new *Stena Hollandica*, dumped our stuff in spacious, air-conditioned cabins with soft beds and warm duvets, and had a delicious meal served by polite, attentive staff, while on the wall hung a poster from the film *Easy Rider*. Now that's what I call attention to detail. Best of all, the simple cardboard cabin key with a bar code on it worked better than most of the plastic ones in five-star hotels.

As we got ready to go to bed, I suddenly realised we had been on the road for almost a week, yet the trip's official photographer and cinematographer hadn't given me any of the four million pics he'd taken.

'Here, Gary, any chance of flinging some pics on a USB stick for me?' I said.

'How do you do that?' he said.

'You mean you don't know?'

'Well, we didn't have any power for three days, so I couldn't practise,' he said, intriguingly.

Still, it was nothing a ten-minute lesson didn't cure, and we finally nodded off, to be roused from our slumbers the next morning by the strains of that well known Dutch air, 'Don't

Worry, Be Happy', followed by the announcement that full cooked breakfasts were now being served in the restaurant.

Outside, the sea mist was just being burned off by the morning sun. Or was it fog?

'What's the difference?' I asked Peter as we were loading up the bikes.

'Fog has a horn,' he said, as I worked out how to change the clock on the bike dash to an hour ahead, using the traditional bloke method of pressing buttons at random until something happened.

'Want me to do yours?' I said to Gary.

'Nah, I'll just do it next time we fill up with fuel.'

'But then you'll be an hour behind, and we'll have to wait for you,' said Peter, then turned to me and said as an aside, 'you do realise that in a few moments you're going to be the only hill in the Netherlands.'

Honestly, there's no end to the wit of these *Irish Times* chaps.

And so, to the continent, by Jove.

Chapter Four

A short history of Holland

16th century
Amsterdam appears out of nowhere as a global centre of commerce creating spectacular wealth and a matching golden age of art led by Rembrandt and a bevy of Bruegels, followed at length by Vermeer, Hals, van Gogh and Mondrian.

1568
The Dutch War of Independence begins. Entire population condemned to death for heresy by the Vatican.

17th century
Dutch East India Company controls large parts of Malaya, Ceylon and Indonesia. Dutch West India Company loses New Amsterdam to the Brits, who rename it New York.

First World War
Dutch remain neutral.

Second World War
Attempts to stay neutral again are slightly screwed when Germans invade and flatten Rotterdam. Just typical.

2012

Tourists banned from smoking dope, indicating that days of coffee shops and brothels may soon be over.

I had forgotten how much I loved Holland. Everything is neat and tidy, and the people are polite, charming, funny yet pragmatic and liberal yet decent.

All around us, impossibly healthy folk cycled to work looking as if they had just emerged from the shower after being scrubbed all over then dusted lightly with sunshine, while others were engaged in that uniquely Dutch pastime of walking the dog by bicycle.

Clancy's first impression was not quite so idyllic: his grumpy mood after an expensive crossing and a lukewarm meal wasn't helped by having to wait two hours on the docks at Rotterdam in the rain while the customs officer was roused out of bed to examine their passes.

He and Storey then managed to lose each other, met up in Delft on the way to Den Haag, missed the signpost for Amsterdam and, after a day of being shaken to pieces by the bumpy brick roads, rode into Amsterdam as darkness fell and climbed wearily off their bikes outside the garage of a friendly Dutchman they had met on the boat.

He came out wiping his hands on an oily rag, greeted them warmly and got them sorted at the Rembrandt Hotel with bed and breakfast for three shillings each.

Clancy would have been moderately stunned by the silky tarmac today, not to mention the cycle paths with their very own traffic lights, complete with red, orange and green bicycles, I thought as we followed his tyre tracks to Delft, best known as the home of the eponymous blue and white ceramics and the painter Johannes Vermeer, who in turn is best known today as the creator of the beguiling portrait of the family's sixteen-year-old maid known as 'The Girl With the Pearl Earring', subsequently a book, a movie and probably quite soon a video game.

When Vermeer died he left a wife, Catharina Bolnes, eleven children and a huge debt to the local baker. Catharina paid this by giving the baker two of her late husband's paintings, before subsequently bankrupting herself trying to get them back.

Other famous historical figures from the area include William the Silent, who is buried in Delft's Nieuwe Kerk church. As an army commander who fought several campaigns against the Catholics, he was a sort of quieter version of his descendant William of Orange, whose escapades in Ireland created the surreal logic which has become the basis for Northern Ireland politics.

Of course, it's no surprise William of Orange was confused: his compatriots call their country the Nederlands, everyone else calls it Holland, their language is called Dutch, the national colour is orange, and the national flag is red, white and blue.

William the Silent, being just as Orange as William of Orange, was assassinated in 1584 by a Catholic fanatic called Balthasar Gérard. Protestant legend has it that the dying William, speaking up for once, asked for Gérard to be treated mercifully. However, since Gérard was then dismembered with red-hot tongs, quartered while still alive and had his heart cut out and placed on his face (although according to contemporary accounts he remained calm throughout) I wouldn't have liked to have seen them treat him unmercifully.

We remounted and followed the Clancy trail to Den Haag, as dull and prosperous today as it was when he passed through, and when in 1859 British poet Matthew Arnold dismissed it in a fashion of which Clancy would have been proud, 'I never saw a city where the well-to-do classes seemed to have given the whole place so much of their own air of wealth, finished cleanliness, and comfort; but I never saw one, either, in which my heart would so have sunk at the thought of living.'

And so to Amsterdam, where the Rembrandt Hotel where Clancy and Storey stayed is no more, though there are two hotels of the same name in the city today. The one on Herrengracht was a private home when Clancy passed through, and the one on Plantage Middenlaan was a house for single Jewish ladies. Today the latter is a pleasant four-storey red brick and cream building with a sign in the door asking guests to not let Bink the cat out – with a photograph of Bink just in case they accidentally let another cat out. Mind you, knowing cats, Bink has probably faked the photo so he can come and go as he pleases.

Sadly, both of the Rembrandt Hotels that Clancy hadn't stayed in were full because it was Good Friday, although after trying another half dozen hotels in vain, we were wondering what was good about it. We finally ended up in an average establishment which charged prices that were anything but: €229 for a room without breakfast.

Clancy and Storey, meanwhile, realising they hadn't eaten since breakfast, piled into the 1898 Café de Kroon for a feast and all the beer they could drink for 60 cents – the only time in the entire journey Clancy mentions getting sloshed.

Still, he was only twenty-two, and his life was filled with the hopes and dreams which don't need booze to sustain them, unlike those of us who end up middle-aged and tucking into a bottle of wine a night to dull the vague sense of disappointment that we have not, after all, ended up as James Bond.

Having said that, James Bond is James Bond, and he still lives on a diet of lethal vodka martinis, so what's he disappointed about? And I know what I'm talking about on the martini front – every time a new Bond movie comes out, we have a party at the house. Everyone turns up in bow ties and best frocks, or dressed as a Bond character, and after some nosh and vodka martinis, we all head off to see the movie, then come back for more fun and games.

The last time, one of our neighbours who hadn't quite figured out that, apart from the olive, martinis are pure alcohol, had four and spent the evening trying, and failing, to speak.

It's not for nothing that American satirist Dorothy Parker said:

> I always have one martini
> Two at the very most.
> After three I'm under the table
> After four I'm under the host.

Still, the good thing for my liver was that after a hard day's motorcycling and writing, it only took a couple of beers in the first floor dining room of the De Kroon – which had been restored to its former glory in 1990, with the addition of Amsterdam's largest disco next door – to create that state of blissful serenity and oneness with the world and everyone in it that Australians call the warm fuzzies.

As we were tucking into a rather splendid boeuf bourguignon with chips and mayonnaise, Peter suddenly straightened and looked out of the window across Rembrandtplein.

'Good grief,' he said. 'Look at the name of that hotel above the Smokey Café.'

We looked. It was the Rembrandt Square Hotel, and it all made perfect sense. If Clancy and Storey had stayed there, they would have emerged hungry, and made straight for the De Kroon across the square.

Sadly, when we crossed the square to make enquiries from the callow youth behind the reception desk, he hadn't a clue how old the hotel was, whether it had been called the Rembrandt one hundred years ago, or who would have a clue. Defeated, we walked home, stopping in several pubs along the way to ease the pain of our disappointing lack of success as Clancy detectives.

'Here, what time does the hotel not serve breakfast tomorrow?' I said as we staggered from the last pub after sampling a disturbingly strong Belgian ale brewed by monks who should know better.

'They don't start serving it at seven, and they stop not serving it at ten,' said Gary.

'So what time will we not have it?' said Peter.

'Let's have a lie in, and not have it at half seven,' I said.

And so we finally fell into bed, after a day of not finding a hotel that was there, and woke the next morning to a breakfast that wasn't.

On Clancy and Storey's next morning, they went for a quick dander around the Rijksmuseum to see Rembrandt's 'Night Watch' – which, as restorers found when they removed the dark varnish in the 1940s, was actually a day scene – then returned to the garage to find their bikes had been cleaned, topped up with fuel and oil, and the tool bags supplied with metric spark plug adapters and a road map, for all of which their good Samaritan refused payment except for a short ride on the Henderson.

It was hardly surprising. The Dutch are model Europeans, and bikers are always friendly to each other, generally stopping to see if another rider stopped by the roadside is okay, and nodding to each other when they pass which, along with the visored helmets, the armoured suits and the gauntlets, always makes me think of them as modern-day knights.

Or possibly ants, the only other species to nod at each other as they pass.

With their machines sparkling in the morning sun, the two men rode south to Haarlem, where we arrived one hundred years later to find the Saturday morning market in full swing. With the pavements bright with trays of tulips, crocuses and daffodils and the air warm with the scent of cheese, pickled herring, sausage and freshly baked bread, and with the rising sun bringing a tremulous ghosting of heat to our faces, we could at last see spring hurrying to meet us, late for an appointment it had been too long in keeping.

After a wander around the vast cathedral of St Bavo – where the eighteenth-century organ which has been played by both Handel and Mozart is, at 90 feet tall and with 5,068 pipes, one of the largest in the world – we emerged to find that I had spoken too soon about spring being in the air, for it was snowing.

As we rode south vaguely hoping that at some stage it would get warmer, we were greeted by a sight that I imagine would have left Clancy mildly mind-boggled: a 747 coming in to land at Schiphol Airport.

However, he had enough on his plate, after a day which began well and went swiftly downhill, with bumpy, slimy roads and unyielding cart drivers eventually sending the unfortunate Storey plunging into a ditch, breaking his starting crank and several spokes and forcing them to creep along until Clancy ran out of fuel.

Sighing deeply in a manner which will be familiar to all motorcycle adventurers both then, now and probably for ever, he walked back a mile and bought some from a cycle shop, and they limped on until rain and darkness finally forced them to call it a day at Het Witte Paard (The White Horse) in Zwijndrecht, a combination hotel, café and amusement hall.

At breakfast, realising they were Americans and therefore obviously flush, the waiter presented them with a bill of 70 cents each for the meal, resulting in an international incident. Clancy demanded to see the proprietor, and when told he was asleep, told the unfortunate waiter that he would pay New York prices in New York, but not in Holland. Taking out his fountain pen and halving the bill, he then left the money and marched for the door with Storey in tow, ignoring the barrage of insults flung after him.

I am glad to say we were greeted in an entirely better fashion when we arrived at Het Witte Paard at lunchtime. The cheery waitress served us coffee and bread cake, then charged us not a penny more than she should have.

'Wow, what a great adventure you guys are having,' she said.

'Want to come with us?' said Gary.

'Absolutely. Let me just phone my boss,' she laughed.

'Hang on,' said Peter, looking at a map and his copy of *Motorcycle Adventurer*, 'I think we're in the wrong Het Witte Paard.'

Indeed, hauling out his phone and doing a spot of Googling, he discovered that the one we wanted was seventeen miles to the north.

After I'd gone outside and given myself a good thrashing with a wet lettuce, then sacked myself as Head of Research, we climbed back on the bikes and rode off to find the real one, only to find that it had been turned into a printers after the war, then knocked down in the 1980s and replaced by an entirely undistinguished old peoples' home in which the residents sat, looked out over the river to the cathedral with its wonky clock face on top, and dreamed of a better past, much as their building did.

'You boys must be freezing,' said Henk te Veldhuis, the owner of the bookshop across the street where Peter Murtagh had nipped in for a chat. 'This is the coldest March in Holland for ninety years.'

Henk turned out to be the perfect man to talk to about the hotel, for he was the author of *The Past in Pictures*, a photographic history of Zwijndrecht which featured several photos of the lovely old building in which Clancy and Storey had stayed, even if their memories of the stay were not quite so lovely.

They took the ferry from Willemsdorp to Moerdijk, which had been running at least as far back as 1838, when John Murray published his *A Handbook for Travellers on the Continent: Being a Guide to Holland, Belgium, Prussia and Northern Germany, and along the Rhine from Holland to Switzerland*. Now there's a catchy title for you.

Today, the ferry's been replaced by a bridge.

After getting Storey's forks fixed, they only made it the twenty-four miles to Zundert, the birthplace and childhood home of Vincent van Gogh, who was born in 1853 in a little house on the main street. The house became too dilapidated to preserve, but its successor and the house next door have been turned into a museum to van Gogh, whose struggle to sell a single painting in his life would have left him sad and bemused to see the stream of Japanese tourists emerging from the house with sunflower handbags, jewellery and postcards. Not to mention the sums his paintings sell for these days.

Nearby is the Dutch Reformed church built in 1806 in which his father, Theodorus van Gogh, preached, and in the graveyard, as neat and tidy as everything in Holland, is the tiny, poignant grave of Vincent's brother, who was born a year before him, named Vincent, and died in infancy.

We stood looking at it for a few minutes, then decamped to Eindhoven and the comfortable suburban bungalow of Howard Bell, a friend of Peter's with whom, in Peter's own words, he had 'biked around Ireland in the late nineteenth century', before Howard, who had worked for Philips in Ireland, was offered a two-year placement with the firm in Holland. Two years became three, four and then for ever, and now, with their children grown up, living nearby and more Dutch than Irish, Howard and his wife Joyce – a nurse as quiet and pleasant as Howard was garrulous and convivial – were here for keeps. Howard's passion for biking hadn't abated over the years, and in their garage sat a rare and immaculate BMW R69S, which he had restored, and a more modern GS.

'Mid-life crisis,' he laughed as we climbed into their Volvo estate and drove to a social evening at the local BMW club where we met several bikers who had been on the same ferry from Harwich as us.

'You're taller in real life,' said one who had made the mistake of reading my *Sunday Times* column to find something out about motorbikes, as we queued for food.

'Sorry about that,' I said, then fell into conversation with Johan Jansen, a fifty-year-old gardener who in 1991 had gone on a grand adventure through Africa on his 1988 GS1000, the first one in Holland, fitted with homemade panniers and top box.

'The shock absorber broke in the Cameroon jungle,' he said, 'and I was standing at the side of the road thinking that the trip was over when a man came along and took me and the bike in his truck to a mechanic who fixed it for nothing. It's still fixed, and the bike has over 200,000km on it.'

It just goes to show, as I've always found, that people are generally good all over the world. As Leonard Cohen said, they'll help you if they can, and only kill you if they must.

As the food was cleared away and the DJ started to belt out Seventies disco classics, the conversation somehow turned to the dark art of counter-steering, of which Peter had never heard.

'So let me get this straight,' he said. 'To go right, you push the right bar, and to go left, the left bar.'

'That's it,' said Gary who, along with all his other careers, had been a former biking instructor.

'Mmm. Sounds desperately counter-intuitive. I'd better have some more wine and think about it.'

The next morning, we turned up for a ride out with the club and found a falconry display in progress, led by an owl with that look of erudite scorn that they have, like a professor to whom you have just handed an illiterate essay, and an eagle whose eyes were full of a savage sadness that he was on a campsite in Holland rather than soaring in the Alps.

Many of the small rural roads around which we pottered that morning were paved with the brick of which Clancy complained long and hard, for while the Beemers soaked them up, they must have been boneshaking on a Henderson with no rear suspension.

In spite of the roads, and their surprise at seeing large dogs pulling carts, small boys puffing on pipes and cigars, and everyone wearing clogs, Clancy was sorry to leave a Holland which he'd found picturesque, free from artificiality and so clean that they often rode past housewives scrubbing cobblestoned streets with soap and water.

We were just as sorry to leave it, too, when the next morning we said farewell to Howard and Joyce and proceeded south towards Belgium with Peter gaily practising his counter-steering on every corner.

So far, it had proved entirely successful in that he hadn't fallen off once.

Chapter Five

A short history of Belgium

Beer, chocolate, bureaucrats, Tin Tin, Poirot and van Damme. Oh, and author Hugo Claus, who said: 'I insist on being Belgian. I want to be a member of the pariah nationality, the laughing stock of the French and the object of contempt of the Dutch. It's the ideal situation for a writer.'

Not knowing that *Douane* meant 'Customs', Clancy and Storey rode blithely across the border until they were stopped by a gendarme and sent back to an irate official.

Using the well-known placid ignorance technique – which Clancy would be pleased to know has served me well at many a border and police checkpoint – they were soon on their way to Breda and Antwerp.

The main road was, unfortunately, as rough and bone-shaking as those in Holland, but the two men sneakily mounted the better paved cycle path and bowled along until they were stopped by a heartless policeman and told to get back to the wretched road where they belonged.

Today, thanks to the Schengen Agreement, the only sign of the border we saw was a white and blue België sign as we passed seamlessly across on our way to Ghent, the ancestral home of

Paddy Minne, the world-famous Franco-Belgian motorcycle mechanic who had accompanied me on my first motorcycle adventure from Delhi to Belfast on two Royal Enfields.

On the way, I noticed that local bikers would stick out a foot to thank drivers who had pulled over to let them pass, but since that looked disturbingly like a dog cocking its leg at a lamppost, I continued to use my traditional method of a cheery wave followed by an undignified wobble as I almost fell off.

When we got to the outskirts of Ghent, and tried to make our way to the old centre, the satnav continued its trick of taking us by the most convoluted route possible, so I switched it off and used the Murtagh Method which Peter had recommended the day before, of heading for the big pointy thing instead.

These are called cathedrals, and have been handy reference points ever since tourists were medieval pilgrims, and Peter had discovered it, rather appropriately, by being a medieval pilgrim himself when he walked the Camino de Santiago de Compostela with his daughter Natasha, a journey which had resulted in the excellent book *Buen Camino*.

When Clancy and Storey got to Ghent and the big pointy thing in the middle, they left their machines at Joseph Houard & Fils at 11 Rue des Vanniers (the street of the basket makers). Joseph had been a bicycle manufacturer since 1888, then in 1901 became a motorcycle dealer for the Belgian firm FN, a company which made an inline-four very similar to the Henderson, was a pioneer of shaft drive in 1903 and went on to achieve success in racing and motocross before finally closing in 1967.

Sadly, the Fils obviously weren't made of the same mettle as Père Houard, for the shop is long gone. As indeed is the street, for in spite of Nancy De Letter in the Ghent tourist office spending a good forty minutes checking the city records and phoning two local historians, she only found that the street had ceased to exist in 1942, and could find no evidence of where it had been.

Clancy and Storey, meanwhile, gave their aching bones a welcome break and took the train to Bruges. The intricate glories of the 1376 town hall sent Clancy into a reverie of delight, as did the Church of Notre-Dame, the spire of which he insisted could be seen from the Spanish Main, making me suspect that he'd bought more in Amsterdam than beer. Having said that, I'm not surprised he was impressed by the town hall, an architectural fantasy so gothic it's almost a parody of itself.

By now it was time for lunch, and so we decamped to La Belle Vue on the main square, where Cate and I had had dinner once. Taking the name as a clue, I greeted the saturnine waiter with a cheery, 'Bonjour, Monsieur'.

'Why are you talking to me in French? Do I look like a Froggie?' he spluttered, then became even more gloomy when we only ordered soup.

'Are we the worst customers you've had today?' I said.

'I've had worse,' he shrugged.

When the time came to call for the bill, we resisted the temptation to hail him with a cheeky 'Garçon!' But only just.

Clancy and Storey, having sated themselves on the ancient glories of Bruges, took the train back to Ghent and gave themselves the shivers at the 'grim recesses and terrifying dungeons' of the Château des Comtes.

Built by Philip of Alsace, Count of Flanders, in 1180, to a design inspired by Crusader forts in Syria, it was fully restored in the late twentieth century but is still satisfyingly grim and terrifying, housing a museum full of weapons and instruments of torture. So bleak was the collection that we were happy to leave it and make our way onto the battlements for a fine view of the river wending its way beneath ancient rooftops which were at last beginning to be warmed by the sun.

Emerging into the winter sunlight, then having their gobs smacked even more by the awe-inspiring St Bavo's Cathedral, the dynamic duo booked a room for a dollar in the Grand Hotel Metropole, which is no more, and at those prices I'm not surprised.

The following day they set off for Brussels – where they stopped just long enough to collect their poste restante mail at the post office – before the attractions of a good, smooth-surfaced road called to them, and they sped on to Namur.

Indeed, I could empathise: the first time I went to Brussels, I had allocated two whole days for sightseeing, but after seeing the Manneken-Pis and the Grand-Place, realised I had only needed forty-seven minutes.

'Here, is there anything else to see in Brussels?' I asked the jolly girl back at the tourist office.

'Well, there is a pub selling three hundred types of beer,' she shrugged.

That was good enough for me. I got on a tram, went too far, got on a bus, went too far the other way and, some hours later, parched for a pint, finally staggered up the street to the pub; only to be greeted by a sign saying 'Closed on Mondays'.

I envied Clancy the fact that his only connection with the world he had left behind was collecting his mail from post offices along the way. The world we live in today, with its mobile phones and broadband, is a blessing in many ways, but it is also a curse. We've become addicted to constant communication to the extent that I remember sitting through a dinner in Los Angeles one night at which almost everyone at the table spent the entire meal answering business emails on their Blackberries.

It also means that if you are in constant touch with home, you are never truly away: as a student, I would often bugger off for the entire summer holidays and never be in touch once, and much as I love my wife, one of my happiest trips of recent years was two weeks riding an Enfield through the Himalayas with no mobile or broadband signal. It was bliss, tempered only slightly by the fear of the tsunami of emails that would await me when I got reconnected.

As for Clancy and Storey, they had no such concerns. Tucking their letters from home into the pockets of their tweed jackets to read that evening, they rattled through the Meuse Valley by moonlight and spent their last night in Belgium at the Hôtel Charpentier in Dinant which, like the Metropole, is no more.

Still, I thought as I sat down in the airy lobby of the *auberge de jeunesse* in Namur that evening to file a blog to the Adelaide Adventures website, Clancy would have taken some pleasure from the fact that, in spite of all the technological changes since then, the qwerty keyboard on my netbook was much the same as the portable typewriter on which he had typed up his notes for posting to the *Motorcycle Review*.

Chapter Six

A short history of France

1375
King Charles VI goes mad, just to prove the English didn't have a monopoly on insane monarchs.

1643–1715
Louis XIV, aka the Sun King. Admired for his wisdom, which he displays by spending entire national budget on building the Palace of Versailles and waging endless wars, then driving out 200,000 Huguenots who were the country's finest artisans, merchants and soldiers.

1789
Revolution replaces useless kings with useless republican leaders such as Napoleon, who in 1804 crowns himself emperor then spends entire national budget on war with Russia.

1815
French monarchy reinstated after Waterloo, placing King Louis XVIII, and then Charles X, back on the throne just in time to create economic crisis.

1848

Another revolution, followed by election of Napoleon's nephew, who maintains family tradition of modesty by crowning himself emperor.

1849

Jean-Baptiste Alphonse Karr sums it all up with: *'Plus ça change, plus c'est la même chose.'*

First World War

France in ruins, and after war builds Maginot Line to stop Germans ever invading again.

Second World War

Germans bypass Maginot Line and invade France through Belgium. Karr turns in grave.

On French roads which were no better than the Dutch and Belgian ones, it took Clancy and Storey three exhausting days of punctures and spills to get to Paris, where they were glad to put the Hendersons into cold storage for 80 cents a month and ride through town on the omnibus instead.

It took us only three hours to make the journey, travelling through Flanders, Ypres and the Somme – names which, when Clancy passed through, were synonymous with chocolate, roses and weekends in the country for the good citizens of Paris or Brussels, but that in two short years became bywords for blood, mud and carnage.

Peter had found a little hotel in the south of the city and we spent the night there before making our way to the destination every tourist wants to visit the moment they arrive in Paris: the Algerian consulate.

Quite.

You see, because we'd received the bike registration numbers so late, never mind the bikes, we hadn't been able to get Algerian visas in time, and a week before we left, I was in Sam Geddis' office banging my head off his desk when he had the bright idea of phoning his MP Ian Paisley Jnr, who turned out to be a mate of the Algerian ambassador in London.

'Leave it with me,' Ian had said. 'I'll see if I can get them a meeting with him as they're passing through London.'

Sadly, nothing came of it, and we'd heard no more by the time we had arrived in Paris.

'Why don't you try just turning up at the Algerian Consulate tomorrow and asking? All they can do is fling you in jail and throw away the key,' said Peter as we tucked into beef casserole washed down with a bottle of red at a little bistro around the corner from the hotel that night.

It made sense, but we thought we'd try it anyway, walking through a derelict security scanner in the consulate the next morning to find a scene of appropriate bedlam, like a microcosm of the country itself.

As we were standing in the queue, my phone rang. It was Nichola at Adelaide with the news that she'd just received the previous two weeks' issues of the *Mirror* (Republic of Ireland edition) and there was no sign of the Clancy spread, in spite of the fact that they had promised twice in writing to run it in both northern and southern editions.

My stress tachometer hit the red line, then bounced off the end stop – the main reason Adelaide had sponsored the gig was to increase business in the south, so coverage in that edition was crucial to the deal, and Sam could now quite easily pull the plug on the whole thing, meaning the trip was over and two years of planning had been completely wasted.

'John Kierans, the editor, is off on holiday, and his deputy, Kevan Furbank, is off today, so I'll call him tomorrow and get back to you. I assume you know this jeopardises everything, since the Irish market is key for us,' she said.

'I know, Nichola. Only too well,' I said.

Even worse, when we finally got to the front of the queue to ask if we could get a visa in one day rather than the usual fifteen, the polite chap behind the desk said simply, 'Where are you from, messieurs?'

'Irlande du Nord, monsieur,' I said.

'Then it is impossible. I can only issue visas for French citizens,' he said with a shrug which showed that the Algerians had picked up more than just the language and a taste for decent bread from the French.

Oh well, at least that answered that question. So all we could do now after Spain, rather than taking the ferry to Algeria, was to ride down through Italy, get the boat to Tunisia, pick up the Clancy trail there and ride to the Algerian border to see if we could blag our way in.

In the meantime, we thought we may as well see the sights of Paris, a city that Clancy and Storey liked instantly, and not just for the architecture – which, they thought, far outshone that of New York or London – nor for the 'vigorous, throbbing life of the French people', but for a born artistry exhibited in events such as the 1912 Salon d'Automobile held at the Grand Palais, which was gloriously lit by electric candles for the event.

In fact, they liked Paris so much that they decided they needed at least two months to do it justice, and booked a room at the Grand Hotel Corneille at rue Corneille 5. There, for $20 a month, they enjoyed the luxury of electric light, steam heating and a valet who every night polished the very boots which were snug in my right pannier as we pulled up outside the very same building a century on. A building that, over the years had been a favourite haunt of many famous Irish travellers – including W.B. Yeats, James Joyce and John Millington Synge.

Today, I found a plump and pleasant workman called Alphonse standing in the doorway at No. 5 in a pair of faded red dungarees, having just finished painting the hallway of the pale stone six-storey building.

'Ah yes, it was a hotel right up until the Second World War, when it was occupied by German officers. Although they got a bit of a shock when a bomb went off inside,' he said, wiping the last of his paintbrushes clean. 'I imagine it was the Resistance, but of course no one knew. After the war, this part of the building became the Bank of France, and the part down to the corner became apartments above, and on the ground floor a bistro, a brasserie and a cheese shop, as you see.'

As I did. Thanking him for his help, we got back on the bikes and rode to the Pigalle district to find another couple of Clancy's haunts. Clancy, for his part, had decided against using the bikes in Paris, declaring that the traffic there, being regulated at only two crossings, was too dangerous. It took a month and a half before he ventured onto the streets on his Henderson, and even then it was only to demonstrate it to potential importers, which he did so successfully that he was able to secure an order for one hundred machines.

It's as well he got his thrills from the traffic though, since he didn't seem to get any during his visits to the Moulin Rouge, the Chat Noir or the Rat Mort. 'None of these amusements inspired a single thrill,' he complained, 'although the black, narrow alleys on either side caused many an involuntary shudder.'

The Moulin Rouge, with the iconic red windmill on the roof, was built in 1889 by Joseph Oller, who also owned the Paris Olympia, and is, of course, best known as the birthplace of the can-can. Originally a seductive dance by the courtesans who worked there, it evolved into a form of entertainment of its own and was copied in cabarets all across Europe.

Today, the place still embodies all the romance of belle époque France, and its admission fees embody all the attraction of emptying your wallet, at a whopping €105 per person, or €175 with dinner, which was well beyond our means.

Down the street was the final resting place of Le Chat Noir, first opened in 1881 at another address by the impresario Rodolphe Salis. It's generally thought to be the first modern cabaret – a nightclub where the patrons sat at tables and drank while being entertained by a variety show on stage, introduced by a master of ceremonies who interacted with people he knew at the tables.

Salis began by renting the cheapest accommodation he could find, a small two-room affair at 84 Boulevard de Rochechouart, a site now commemorated only by a historical plaque. Small and bijou it may have been, but before long it was packed with radical young writers and artists who called themselves Les Hydropathes (those who are afraid of water), led by the journalist Émile Goudeau.

In spite of the notoriously bad wine and shabby décor, guests were greeted by a Swiss guard, splendidly bedecked and covered with gold from head to foot, who was supposedly responsible for admitting the painters and poets who arrived, while barring 'infamous priests and the military'.

In June 1885, having become incredibly popular, the club was forced to move to bigger premises: the sumptuous former private mansion of the painter Alfred Steven, only a few doors down from the original. It eventually moved again, to 68 Boulevard de Clichy, but closed in 1897, not long after Salis' death, much to the disappointment of Picasso and others who looked for it when they came to Paris in 1900 for the Exposition.

Today, the old Chat Noir building has been transformed into a hotel and bistro, retaining the name of its raucous ancestor, while the neighbouring buildings reflect more of the debauched spirit – housing an erotic museum and various sex shops, lap dancing clubs and houses of ill repute.

By now, it was lunchtime so we secured an outside table in the sun at the bistro and had a coffee and a pear tart, since we were happily married men on a budget and the tarts up the street were beyond our hearts and wallets.

Le Rat Mort, another club which Clancy and Storey visited, was a favourite of American Harry Thaw, who inherited four million dollars from his father, William Thaw, the railroad and coal baron. Harry spent half of the inheritance on drugs and prostitutes, and squandered the rest – lit cigars with $100 bills, coined the term playboy, murdered his love rival Stanford White, then got off on grounds of insanity, threw a party costing $50,000 when he was in Paris, and otherwise lived a quiet and unremarkable life until he died aged seventy-six.

Le Rat Mort was also a famous lesbian haunt, but since I'm not one and Gary and Peter weren't sure, there seemed little point in going.

Oh well, even if Clancy found more excitement in the traffic than the can-can, at least he noted approvingly that Paris was the cheapest of all cities for good food, and they could live comfortably there on a dollar a day – particularly since they tracked down a small restaurant on the Boulevard Saint-Michel where they could get a five-course feast with wine for 25 cents.

Excuse me while I sob gently in the corner for a bit.

Apart from that, and in spite of the fact that he initially raved about Paris, after two months he decided that it was a city with a great future behind it, and could see no reason for its existence other than for the world's rich to come and spend money, since it seemed to produce nothing.

'Indeed, I believe this is why the whole French nation is on the decline – it is not sufficiently productive, except of aeroplanes, one or two of which were to be seen sailing over the city nearly every day,' he said.

Sadly, it was just as they were preparing to leave Paris that Storey made his decision to return to the States – a loss that, remarkably, Clancy dismisses in only a couple of lines:

'At this point Storey was imperatively called back to America and, knowing no one to take his place, I determined to continue all alone,' he said, then sold Storey's Henderson to the new French importer. He set off the next afternoon with a heavy heart; not because he was leaving Clancy, but because he was leaving Paris, which he only realised how much he loved as he was leaving it.

Men, they're all the same.

Ironically, as we rode away from the hotel the next morning, I noticed that the shop across the road was called Alegria. It was probably the closest we were going to get to Algeria, although with Gary's dyslexia, it was probably much the same thing. And if you think I'm being cruel to him, he'd laughed his leg off the night before at one of my favourite jokes, about the dyslexic bank robber who ran in and shouted: 'Air in the hands, motherstickers! This is a f**k up!'

Reaching Chartres that night after fifty-five tough miles on muddy roads, Clancy stayed at the Grand Hotel de France, of which I could find no trace. Though this was possibly no bad thing, since Clancy was really grumpy that, not only did it cost twice as much as a Paris hotel, but they wouldn't give him a 10 per cent discount for his Touring Club de France membership. He wasn't entirely surprised though, as when he had mentioned it elsewhere, the price would immediately be raised to cancel the discount.

'Still, membership costs but a dollar and secures unlimited touring information, so I am well pleased anyway,' he concluded.

For us, the twin spires of Chartres Cathedral slowly appearing out of the mist were as astonishing as they must have been to medieval pilgrims; as they were to Clancy; and as they were to me the first time I saw them, Inter-Railing around Europe in September 1975. I wish that I had been able to enjoy the sight more, but as we rode, my mind kept straying to the thought that if the *Mirror* fiasco didn't get sorted out, Sam at Adelaide could well pull the plug on this whole trip.

Outside the cathedral, a man in a flat cap was singing Bach's 'Jesu, Joy of Man's Desiring' and offering daffodils for small change, although his air of sanctity was somewhat diminished by the cigarette dangling from his lower lip.

The cathedral itself was more impressive. Built relatively quickly between 1194 and 1260, it is therefore a much more harmonious whole than many of its peers, which often took centuries to construct, and so encompassed several architectural genres resulting in a marriage which is not always a happy one.

In a small side chapel dedicated to the Sancta Camisia – the robe allegedly worn by Mary when Christ was born (although these days it is not on public display in the cathedral) – a small mass was being held and, as the voices of the priest and the faithful singing the 'Te Deum' rose and echoed in the still, high spaces, it still sent a shiver up my spine, as it must have done for over eight hundred years to the many visitors to this place.

We saddled up, and rode on towards Blois, stopping for lunch in La Toque Blanche, a little roadside restaurant in the attenuated hamlet of Marboué. The waiter, quite rightly, ignored our pathetic appeals for soup or omelettes and brought us the *plat du jour* – earthy terrine, followed by steak with pepper sauce, then chocolate mousse with delicate crème anglais, and a tiny cup of coffee as dark and bitter as a widow's curse on the tongue, then like an electric shock to the heart.

'It always amazes me about France that you can close your eyes, walk into any little restaurant and find deeply satisfying provincial cooking. Why is that?' I said.

'It's because after the Revolution all the chefs who cooked for the aristocracy were out of a job, so they all opened restaurants. Any chance of some more bread?' said Peter.

The soundtrack as we ate came courtesy of Bob Dylan, Van Morrison, Elvis, Aretha Franklin, Simon and Garfunkel and the Blues Brothers, finishing off with the theme tune for the *Pink Panther* and 'If You're Going to San Francisco'. At that stage I didn't know whether we were or not, but after half an hour of riding through some heavy rain, we were rolling into Blois, where Clancy had stayed in the Hotel de Château. He had parked the bike in one of its old wine vaults, climbed the terrace for his first view of the Loire, and felt as if he was 'at the very front door of history'.

Today, the only hotel of that name in Blois is the Best Western Blois Château, but when we asked the small, dark, nervous girl on reception – although possibly the only reason she was nervous was because three motorcyclists were dripping all over her lobby and asking strange questions – the hotel had only been there three years and she hadn't a clue where the previous Hotel de Château had been

As we emerged, my phone rang so I looked at the caller display. It was Nichola from Adelaide. I took a deep breath, and pressed answer.

'Good news,' she said. 'I've just talked to Kevan at the *Mirror*, and he knew nothing about the agreement, but he couldn't have been more helpful. He's running the prelim piece and the first two pieces in the southern edition next week, then everything in both after that.'

I thanked her, breathed a very large sigh of relief, and hung up. We were back on the road, even if it was an increasingly soggy one, and as we followed the path of the Loire I thought about how lovely the journey would be on a good day. As it was, there was not a single motorcyclist in sight, and I don't blame them, since on a day like this anyone with any sense would be tucked up in bed with a hot chocolate and a warm Labrador.

I did think I caught a glimpse of another biker as we bounced over the cobbles in one village, and was just about to give him a wave when I realised it was me reflected in a shop window. I gave myself a little wave anyway just to cheer myself up, since I looked a bit glum.

Since it was still the middle of winter when Clancy was in Blois, he had a gloomy wander around the Royal Château de Blois by himself, with hail battering the windows and the wind howling down the chimneys. Later that day, when the rain had subsided, he set off for Chaumont, a chateau remarkable for the fact that its stables were lit by electric lights before the main house was. Clancy immediately declared it as his favourite, exactly what in his childhood he had imagined a French chateau to be. 'Sometime I hope to buy it,' he mused, climbing back on the Henderson and motoring on to the Château de Chenonceau.

With its arched river bridge, Chenonceau is the most recognisable of the chateaux of the Loire owing its exquisite beauty to the influence of two women – Diane de Poitiers, the mistress of King Henry II, and then Queen Catherine de' Medici, his wife.

On Catherine's death in 1589 the chateau went to her daughter-in-law, Louise de Lorraine-Vaudémont, the wife of Henry III, who after her husband's assassination in 1589 spent the rest of her days dressed in mourning clothes and wandering aimlessly along the chateau's corridors, which were draped with black tapestries stitched with skulls and crossbones.

In 1864, Daniel Wilson, a Scotsman who had made a fortune installing gaslights throughout Paris, bought the chateau for his daughter. In the tradition of Catherine de' Medici, she bankrupted herself on elaborate parties and the chateau was seized and sold to José-Emilio Terry, a Cuban millionaire, in 1891. Terry sold it in 1896 to a family member, Francisco Terry, and in 1913, the Menier family, famous for their chocolates, (even if they didn't invent the chocolate orange like the Terrys), bought the chateau and still own it to this day.

Clancy had hoped to call in with the Terrys, but found them wintering in Cuba, as one does.

It is easy to see that women were involved in creating Chenonceau, for in spite of its scale, it is an expression of refined, delicate beauty rather than masculine pride, and the rooms are small and intimate, for conversations and reading, rather than vast bombastic spaces which are impossible to heat.

Possibly the most exquisite part of this exquisite building is the long gallery over the Loire, which makes your heart sing wherever you look – at the chandeliers tinkling above, the white walls, the view through the tall windows of the river rolling past below, unperturbed by all that has gone on above, or the chequerboard floor beneath your feet, which once echoed to the steps of kings and queens, and now does the same to the loafers of Japanese tourists and American coach parties, and the weighty clump of bikers in boots, such as Clancy and ourselves.

Undeterred by the fact that the Terrys were not in residence, Clancy declared Chenonceau a fairy spot and motored on to Amboise, the town where Leonardo da Vinci spent his final years and is now buried.

At the chateau there, a guard 'without a drop of sporting blood in him' refused to let Clancy attempt a ride up the steep roadway to the Tour de Minimes to test the Henderson's mettle.

The rain had turned to drizzle as we rode into the town through trees glistening with clumps of mistletoe. We stopped at a café into which the owner had piled so many seats that it was almost impossible to sit down, and feasted on croque monsieurs and hot chocolate. And then, since the grandson of the unsporting guard was nowhere in sight, we roared up and down the roadway to our hearts' content before speeding on to Tours, where Clancy and the Henderson had stopped the traffic and created such a crowd that several gendarmes had to clear a path to a hotel for him.

Arriving at twilight, as he had, we found a similar crowd;

except they were a crowd of solicitors in town for a conference and they had booked every room going, damn and blast their pinstripes.

Since it was now chucking it down as if rain was going out of fashion, we sought refuge in Paddy Flaherty's Irish bar, where a stern notice above the bar announced that no coffee would be sold on Saturdays.

Behind the bar was a sweet girl with a forest of dark curls who looked about sixteen, but was in fact the manager. Her name was Ophelie, and after she'd rustled us up three coffees, since it was still only Friday, she got on the blower to a mate who owned a little hotel out of town to see what he could do to help. Half an hour later, after a brief visit to a bike shop to book Peter's bike in for a new front tyre, since he'd worn his out practising counter-steering, we were ensconced gratefully in a room that was warm, and most important of all, dry. We changed, hung up all our soaking kit and tumbled into a nearby restaurant just in time for last orders.

The next morning, I was busy writing the story for next week's *Mirror* when I realised that I needed a photo from Gary of the Ace Café in London.

'Do you want me to email or put it on a USB stick?' he said.

'Whatever's handy.'

'How do you email pics?' he said about five minutes later.

'Gary, I don't know. It's your machine. Didn't you learn any of this stuff before you left?' I said, counting to ten, and then to eleven just to be on the safe side.

'Sorry. Life's been a bit chaotic lately. Or possibly forever,' he said.

Still, the next night he managed to download three pics in a minute flat, so at least he was a fast learner. And even better, he turned out to have a great eye for a shot, so all his photos and footage were turning out rather splendidly. Even if Nichola had told him to ignore interesting background items like the Eiffel tower, Chartres Cathedral and so on, and just concentrate on the Adelaide stickers on the bikes.

We spent a night in a soulless hotel in the soulless town of Poitiers, then rode south the next morning, our armoured suits bejewelled with mist, like chain mail of old, and the temperature refusing to rise above four degrees. Still, at least we were remaining true to the spirit of Clancy, who had ridden through here in similar temperatures in February 1913.

After a while, the mist got fed up hanging around and turned to rain, which turned into a torrential downpour as we rolled damply through the valley of the river Aude and into Carcassonne – the walled city where, in the thirteenth century, the Cathars had sought refuge – at which point the satnav had its finest hour yet. After trying to take us up several one-way streets in Poitiers the day before, it now led us up a muddy track to the locked gate of a private house.

Eventually, we found the youth hostel, an oasis of warmth inside which Michael the patron was greeting guests in half a dozen languages. He checked us in, recommended a restaurant called the Auberge des Lices around the corner – in which we later had a superb meal for €19.50 each plus wine – then started chatting to another guest in fluent Arabic.

Sitting in the lobby was a ruddy-cheeked man in his thirties in a tweed jacket and a flat cap who, after hearing our accents, wandered over for a chat. His name was Tony and he was German-born, but as a child he had developed a romantic passion for Ireland. He moved to Limerick to answer it and was still based there, teaching languages.

'There wasn't a lady involved, or anything,' he said in answer to the question I hadn't asked. 'Although, I could have possibly picked a more romantic spot than Limerick.' He paused, and looked out at the rain streaming down the window. 'And possibly a dryer time of year to visit Carcassonne, or maybe I've brought the weather with me.'

Clancy, by all accounts had had a somewhat less soggy time of it: in the delightful, picturesque foothills of the Pyrenees, where 'miles of vineyards basked in the cordial sun and lazy, dark-skinned peasants were pruning the winter's growth of sprouts,' he waited for five minutes at a level crossing for a train that was nowhere in sight. Finally losing his patience, he pushed the Henderson across the track, whereupon the female guard burst into tears and ran away.

He rode along the track for miles, watching for the train that never appeared, but he hardly cared, for he was finally bidding farewell to the mud of northern Europe, and hello to two months of heat and dust.

In the valley of the Aude, he passed endless lines of two-wheeled carts piled high with hay or casks of wine, drawn by gaunt horses and with their drivers to a man fast asleep. Then, as he wound his way through almond groves up the mountains and through Limoux, Quillan, St Paul and Estagel, the temperature fell and he met locals wrapped up against the chill wind, in baggy corduroy trousers of dark brown or green, with jaunty red sashes and matching caps.

As we followed the same road the next morning, the sun finally appeared after all the days of snow, rain and biting wind; at first peeking shyly from behind the clouds, and then, emboldened by its welcome, flaunting itself gloriously for the rest of the day.

The bad news was that Gary and I were both flashed by a speed camera on the road to Perpignan, but the good news is that since it was a rear-facing one, it got a lovely shot of the Adelaide and IAM stickers on the front of the bikes, but not our numberplates.

We found the very railway track along which Clancy had ridden and, beyond it, the glittering sea, as thrilling a sight as it was on childhood summer holidays to Rossnowlagh in County Donegal, our buckets and spades piled into the back of the family Cortina; or as it was when Paddy Minne and I had seen it on the north coast of Turkey after the long days riding across the burning sands of Persia on the way home from Delhi; and as it was when Clifford and I had seen the Pacific as we swooped down into San Diego on our way from Chile to Alaska.

How lucky I was, I thought, to have seen such things, as we got our first sight of the soaring Pyrenees, snow-clad even in April. But then we were used to snow, having been to Birmingham.

It was a shock to see the mountains rising suddenly out of the coastal plain, as if the earth had been overcome by a spontaneous desire to become the sky, but found no matter how high it soared, it was still earth.

We stopped for coffee and pain au raisins in a little café in Perpignan, sitting outside and letting the heat of the sun soak into our bones.

Clancy had arrived here to find a carnival in progress and the streets thronged with masked and costumed revellers, but not even a fireworks display starting at 11 p.m. could keep him awake as he collapsed into a downy bed and fell fast asleep for his last night in France.

Chapter Seven

A short history of Spain

721
Moors conquer country.

1492
Christians get it back, and celebrate by sending Columbus off to discover America, leading to centuries of Spanish colonisation of an entire continent noted for its kind, gentle empathy with native culture. Back home, same spirit of tolerance is shown towards Jews in the Inquisition.

1923
After centuries of rule by Habsburg and Bourbon royals, economic chaos and riots lead to military coup, followed by economic chaos, riots and civil war.

1939
Franco seizes power, kills or imprisons up to two million opponents, and plunges country into decades of austere isolation.

1975
With a growing tourism industry, Franco's death paves the way for a return to democracy.

1990s

Everyone in Ireland buys off-plan holiday villa on Costas, paving the way for construction boom.

2008

Celtic Tiger dies. Spanish construction industry follows suit, paving the way for economic meltdown.

At the border crossing at Le Perthus, Clancy ran into trouble.

'A villainous Spaniard, bedecked in the most dressy of uniforms, blocked my entrance into sunny Spain,' he fumed in his diary that night. This 'veritable brigand' then charged him a whopping $55 customs deposit, or almost a month's wages back home, in import duty, then had the audacity to demand a tip.

Giving him six cents, Clancy was allowed into Spain, only to be stopped twice within a mile and asked for his papers. When he finally set off on the 120 miles to Barcelona; it was only to be slowed to fifteen miles an hour by the conditions.

'I had expected poor roads in Spain, and was not happily disappointed. To all those who are planning to motorcycle in Spain, let me give one word of advice – don't!' he wrote grimly.

Then, a broken crankshaft bearing – caused by poor oil he had been forced to buy in France – obliged him to spend the night in Figueras, where his complete lack of Spanish resulted in him being led, with half the town at his heels, to a hotel instead of a garage, and, later that night, the waiter in his hotel bringing him a bottle of wine when he asked for the bill.

Salvador Dali, the master of surrealism who was born there in 1904, and whose museum is one of the highpoints of the town, would have approved.

Today, Le Perthus is a long, steep street lined with shops, off-licences and tattoo parlours, every parking space filled with Sunday bikers, muscle cars and estates, and its pavements hiving with shoppers carting crates of cheap booze back to France, while the entire scene is watched over by a disturbingly glamorous blonde policewoman.

'I wonder how I could get myself arrested and strip-searched,' said Gary as an elderly Frenchman came over for a chat.

He turned out to be Maxim, an eighty-year-old former postman whose father had been a wartime pilot with the French Air Force under De Gaulle. 'Le Perthus has been like this since the Fifties, and it's no surprise,' he said. 'I've just bought a case of Marlboro for 46 euro, and back home it would have cost me 65.

'Nice bikes, those. I had a Norton Commando and a Triumph 650 when I was young, and I toured all over England and Scotland. I was surprised at how good the food was, for everyone said it would be terrible.

'But you know what? I'm glad Churchill took over from Chamberlain, because he would have surrendered, and today, all of that, and all of this, would have been German.'

He shook our hands and pottered off to drive home, and we looked in wonder at a scene in which the only thing Clancy would have recognised is the ancient customs post at the bottom of the street, the blue sign above the door saying *Bureau des Douanes Francaises* slowly fading in the sun, and inside a desk and three chairs which had not been used for many a long year.

As we rode into Figueras, we passed the appropriately surreal sight of hundreds of caravans sitting in a mobile home graveyard, and then the Dali Museum itself, designed by the great showman and in which his body lies today, still at last after a life of relentless self-promotion in which I suspect he was generally having a laugh at us all.

It's hard to miss, with its giant eggs on the roof and walls studded with loaves, but since I'd been before (and after about an hour got fed up with telephones which were bananas and women who were either Abraham Lincoln or giant sofas, and had decamped to a nearby bar where a beer was just a beer) I left Gary and Peter to it, sat on a park bench in the sun and read over my notes on Clancy's progress through here.

Or lack of it. Leaving the Henderson in Figueras to be repaired, he boarded a 'wretched hencoop train' which took seven hours to get to Barcelona. Given plenty of time to observe Spanish customs and character, he decided that he preferred the Spanish to the French both in looks and temperament, and that they were 'even more gay than the Italians in nature'.

Ah, how the language changes. If we'd told any of the Spaniards we met that they were more gay than the Italians, a riot may well have ensued.

Wandering around Barcelona the next day, Clancy felt refreshed by the constant laughter and play of children, and deeply impressed by the fact that the hard dirt streets were swept and sprinkled with water every night. Most enchanting of all, though, was the *paseo*, or evening walk, in which the citizens strolled hand in hand or arm in arm along Las Ramblas.

He would be pleased to know that both the *paseo* and the sprinkling of streets are customs maintained to this day, and although the children he saw laughing have grown up and old and died, their grandchildren are laughing still.

'Everyone seemed to be promenading – and to be happy!' he wrote in his diary, before going on to admire the 'mountain peasants with their queer red caps perched jauntily on one side' who would burst into a snatch of opera on a whim, the weatherbeaten sailors, smart looking soldiers, entreating flower girls, prosperous merchants with their families, laughing and playing children, dainty white-gloved grandmothers, and 'soft brown-eyed, black-haired senoritas who would inspire a serenade from almost any lad of spirit'.

He must have been quite taken with the senoritas, since he

didn't even mention those fabulously lunatic Antoni Gaudí creations, the Sagrada Família, Park Güell and Casa Batlló, all of which were in existence in 1913. Although the Sagrada, which will finally be finished one of these decades, was still a modest construction when Clancy was there, compared to the soaring tribute to unbounded inspiration it is today.

In any case, he went to bed a happy man and next morning took the train back to Figueras to see how the repairs to his Henderson were coming on, only for an 'exasperatingly slow mechanic and his two ornamental assistants' to take three days for the job, leaving him with only twenty-four hours to ride the 120 miles back to Barcelona port for the boat to Algiers.

What then followed was the worst ride of the trip so far.

He set off at 5.30 p.m. on 'wretched roads' that shook him to a pulp, and by the time darkness fell at nine, he had only covered 60 miles. After an hour in which he saw neither a living soul nor a house, and now unable to see the holes and rocks in the road let alone avoid them, he fell twice, the first time smashing his light and the second almost breaking his leg.

He pressed on into the night, pushing the bike across countless rivers, until his nerve was badly shaken when the shadows at the bottom of a steep descent suddenly turned out to be a raging torrent.

'After a while I got so I didn't care – philosophically reflecting that one must die sometime and to die with one's boots on is very noble; so I rushed all the fords that came later, and surprised myself each time by reaching the other side alive. My dear old Henderson seemed to enjoy the excitement,' he wrote in his diary.

With no moon and no lamp, he had to quit at last, and found a bed for the night in the 'crumbling village of Tordera' where, watched by the entire village, he had a late supper of coffee and toast.

I wonder what he would made of the eight-lane motorway

along which we sped at 80mph, or the smooth-surfaced side roads, bright with rapeseed, that led into Tordera. Which, by the way, is still crumbling away nicely.

Eschewing coffee and toast, we sped on to Barcelona, where we proved that we could be just as stupid as the satnav. Stopping at the address it indicated and seeing no sign of the youth hostel, we asked a bevy of local girls if they knew where it was, got directions to half a mile down the street beside a large church, then rode around in circles for half an hour before we finally found the hostel 20 yards behind where we had stopped, hidden down a flight of stairs.

Piling gratefully into our ten-bed dorm, we found it occupied by a middle-aged American with a saturnine and baleful air about him.

'You English?' he growled.

'Irish,' said Peter.

'Irish! I spent three months in Dublin, and they violated my human rights and treated me like a piece of shit. Made me ashamed to be called O'Flaherty. I'm going to find me another room,' he said, gathering up his belongings and storming out.

Oh well. At least it left more room for us.

In the afternoon, we rode to the statue of Christopher Columbus in the Mirador de Colom to meet up with Adelaide director Sam Geddis and his wife Gloria.

It was an appropriate place to meet, not only because Columbus was an adventurer, but because we were also being watched over by the ghost of Clancy, since he'd stayed in a two-room apartment overlooking this very spot.

And there they were at the statue; Gloria looking immaculate as ever, since when she and Sam had ridden with us for the first three weeks of the Adelaide adventure around Oz, she'd managed, by my reckoning, to fit 4,386 changes of clothing into a single suitcase.

'Geoff, great to see you. Fancy a Magnum?' she said.

That's right, I'd forgotten: one of the rituals in the baking heat of Oz was the daily stop for a Magnum, possibly the finest ice cream bar on the planet.

'Gloria, are you mad?' I said. 'I've seen enough ice in the past fortnight to last me a lifetime.'

'Nonsense. It's a lovely day,' she said, nipping off and returning with Magnums for all.

After posing for some photos in front of the statues, Gloria and Sam nipped off to do a bit of sightseeing and I took Gary on a motorcycling tour of the sights of the city: the Sagrada Família, Casa Batlló and Park Güell, that trilogy of tributes to organic lyricism.

That night, we all met up again for a slap-up meal in Los Caracoles, the antiquated restaurant in the old quarter that Peter and I had suggested simultaneously, and after the usual argument, Sam ended up picking up the bill, as he does.

The next day was Peter's last with us, and how poignant it was to say farewell to him that morning. Not just because it also happened to be his sixtieth birthday, but because, witty, erudite, kind and endlessly enthusiastic, he had been the perfect travelling companion. Apart, perhaps, from a rich twenty-five-year-old Japanese nymphomaniac contortionist.

Before we climbed on the bikes and went our separate ways, we hesitated for a second at shaking hands, then exchanged hugs using the strict principles of the man-hug: shoulder contact only, accompanied by hearty back-slapping, then lots of talk about rugby afterwards.

And then, how glorious that feeling of threading our way through rush-hour traffic and breaking free of the city to see the open road stretching before us; and what a lot of open road there was for, since Plan A for Algeria had failed, we were on Plan BB for Bugger off from Barcelona for four long days south through Italy to catch the weekly Saturday morning sailing from Palermo to Tunis.

The plan then was to pick up the Clancy trail at the Tunisian–Algerian border and see if we could blag our way in. If not, the worst-case scenario was to get a visa when we got home, fly out to Algiers and at least retrace Clancy's route through Algeria in a hire car.

Clancy had a slightly less glorious departure from Barcelona than we did, for his days of being ripped off by the Spanish were not yet over: the next morning, he was charged a record 90 cents a gallon for fuel, almost five times what it was back home, and then when he pulled up outside the Customs office in Barcelona to get his $55 deposit back, he found it closed for a three-hour lunch break.

When they finally opened the doors again, they told him that the refunds department only worked in the morning, and in any case, he couldn't get his refund until he got signed confirmation from the captain of the ship to Algiers that the bike had been loaded.

Exasperated beyond measure, he repaired to 'the haven of refuge of all American citizens in foreign cities, Thos. Cook & Sons office', and was told that since the boat called in Spanish-owned Palma before sailing on to Algiers, he could get his deposit back there.

'With great rejoicing and hallelujahs in my heart, I finally got the machine and all my possessions on the boat, and for the first time in seeming ages, relaxed!' he noted in his diary as the boat finally steamed away from Barcelona.

In Palma, though, his troubles with Spanish bureaucracy were far from over. Finding the customs office closed, he went off and had a breakfast of eggs and coffee, then returned to be told that he couldn't get his deposit back because the office didn't have $55, and if even if it had, it would have to write to the brigand back at Le Perthus and get a reply before paying up.

'Insanity of insanities! ... I was stunned by the idiot way in which the Spanish government does business,' he railed in his diary, then, feeling somewhat better for having at least expressed his feelings to his notebook, he wandered back to the steamboat office and presented his case to an imposing official there.

The official, busy reading his newspaper, told him to come back at 11 a.m., so he went off and kicked his heels in the cathedral, and almost three hours of paperwork later, was handed back his deposit minus a $4 unexplained official fee.

His spirits restored, he boarded the boat to Algiers, and was so seasick for the entire fourteen hours of the journey that several times he wished he had died on that night ride from Figueras.

Leaving his ghost behind us for the moment, we rode north before cutting east across the bottom of France and, as we were filling up with fuel outside Narbonne, a French kid came wandering across the forecourt with baggy trousers around his knees, several gold chains, a Puffa jacket and a baseball cap worn at a rakish angle.

'Does he realise that makes him look like a dick rather than cool?' I said.

'No, man, he is getting down to some serious rap with the boyz in the hood,' said Gary. 'I know because I is Gary G and I is black.'

'Aye, right. It's your turn for fuel.'

In Nice, we found a little hotel that was a tad more pleasant than the youth hostel I stayed in during my first visit to the city, where my roommate had been a large, if friendly, rat.

Then we were riding into Monaco, where it is apparently compulsory to drive a Ferrari, a Bentley or a Rolls-Royce, although I did see a few poor people driving around in Aston Martins, wearing sunglasses so their friends didn't recognise them.

Women with foreheads as tight as snare drums walked small, yappy dogs that were just as small and yappy as they are everywhere, and even the air smelt rich, although with a slightly sour top note of tax avoidance.

In the harbour was a fleet of extravagant yachts, most of which were the size of houses and all of which seemed to be based in the Cayman Islands. Still, it was nice to see their owners getting out and about and travelling a bit, even if they were nowhere in sight – the only occupants were crew in various states of ennui.

Resisting the temptation to spend the entire trip budget on a shared coffee, we rode east, then turned south into Italy.

In Carrara, we marvelled at the great blocks of marble glistening in the roadside sun, and in Pisa we accidentally rode past the hotel we were aiming for, realised that the one we had arrived at, the Villa Kinzica, was much nicer and checked in there instead. Fabio, the Vespa-owning manager, was as young and charming as his building was old and quaint.

Resisting the kind offers of the several Senegalese gentlemen outside to sell us genuine fake Rolexes and Breitlings for 60, 40, 30 then 20 euro, we went for a *passeggiata*, or evening stroll, amusing ourselves by walking at an angle past the famous tower so that American tourists arriving by coach might think it had been straightened and go straight to the rep to ask for their money back.

The next morning, villages slumbered on the hills of Tuscany, oblivious to the passing of either time or us, and the countryside, shimmering in the hot sun with the iridescent green of spring, was so delicious that if it was a woman you would want to marry it and have its children, never mind the pain. In one rolling meadow, a girl in a yellow pullover waved, and I waved back, in a moment loved and lost.

South of Rome, an accident on the road ahead caused a mile-long tailback, but one of the great things about bikes is that you can always filter to the front, so when the cops gave the all-clear we were first away.

With the autostrada empty before us and a queue of cars and trucks coming the other way, it was like a perfect advertisement for motorcycling as we swooped and dived through bends as fast as we dared.

In the next half hour we were passed only once, by the driver of a scarlet Alfa who swept past us with a wicked grin, doing at least 130mph. As we were filling up at the next service station, a police car pulled up and the driver got out and walked over. Whoops, I thought.

'Nice bikes, guys,' he said in flawless English. 'The corners south of here are great, so enjoy them.'

We laughed, and thanked him, and half an hour down the road we saw him pulling over a driver with Swiss plates, presumably to fine him for obeying the speed limit and then send him home for being more interested in money than the important things in life, like love, beauty and who won the football last night.

We spent the night in Padula, and the next morning faced endless roadworks and diversions up winding mountain hairpins; not that it stopped the local in the white Corsa overtaking on blind corners while smoking a cigarette with one hand, talking to his girlfriend on his mobile on the other and chatting to his mates in the back. The police in the car behind were completely unconcerned.

When the road finally opened up, soaring and dipping between verdant mountains, my thoughts turned to Cate, who I always imagine is on the pillion seat, watching over my shoulder, and whose little silk bag of silver good luck charms I carry always in my right pocket on trips like this, augmented this time by a lucky silver cat from my mate Gerry.

At 2 p.m., we were on the ferry to Sicily, and by late afternoon were sweeping between the glittering sea to our right and rugged hills to the left on which the cypress trees of the mainland had given way to the palms of the Mediterranean. In the far distance, a snow-clad Etna steamed gently.

The temperature had climbed to the giddy heights of 26 degrees, and when we stopped for a drink, I swapped my heavy gloves for the pair of Italian tan leather ones I'd bought for the Delhi to Belfast adventure back in 1998.

'Those look a bit like gay cowboy gloves,' said Gary as I put them on.

'Well, if you've seen *Brokeback Mountain*, you'll know you're in for a treat later,' I said.

By now, I was completely tuned into Gary's riding style. I knew that he would always ride at least 10mph over the speed limit, and way beyond that if he could get away with it. I knew exactly when he would indicate to overtake, and knew that he would overtake everything in sight.

He was, in short, Italian, or more specifically Sicilian, as he proved when we entered Palermo during rush hour – which I wouldn't recommend for the faint-hearted – and he rode past half a mile of gridlocked cars on the wrong side of the road.

We found a little hotel called the Letizia, and after a flurry of phone calls from the man next door, a chap called Johnny rolled up on a scooter to unlock the garage so we could store the bikes there safely for the night. We parked beside the immaculate 1971 BMW R75 owned by a charming man called Antonio who then bought us a beer.

So the next time someone tells you Sicilians wake up every morning with a horse's head in the bed and another dry cleaning headache, tell them to go to Palermo immediately. Except maybe not in rush hour.

'Loved those roads today,' said Gary as we sat down for something to eat. 'You know why there are so many corners in Europe? It's because donkeys are lazy but curious, so the only way to get them to pull a cart down a road is to put a corner in it. They'll go to that corner to see what's around it, then when they see another corner, they just keep going for ever.'

The next morning, the ferry was three hours late, but we spent the time chatting to Manlio Caliri, a Sicilian biker heading for three weeks in Tunisia with two of his mates. When the ferry finally arrived, our designated seats were in a gloomy lounge filled with several families who were asleep on the floor, a crying child in one corner, and a barking dog in the other.

'Well, I'm going to listen to some music and chill out,' said Gary, plugging earphones into his iPhone.

I wrote an article for the *Sunday Times*, then went to see if I could get some cash for Tunisia and access to the wi-fi so that I could get a phone number for our hotel in Tunis to tell them we would not be there until 11 p.m., but there was no bureau de change, and the wi-fi was not working.

Then I thought of calling Cate and asking her to Google the number, but my phone battery was dead, and when I found a socket and charged it, the touchscreen refused to work, presumably as a result of the soaking in French rain, since our state-of-the-art BMW suits seemed to have a disturbing lack of ability to repel water.

I returned to our gloomy lounge to find Gary fast asleep, and felt a brief wave of annoyance at him, and a sudden tiredness that I had to organise everything. But then, what could I ask him to do? I had taken this on myself, and he was so dyslexic that he'd struggled with the visa forms and had had to delegate them to his wife Janet.

And I knew that, under the constant swearing, farting and crudity he'd learned as a teenage apprentice at the ill-fated DeLorean car factory before he became a racer, actor and now theatre and film rigger, he had a good heart and not a bad bone in his body.

A few nights earlier I'd seen how much of a problem dyslexia was to him when I found him struggling to transfer some money online to his wife at home.

'I've tried this three f**king times and it won't f**king let me,' he muttered, whacking his hand off his forehead in exasperation.

'Here, let's have a look. Where are you getting stuck?'

'At this bit, where it says enter at least four digits of the account number.'

'No, it says the last four digits.'

'Oh …'

You see, I lived in a world of words. They were my lifelong friends, and I loved their power and beauty, and their ability to conjure up an entire universe of emotions in a few well-chosen syllables. But for Gary, they were a minefield through which he walked one painful step at a time, so it was no wonder he retreated into the known world of loving his wife, his kids and motorbikes.

And farting and swearing, of course.

Anyway, if funds ran low, there was a simple solution in Gary: fit a swear box to his bike, and we'd be quids in.

Mind you, I could tell how important the securities of home were to him as, when he Skyped Janet, their sons Luke and Buddy and the dogs every evening, the strongest word that escaped was an occasional 'flip!'.

I went for a wander and found a nicer and almost deserted lounge with window seats where, suddenly, my phone mysteriously started working again.

I called Cate, and hearing her voice for the first time in weeks was a balm for my soul. She found the hotel number, and I rang them, then hauled out my own little-used iPod, listened to k.d. lang and Leonard Cohen, and all was well again in my little world.

In Tunis, our new friend Manlio was endlessly helpful in getting us through the paper trail of customs clearance and we were done in an hour.

'Thank you so much for your help,' I said as we bid him farewell. 'Italians are great: so helpful and friendly, and with such a love of life, beauty and fun.'

'Yes, Italians are good people, but our image is tainted by Berlusconi. When I say I am Sicilian, people always think Mafia, but given the choice between Mafia and Berlusconi, give me Mafia any day,' he laughed.

It was half past midnight when we finally arrived at our hotel in Tunis, so we dined heartily on the last bag of Clancy's Nuts, washed down with tap water, and finally fell gratefully into bed.

The next morning, we rode to the Algerian border in a last attempt to get a visa, only for our polite requests to be greeted with a baffled: 'Ian Paisley who?'

We stood there for a few minutes looking across the border at Algeria in much the same way as Armenians look across the border into Turkey at their sacred mountain of Mount Ararat; so near, so unattainable.

Oh well. I would give it another shot through the Algerian tourist board when I got home, even if I had a suspicion that their office might be like the complaints department in the Carlsberg advertisement: a cobwebbed room, a dusty desk and a phone that never rang.

For the moment, though, Algeria would have to wait for another day, or possibly forever, which seems like a good point to return to Clancy's arrival there.

Chapter Eight

A short history of Algeria

1000BC – 1945AD

Algeria variously occupied by Berbers, Romans, Arabs,
Ottomans and, from 1830, the French, producing an eclectic
architectural heritage and a thoroughly baffled people who at
least can comfort themselves with fresh baguettes and decent
coffee.

1945

After 115 years of repression by wealthy French settlers,
Muslims stage a march for independence. French think about
it, then kill the protesters, sparking a civil war which kills up to
a million and leaves the country in ruins.

1962

Independence. Algerians celebrate, then realise that the
wealthy settlers were the managers, civil servants, engineers,
teachers, doctors and skilled workers of the country, and they
have now fled, leaving chaos and 70 per cent unemployment.

1991

More civil war, with bombings, burnings and beheadings.

1999

New president Abdelaziz Bouteflika secures amnesty and promises peace. Algerians cross their fingers, and put on the kettle for a nice cup of coffee.

'One who does not take a motor into Algiers misses half the opportunities the colony offers for exciting adventure,' said Clancy, which must have been the understatement of the century.

First of all, scores of swarthy, bare-legged Arab boatmen swarmed up the gangplank and manhandled his Henderson ashore in spite of his protests that he could do it perfectly well himself. Then, their chief, 'a splendid, fez-capped specimen about six and a half feet high', tried to charge him twenty-five francs, or $5.

Clancy refused to pay more than five francs and, when no accord could be reached, pocketed the money and set off for his hotel. The chief followed and for the next two days, while the Henderson was being cleared through customs, he and his mob followed Clancy around the town, harassing him at every turn.

When Clancy finally got the Henderson out of customs, he grabbed at the chance to escape his antagonist, and raced off – only to have the gateway out of town blocked by the fez-capped chief. Eventually, the chiefs of police were called, decided that eight francs was enough, the matter was settled, and Clancy was free to take in his first proper impressions of Algeria.

He stayed for seventy cents a night at the Hotel Regina, which still exists as the Grand Hotel Regina, then set off east with some trepidation, since several people had told him it was not safe to travel alone.

'Still, with my ten-shot quick Savage in my hip pocket, a big new horn, the Michelin guide for my pilot and two road maps, I resolved to take the chance,' he wrote in his notebook.

Today, with Algeria in the midst of a civil war that has claimed 100,000 lives since it began in 1992, things are much the same – right down to the fact that Michelin still makes a map of the country.

The Foreign Office, of course, had warned us that if we went there we'd probably be kidnapped and shot, but then the Foreign Office probably says the same thing about Glasgow. It had certainly said the same thing about Baluchistan and Colombia, and the people I'd met when I rode through both places had been the friendliest on the planet.

In fact, I'd lost count of the people in Colombia who, when I told them I was from Belfast, said: 'Wow. Is that not really dangerous?' Then tried to sell me a Bobby Sands T-shirt.

As for Clancy, if he was expecting the burning sands of Arabia, he was in for a shock, for on leaving Algiers he was first of all frozen by a hailstorm, then doused by torrential rain which lasted all day. Forced to haul out his waterproof suit and a warm pullover, he pressed on with his tweed cap and his boots soaked through, fearing that at any minute the engine would cut out under the deluge.

But the Henderson didn't let him down and he battled on through the bad weather, not even stopping when the locals of the town of Azazga told him that the road ahead was impassable due to heavy snow. He rode on, his twin mottos of never believing what you hear and never taking anything for granted firm in his mind, and found the high pass muddy but rideable. The Azazga locals were obviously employed by the Foreign Office.

Up and up the road climbed, with the sharpest turns marked by the Touring Club of France, foaming torrents rushing down the mountain and the wind roaring and sighing through the forest as if nature's grief was inconsolable.

Rounding one corner, he came upon a group of horsemen who were as surprised at the sudden meeting as he was, and as he rode on over great bridges which spanned huge waterfalls, darkness gathered and the wind and rain doubled their ferocity, blowing out the last of his matches and leaving him creeping in pitch darkness along a road that had been dug up and never repaired. Once, mistaking a streak of snow for the road, he edged along it, only for the sound of rushing water in the gorge below to bring him to a halt inches from certain death.

Finally, aching with cold and having had nothing to eat but a sandwich at seven that morning, he saw a light glimmering in the distance, and then another, heralding the village of El Kseur.

'Never before had a village looked so good to me,' he wrote. 'And as I dried my clothes before a wood fire and drank pints of steaming coffee, I had indeed reason to be thankful.'

And reason to be proud of himself, although that wouldn't have been in his nature, for in spite of conditions which would have broken a lesser man, he had ridden 151 miles that day.

The next day, he was up early and on the road again, passing through Bougie (now Bejaïa) on his way to Sétif, the small market town which, in 1945, saw a series of widespread disturbances and killings now collectively known as the Sétif massacre.

On VE Day, 8 May 1945, about five thousand of the Muslim Algerian population of Sétif gathered to celebrate the Nazi surrender in Europe and to express their desire for independence from the French administration. Gendarmes tried to seize the banners which attacked colonial rule and there were clashes in which many of the protestors were shot.

The next five days saw a series of attacks on French settlers in the neighbouring countryside and over one hundred people were killed. After five days of chaos, French military and police restored order but then, aided by settlers, carried out a series of reprisals, lynching prisoners taken from local jails or randomly shooting Muslims – historians estimate that at least six thousand people died. Nine years later, in March 1962, a general uprising led to independence from France.

Clancy passed through the village of Kerrata without even noticing it, and at El-Ouricia, trying to get to a garage for fuel, he was pestered for money by a bunch of local boys, one of whom grabbed hold of the handlebars and would have had Clancy off had he not been dispatched with 'a lusty kick'.

On the road to Constantine, he was so impressed by the splendid Algerian roads that, for the first time on the trip, he cranked the throttle of the Henderson wide open.

'The machine leaped and tore away so fast that I could barely hang on, and the air roared by my ears so loud and the tears streamed from my eyes, so that I concluded sixty miles an hour was not what it was cracked up to be, and dropped back to a more comfortable gait,' he wrote.

After fixing a fuel leak caused by driving over a large stone, he arrived in Constantine and, exhausted after riding 165 miles that day, walked into the Grand Hotel, the first one he saw, and got a bed for the night without asking the price. He regretted it the next morning when he was charged $1 for the room, 90 cents for dinner and 45 cents for breakfast – double his usual budget.

On his way out of Constantine, Clancy crossed the Rummel Gorge over the brand new Sidi Rached viaduct, which at 336ft high and 1,467ft long was one of the largest concrete arch bridges in the world, in a town which is famous for them. Constantine is known as the City of Bridges thanks to the many impressive and picturesque bridges which connect the mountains that the city is built on – the four built over the deepest section of the river Rummel all come in at over 328ft high. The Sidi M'Cid bridge, which also opened in 1912, was the highest bridge in the world at 575ft until the Royal Gorge bridge opened in 1929 in Colorado.

Leaving Constantine and finding his horn useless at persuading slow-moving stagecoach drivers to get out of the way, he overtook one then fell off in soft sand in front of the leading horse. He was fine, but the useless horn was wrecked, making it even more useless.

He had his customs documents stamped by the French officials in the picturesque port of El Kala, ten miles west of the Tunisian frontier, where they kept him waiting an hour, but at least only charged him three cents, then told him he would have to cross the border at Aïn Babouche.

The twenty miles there led over a steep, high pass, at the top of which he found several women, with their children playing about, side by side with huge black men breaking stone by the roadside.

'Tiny donkeys driven by the older children brought the large stones from the side of the hill in woven rope baskets hung on each side, and all day long these poor, bare-legged creatures pounded away in the hot sun,' he wrote, then put his pen away for the day, and entered Tunisia.

A short history of Tunisia

814–146 BC
Region ruled by Phoenicians, who build fabulous city of Carthage.

146 BC
Romans destroy Carthage and plough salt into the ruins to make sure nothing grows again. Talk about overkill.

439 AD
Vandals arrive, vandalise everything, and are at length replaced by Byzantines, Aghlabids, Fatimids, Zirids, Almohads, Almoravids, Hafsids, Ottomans and Husaynis.

1881
French arrive and act much as in Algeria.

1956

Independence. New government takes one look at what's happening in Algeria, and starts food, house building and schools programme to create stable, educated middle class.

2010

Stable, educated middle class realise there are no jobs for them and, inspired by suicide of fruit seller Mohamed Bouazizi, revolt to start Arab Spring.

2011

President Ben Ali flees country. Watch this space.

At Aïn Babouche, the Tunisian border officials courteously stamped Clancy's documents without charge and showed great interest in the Henderson, which was the first motorbike to cross the border.

He rode to Tabarka, looking to refuel but could find none of his favourite Vacuum oil, and he only got petrol after persuading the owner of the only car in the village to siphon some from the tank.

He would not have had the same problem today, I thought, as having ridden down through Italy, got the ferry from Sicily to Tunis then picked up the Clancy trail where he crossed the border from Algeria to Tunisia, we rode past a well-equipped Shell station on our way into Tabarka, today a popular resort compared to the the sleepy backwater town it was at the time of Clancy's visit.

As we rode along the very same road that Clancy had taken from Tabarka to Tunis, there were many things that would not have changed in the hundred years that had passed.

The road itself, as good as it was a century ago, still wound its way through green hills, oak, juniper and olive groves and daisy meadows, their beauty doubled by their reflection in deep blue lakes. Dotted along the route were the same white stone distance markers, topped in red and with the kilometres marked in black. There were farmers, still ploughing their fields by horse, and donkey carts piled high with jasmine. An old man sat on the verge, wrapped in a great maroon cloak, selling chillies from the mound beside him, his battered brass scales on the ground in front of him to weigh them. The swallows overhead still dipped and soared in the eternal blue of the Tunisian sky.

As we neared Tunis at teatime, we passed a number of ancient white Peugeot pickups – there to collect the women who had been working in the fields – and several shepherds who were gathering in their flocks.

I slowed for one of them, a venerable bearded sage who looked like a slightly younger Charlton Heston, but with a wicked grin and a twist of his right hand, he indicated that I should do exactly the opposite.

At junctions, the traffic police, immaculate in petrol-blue uniforms and white caps, would either stop us for a chat or give us a cheery wave as we rolled past. Clancy would have approved, and it was all delightfully heartening, especially if your view of Tunisia is that it is the thin end of the wedge of heat, dust, noise and chaos that is Africa.

As darkness fell, we entered Tunis, described by Guy de Maupassant as the most striking and attractive town in Africa, and when Clancy emerged next morning to find what seemed like most of its 100,000 Arabs, 50,000 Israelis, 44,000 Italians, 17,000 French and 5,000 Maltese inhabitants jostling for space in the streets, he had to agree.

Wandering through the narrow, winding streets of the Arab Quarter past the barred windows of harems and with the warm air redolent with sandalwood and myrrh, he declared that here 'was the Orient in all its purity ... the Arabian Nights come true'.

The men, with their jaunty fezes, he decided, looked 'more intelligent, clean and handsome than their Algerian cousins, (probably because their many wives take better care of them),' although the few women he saw in the streets had their features hidden by 'gruesome black veils'.

Barred from the Grand Mosque by 'a sign in four languages, forbidding entrance to all not professing the Mussulman faith', he wandered off again and found himself in the souk, with richly costumed, dark bearded merchants sitting cross-legged in dozens of tiny stalls, 'sewing industriously on fine silks, working beautiful embroidery or executing delicate engravings on ivory, brass or steel'. It was the first time on the trip that he wished he was not on a motorbike and a budget, so he could buy it all and take it home.

It's a shame he didn't get into the Grand Mosque, for the following morning, as we stepped gratefully into the marble vastness of its central hall – wearing long-sleeved shirts in case the sight of our manly forearms drove the local girls into a frenzy – we found an oasis of coolness and calm from the bustle of the medina outside, whose narrow souks have changed little since Clancy's day.

In fact, as we'd stepped out of a taxi earlier at the Sea Gate – outside which the Beys once hosted daily matches between oiled Turkish wrestlers in the month before Ramadan – we'd been immediately befriended by a chap called Abdullah, whose friendship inevitably led to a visit to his brother's perfume shop and his other brother's carpet shop. He claimed that the latter was located in the king's former palace, and had a vast bejewelled bed upstairs in which the king allegedly slept with his four wives.

'Only four?' we said, and Abdullah and his brother laughed, although their laughter wore a little thin when it became obvious that we were not going to buy any carpets, 'special discount and shipping' or not, that day or any other.

The souks of the most honourable professions, such as gold, cloth and perfume, are closest to the Grand Mosque, with the noisy and less exalted ones such as dyeing and metalwork relegated to the outskirts, and somewhere in between is the ancient Souk of the Genuine Fake Watches, where we were approached by a chap called Mohammed, in his mid-forties and wearing a pullover which had seen better days.

'Forgive me, monsieur,' I said, 'but the only fool bigger than the fool who buys a fake designer watch is the fool who buys the real thing.'

'Of course, monsieur, but luckily for me, there is one born every minute,' he said, glancing at my wedding ring. 'Now, can I interest you in some jewellery or silks for your wife? My brother has a little shop just around the corner …'

On the outskirts of the medina, a street full of shops selling figs, dates and dried olives tempted Clancy with pleasures more within his means, but his motorcycle suit attracted such uncomfortable attention there that he decided to scarper. Then his plans to motor the twelve miles to the ruins of Carthage were scuppered when, instead, he spent the entire afternoon growing increasingly hot under the collar at the 'despicable Italian officials of the steamboat line to Naples' who, knowing they had a monopoly, tried to charge him $12 for a second class ticket and $20 for the Henderson as a luxury item.

Considering that the Barcelona to Algiers fare had been only $2, he was understandably outraged, and by the time he'd bargained them down to $10, he was in no mood for Carthage, particularly when he emerged from the shipping office to a torrential downpour.

Still, he didn't miss much, since there is little there to miss of the city founded by Dido, Queen of the Phoenicians, in 814BC. According to Virgil's *Aeneid*, she came home from hard days on the building site, threw off her hard hat and jumped into bed with Aeneas, sole survivor of the Greek destruction of Troy.

This is usually taken as myth nowadays, since Troy fell five centuries before Carthage rose, although it could just have been typical builders: 'Listen, Mrs Dido, I know we said three hundred years, but those architraves are a bloody nightmare.'

In any case, it grew to become the glory of Africa, until the Romans arrived in 146BC and, determined to teach those uppity Phoenicians a lesson, created a wasted land which is made all the more poignant by the sight all around it of chrysanthemums and poppies blossoming wild and, dancing in the breeze above them, goldfinches and swallowtail butterflies.

Today, virtually all we know of Carthage, the glory of ancient Africa, is that its noblest citizens sacrificed their favourite children to the god Baal, and that Hannibal left it with his elephants to cross the Alps. But all that remains of it is a little collection of self-effacing statues in a comer room of the Bardo National Museum in Tunis.

As a result, it has become the James Dean of cities, its mythical glories forged almost entirely in the crucibles of our imagination. So if we imagine it at all, we imagine it walking down a wet New York street, its collar up and a cigarette clamped between its teeth, or driving its Porsche down a sunlit road, blithely unaware that the Romans are hurtling towards the junction in a truck.

As for Clancy, he took the night boat to Italy, his hatred of the shipping line honed even more keenly when the captain told him that his fare didn't include dinner.

Chapter Nine

A short history of Italy

600BC

After general fiddling about by Etruscans and Greeks, Romans roll up their sleeves and establish an empire that lasts for almost a thousand years until Caligula starts period of decadence and decline briefly interrupted by Marcus Aurelius then continued by Commodus. See *Gladiator* for details.

5th Century

Empire finally falls. Barbarians, Byzantines, Lombards and Franks step into the breach.

1401

Renaissance started by men like Filippo Brunelleschi, who invents perspective in architecture and painting, allowing Italians to walk to the end of the street for the first time, although because of the multitude of dialects, no one can understand them. After several years of people wandering around going *'Eh?'* Tuscan dialect adopted as national language and Renaissance steps up a gear, led by chaps like Leonardo da Vinci, the original Renaissance man.

1915

Italy enters First World War totally unprepared and with outdated equipment. After the war, Italians disillusioned with debt, inflation and unrest elect Mussolini. See Hitler for details.

1941

Italy enters Second World War totally unprepared and with outdated equipment. See Jean-Baptiste Alphonse Karr for details.

2011

Prime Minister Silvio Berlusconi, seventy-six, accused of entering teenage nightclub dancer Karima El Mahroug totally unprepared and with outdated equipment. Berlusconi, realising he needs to take a more mature approach to life, then announces engagement to twenty-seven-year-old.

One of Clancy's most admirable qualities was that although he often went to bed with a grudge, he never woke up with one, and although he had been driven to distraction by the Italian shipping company ripping him off then refusing him dinner, he was so delighted by the sight of Palermo the next morning that, while the boat made a five-hour stop in the harbour he went for a wander, enjoying the brightly painted donkey carts with their elaborate Biblical motifs and the novel beauty of the cathedral.

As for us, despite how easygoing and free of hassle Tunisia had been, how pleasant it was to ride off the boat into safe, secure Sicily; and whoever thought we would say such a thing?

Today, the donkey carts of Palermo have gone, replaced by a permanent traffic jam in which drivers sit and honk their horns for hours, then give up, get out and walk home, but the cathedral is still both beautiful and novel, with the menacing turbaned statues at its entrance marking the Tunisian escapades of Charles V.

Polishing off a glass of freshly-made lemonade and happy with life again, Clancy was back on board in time for the sailing to Naples, waking next morning to the glory of its bay and the sight of Vesuvius wreathed in cloud.

But then, he was bound to love Italy, since his research had convinced him that it would be the most picturesque and historical country on his journey; a land of love, romance, beauty, architectural wonders, lakes and valleys flooded with sun or bathed in moonlight. After all, it's probably the only country in the world which could have a word like *asolare*, meaning to pass time in a delightful but meaningless way.

As I did after we took the ferry from Tunis to Palermo, then rode north towards Naples. For a while I marvelled at the way in Italy, even the meadows are art, with the trees apparently arranged just so to cast exquisite shadows as the day goes on.

I spent the rest of the journey waving cheerily at the locals and, just as I had tired myself out, we arrived at an Autogrill, our favourite Italian autostrada stop. It was coming up to 11 a.m., and we were just in time to order cappucino, since anyone asking for one after that is immediately beaten to death, in the same way that Italian mothers will leave ugly children out in the sun to die.

Outside, a sign in four languages warned, 'Attention. Distrust abusive retailers of various articles (Watches, necklaces, textiles, transistor radios etc.).' Needing none of the above and therefore free from abuse, we finished our cappuccinos and rode on up the Amalfi Coast through Sorrento and past the isle of Capri, and I defy anyone to take this route without singing 'That's Amore', even if the lyrics are gibberish. I mean, 'when the moon hits your eye, like a big pizza pie'? Honestly, Dean. You've been on those martinis again, haven't you?

In Naples, even the dirty, noisy inhabitants failed to quench

Clancy's happiness as he hopped on a tram and, in a trance, rattled past the Royal Palace, the church of San Francesco di Paola, the church of San Ferdinando and the Castel Nuovo on his way to the National Museum to gaze in wonder at relics recovered from Pompeii, Herculaneum and the Forum.

Coming from a country whose history is measured in a handful of centuries rather than millennia, his vivid imagination found joy in the smallest things, like the bunch of grapes, the charred English walnuts and a half-baked loaf of bread recovered from Pompeii – 'all carbonized into immortality, and each with its own story of the end of its world'.

The loaf, the walnuts and the grapes are still there, and still looking almost good enough to eat, even though they're 1,934 years past their sell-by date, but how strange it felt to stand there in my own boots on the very spot on which Clancy had all those years ago. He would, I hope, have approved of mine, for they were in the same timeless vein as his: a pair of Altberg Clubman's Classic boots for the gentleman motorcyclist, with a single buckle at the top of each.

As for Naples, it was as dirty, noisy, crime-ridden and lovable as it was in Clancy's day. In Garibaldi Square, it is said that, at any one time, one in three of the occupants are major criminals, and the other two haven't been caught yet, and the Neapolitans will tell you with some pride that the street urchins will unscrew your car number plate at one set of traffic lights and sell it back to you at the next. It actually happened to a friend of a friend of theirs, in fact.

To get to the city, you drive through countryside where more escaping British prisoners of war were caught than in any other European country. Their home-made suits had fooled the Germans, but the Italians took one look and knew that not even Germans could dress that badly.

And when you get into the city, you emerge at the end of every street surprised to be alive, thanks to the fact that at any given moment a Fiat 500, Vespa, pedestrian or crazed dog will leap out in front of you without warning. It would be far too uncool, of course, for any of them to have even glanced in the direction of the oncoming traffic.

The last time I was there, I was shown around by a guide called Antonio who, with his shaven head, luminescent green eyes and slightly pointed ears, looked like the result of a night of unexpectedly illogical passion between Sinead O'Connor and Mr Spock.

'It's a bit unfair the way the city is perceived,' he told me. 'No matter what its social and political problems are, it had a very cultured and civilised reputation until after the Second World War.'

Sadly, my concentration on his subsequent eulogy about the city's moral worth was disturbed at that stage by the sight of a passing pigeon so devoid of self-worth that it had given up flying and was hitching a lift on top of a bus.

'Of course, you must be careful with your belongings when walking around,' Antonio had continued. 'It's understandable – we have a large number of unemployed people, and they can't eat air. But since Antonio Bassolino was elected as mayor in 1993, things have become much better in the city. For example ...'

Tragically, what he had been about to say – that Bassolino had cleaned up the city centre, dealt effectively with its traffic problem and was tackling the stranglehold of organised crime – was drowned out by a group of well-dressed businessmen nearby shouting at each other at the tops of their voices while waving their arms around so extravagantly that it could only be a matter of time before one of them took off and rammed one of the few pigeons who still bothered flying in Naples.

'What are they arguing about?' I'd asked Antonio.

'They are not arguing. They are discussing last night's football match,' he'd said over a constant racket of honking horns and policemen blowing whistles at Swiss motorists who had actually stopped for a red light rather than, like local drivers, accelerating through it.

Like Clancy, we rode south for a few miles and took refuge in the cypress glades of what was once Pompeii, where he paid 60 cents admission and, armed with a local guidebook and a well-thumbed copy of Edward George Bulwer-Lytton's *Last Days of Pompeii*, fought off a horde of guides offering to show him around for a mere $20.

Indeed, I shared with Clancy a soft spot myself for Bulwer-Lytton, the best-selling Victorian penny novelist, since, like Snoopy, I had always wanted to start a book with 'It was a dark and stormy night' as Bulwer-Lytton had in his 1830 novel, *Paul Clifford*. I can now say that I have finally succeeded, as you may have noticed.

Only time, and possibly Snoopy, will tell if I have gone on to do better than Edward, since the rest of *Paul Clifford* was so bad that there is now a Bulwer-Lytton competition to find the worst opening sentence to a novel in the world.

Ironically, along with 'the great unwashed' and 'the pen is mightier than the sword', Bulwer-Lytton also coined the phrase 'the pursuit of the almighty dollar', the very thing from which Clancy was escaping when he set off on his adventure. But Clancy's time at Pompeii had left him rattled and, as he emerged in a dream from the city of death into modern life again, his thoughts turned to home, and he found himself wondering what New York would look like two thousand years from now.

I'm not surprised he was shaken, for Pompeii is astonishing. Although 20,000 people lived there, after several days of ominous rumblings from Mount Vesuvius most of them had scarpered, and it was only the city's 2,000 optimists, who had put the noise down to indigestion, and were in any case reluctant to leave a town containing twenty-five brothels, who were left.

What the eruption in 79AD did leave behind, apart from 18,000 smug pessimists, was the world's most perfectly preserved

Roman town, buried under 27 feet of soft ash which, like an early neutron bomb, killed the people and saved the buildings.

And happily, the optimists did not die in vain, because even their most gloomy counterparts today are bound to be astonished by Pompeii, with its almost complete forum, basilica, baths with detailed stucco and frescoes, its streets of shops staffed by Greek slaves, its amphitheatre, gymnasium and stadium where Gladiators II v Barbarians Thirds would draw capacity crowds every week.

You cannot help but be astonished – by its scale, by its beauty, by the spooky feeling as you round every corner that you will come face to face with a fully armed centurion, looking just as surprised as you do. But there are no living people in Pompeii today, apart from the tides of tourists who ebb and flow. There are just the plaster casts of the bodies caught as they swam or napped, or curled up to escape the fatal rain of ash.

There is a woman clutching her child, and another her valuables, and although the faces of some are contorted in agony, others have the strangely peaceful expression which can only be gained from the sort of optimism which takes the rumbling of a volcano as a spot of indigestion.

In any case, it was time for us to leave for Rome, since Vesuvius, apparently the only volcano in the world designed by Germans, has erupted with clockwork regularity since it buried Pompeii and was just about to pop again, as a result of which a team of scientists monitor it twenty-four hours a day.

We tootled down the autostrada, found our way into Rome, and were pleasantly surprised to find the drivers there a lot more civilised than in Naples. At the first set of traffic lights in the centre, a man who looked exactly like Sir Anthony Hopkins, although it probably wasn't him, amused the waiting drivers by heading a football continuously for the two minutes the lights were at red, then bowed and collected a handful of change and a round of applause which was rapidly replaced by a cacophony of horns when the drivers behind got fed up with being amused and decided they needed to be at the next red light five seconds ago.

At length we rolled up outside a hotel called Fawlty Towers, run by two young Romans with a sense of humour. Well, it had to be done, and in my defence, all I can say is that I once rode 120 miles out of my way while in Alaska to see a place called Chicken, then rode even further to find Gobblers Knob, even though there was nothing there except a sign, a raven and the world's most outside toilet.

Sadly, Fawlty Towers was full, and the two young chaps who ran it said it would be absolutely impossible to find a room in a hotel anywhere in Rome on a weekend in April. Naturally, we found one at the hotel next door.

As we were unloading the bikes, a local man pulled up on a dusty Africa Twin and came over for a chat. 'Nice bikes, guys, although I prefer mine for off-roading,' he said. 'What are the wheels on those?'

'The back's 17 inches, and the front's 19,' said Gary.

'Hang on,' I said, 'does that mean the back wheel goes around faster and overtakes the front?'

'Aye, and it's happened to me several times.'

Clancy, meanwhile, had left the Henderson in Naples and hopped on the express train for the four-hour journey to Rome after declaring the roads in Italy too wretched to even consider motorcycling because of the huge, square slabs left behind by the Romans and the dust which, when it was dry, clogged up the engine, and when wet turned to treacherous mud.

He would have been slightly surprised by the volume of traffic today, in a country whose government boasts a fleet of 629,000 official cars, ten times as many as the US government. And he would have been stunned to see the amount of motorbikes in Rome, from burbling Moto Guzzis through snarling Ducatis to the squadrons of buzzing Vespas.

To be honest, we should have parked the Beemers and gone exploring on a Vespa, but Gary would have wanted to be Gregory Peck and I refused to be Audrey Hepburn.

Surprised to find the ancient Rome of his dreams now a bustling modern city, Clancy made straight for the Forum, which he found packed with 'Americans of the noisy tourist type', all being ripped off by guards who would only brush sand off to reveal the floor mosaics when paid.

Finding the Palatine Hill surrounded by an iron fence, and not wanting to look for another brigand to fleece him, he remembered he was still young and simply climbed over it. Mission accomplished, he then ticked off St Peter's Basilica, the Colosseum and a night at the opera, where he was surprised at how small the audience and how bad the acting was, but delighted to find the singing much better than back home.

He was lucky: the last time I was in Rome, I found myself one night by accident at the Fantasie Theatre, where on stage several chaps in drag and women in authentic polycotton peasant costumes were singing a medley of Italian marching opera, folk, and pop songs to an audience which consisted entirely, apart from me, of Japanese people politely chewing salami.

It was so surreal that the only answer was to drink several glasses of wine very quickly and slide under the table, as all around members of one of the most ancient, civilised nations in Asia, who had abandoned their spiritual inheritance for a pair of Gucci loafers and a Burberry scarf, watched as members of one of the most ancient, civilised nations in Europe, who had abandoned their cultural inheritance for a pair of yellow stockings and brown velvet knickerbockers, belted out 'O Sole Mio' into a Sony microphone.

St Peter's impressed Clancy more as a beautiful, rich place than as a house of worship, and it still seems like a monumental tribute to man's sense of his own importance and far removed from the humility of Christianity's roots.

Today, to get in you have to pass through airport-style scanners which presumably remove all traces of Protestantism, and inside, the opulence is as stunning as Clancy found it. Almost as stunning, and since Clancy doesn't mention it we can only hope he was spared it, is a souvenir shop where the Italians' normally impeccable sense of style has momentarily deserted them.

Here, you can buy everything from 3ft high plastic virgins to holograms which turn from Jesus to Mary and back again.

From far above, if you listen, you can hear God weeping quietly.

That aside, the thing that still impresses me about Rome, even after several visits, is the sheer scale of the public buildings such as St Peter's and the Colosseum. Even the bare statistics are mildly mindboggling: to build the Colosseum, 70,000 Hebrew slaves hauled 50,000 cartloads of pre-cut stone from the quarries at Tivoli, 17 miles away. When they weren't singing, that is.

When it was completed (in a remarkably nifty eight years), there was room for 70,000 spectators, and it was so well designed that they could all enter and be seated in minutes for the celebratory games which lasted one hundred consecutive days.

At the equally impressive Vatican, we'd hoped for a private audience with the Pope, but in spite of mentioning our special relationship with Ian Paisley Jnr, we were turned away as peremptorily by the Swiss guards as we had been by the Algerian border police. Honestly. Your dad calls the Pope the Antichrist once, and they never let you forget it.

As for Clancy, he left Italy with both longing and regret that he had not studied more of its history and learned the language so that he could have appreciated it more. Although, it's doubtful that either could have compensated for his main regret: that the Italians were an unattractive people who were only amiable and obliging after he'd satisfied their endless desire to wring every last penny out of him.

We could empathise: in one day alone, autostrada tolls cost us €140, not to mention another €98 to fill the bikes with fuel, although with the big 33-litre tanks on our Adventure versions of the GS, that had got us over 300 miles on a tank.

All in all, as we came to the end of the European and African leg of the trip, the bikes had proved perfect workhorses, so reliable that we hadn't once needed to put air in the tyres.

The only real fault had been a seat that was fairly hard on the buns after long days in the saddle, but that was nothing that couldn't be cured by taking a break after an hour and a half.

The Rallye 3 jacket and trousers, meanwhile, were really well designed in terms of comfort, pockets, zips and vents, but remarkably unwaterproof for such expensive kit. Not that we or Clancy needed to worry about rain for a bit.

His original plan had been to sail to India and ride across it to Calcutta and then on to China through Shanghai, and he had already gone as far as getting an estimate of $12 for crating the bike and $14 for shipping it from Naples to Bombay. But then he met an Englishman in Naples who had lived in India for ten years and who had told him that crossing India by motorbike would be absolutely impossible, with few roads, bridgeless rivers, prostrating heat, dangerous fevers and petrol only available 300 miles apart, which was twice the range of the Henderson even with spare cans on board.

Dismissing a crossing of Turkey into Persia as impossible, presumably because of the First Balkan War in the former, he decided to sail to Ceylon (modern-day Sri Lanka) and travel up to Madras (modern-day Chennai) and back for a taste of India.

Decision made, he headed for the Naples docks filled with sadness that, because he was running low on money, he couldn't afford to buy the cheap coral jewellery and kid gloves on sale everywhere as presents for the folks back home.

You can imagine his despair, then, when he arrived at the docks and discovered that, rather than being crated, his Henderson had been left sitting outside all week.

Then, when he went to buy a third-class ticket to Ceylon at the North German Lloyd's office, the manager charged him a whopping $95 for the two-week sailing, then refused to accept his American Express traveller's cheque.

Through the intervention of the American consul and the kindness of Thomas Cook & Son, who cashed the cheque, he finally got his ticket, walked up the gangplank of the *Lutzow*, and watched the Henderson being swung aboard.

In the end his troubles in getting the bike to the Far East were minor compared to ours: after contacting every shipping company in the known universe to try to get them to ship the bikes to Sri Lanka then on to Kuala Lumpur and Japan, then from Japan to San Francisco and from New York back to the UK, I'd begun to think it might be simpler to leave the bikes in Belfast for the grand leaving and arriving ceremony and just buy two round the world tickets, ask BMW if they could just provide a set of matching bikes with stickers in each country en route, or dismantle the bikes and post them by FedEx.

In the end, since the only riding Clancy had done in the Far East due to lack of roads was in Sri Lanka and Japan, our simplest and cheapest solution had been to ship the BMWs to LA at the end of the European and north African legs, and rent or borrow bikes in the Far East so that at least we stayed true to the spirit of following his route.

Still, at least the fish curry on our Sri Lankan Airlines flight to Colombo was better than Clancy's daily diet on the *Lutzow* – a breakfast of pork and potatoes, washed down by 'wretched coffee', was followed by lunch of soup, pork and potatoes, and supper of pork, potatoes and tea. All of which, he noted carefully, tasted more or less of sawdust.

Bereft of fine dining, he entertained himself by playing whist, losing a shilling after betting a Scotsman that his cabin mate could get out through a porthole, only for the man to get stuck halfway, and buying a pith helmet when the ship made a stop in Port Said.

And so, as the *Lutzow* slid down the Suez Canal and into the Indian Ocean, and he stood on deck of an evening admiring the flying fish and the increasingly astonishing sunsets, with all the colours of the spectrum shimmering on the calm water like a rare oil painting, Carl Stearns Clancy slowly turned his back on the grey clouds of a Europe preparing for war, and turned his face towards the fantastic, unknown Orient.

Chapter Ten

A short history of Sri Lanka

Mythical version
Waves of immigrants arrive from northern India in fifth century BC.

Real story
Islanders descended from result of one night stand between lion and northern Indian princess in sixth century BC. Princess gives birth to twins, but one, Prince Vijaya, grows up to be such a pain that he and seven hundred of his mates are banished to the island to found Sinhalese nation centred on the great city of Anuradhapura.

300 BC
Buddhism adopted by Sinhalese. Er, apart from Queen Anula who, during her five-year reign from 47–42 BC, marries then murders thirty-two husbands.

67 AD
Sinhalese royals start vast irrigation projects which transform arid plains into fertile land, leading to almost a thousand years of peace and prosperity until Anuradhapura is destroyed by Tamil invaders from India in 993.

1497

Portuguese fleet ends up on the island after being blown off course, is welcomed warmly by the natives, and responds by taking over.

1602

King Dharma Suriya invites Dutch captain Sebald de Weert around for drinkies to see if he fancies helping him get rid of the Portuguese. Sebald offers the king a tour of his ship. King says he doesn't want to leave queen alone. Sebald, slightly tipsy, says from what he's heard about the queen, she won't be alone for too long, and gets hacked to death for his trouble.

1658

Having learned some manners, Dutch return and seize island to control lucrative trade in spices, elephants and pearls, although not all in same shopping basket.

1794

With Netherlands looking the other way due to war with France, British nip in, take over the island, establish coffee then tea plantations and, in 1942, Lord Mountbatten's base for Asian war operations.

1948

Independence, followed by the usual civil war after Sinhalese Prime Minister Sirimavo Bandaranaike, the world's first female PM, deports half a million Tamils.

2002

Ceasefire.

2004

Tsunami devastates island. Huge international appeal raises millions of dollars, most of which disappears.

2008

After four years, government decides to ban anyone from living within 100m of the sea to avoid future disasters. Anyone with money bribes officials and ignores ban. Civil war restarts, then ends in 2009.

As our plane arced south-east through the night on its way to Colombo, the stewardess flitted about in a peacock-bright sari, dispensing food, wine and goodwill to all and sundry. With her wide smile and tiny pointed ears, she looked like an exquisitely surprised elf.

At noon, having had our fill of wine, food and general goodwill, we caught the first sight of the island which has been likened by travellers to a teardrop or a pearl at the southern tip of India, and by those romantic Dutch to a leg of ham.

At first there was only the deep aquamarine of the ocean, then an endless golden strip of beach, and beyond that the verdant smack of jungle punctuated by the terracotta roofs of colonial-style bungalows.

In the tenth century the island was called Serendip, and it was the setting for the Persian fairy tale, *The Three Princes of Serendip*, in which the heroes repeatedly discovered things they had not been seeking. It is from this story that we get the word serendipity, the art of happy coincidences, and indeed we had experienced one of those ourselves thanks to Grant Johnson at the bike adventure site Horizons Unlimited who put us in touch with Alfons van Hoof, a Belgian ex-teacher who was going to take a few days off from his job as a freelance translator and show us around.

As we stepped off the plane, the pre-monsoon air was so hot and moist that even breathing was close to an erotic experience, but since the only potential candidates for consummation were each other, Gary and I collected our bags and a minute later were shaking hands with Alfons, whose father had travelled all over the world as a cellist with a cruise line orchestra, then died suddenly at sixty when Alfons was only eight.

'We were just having dinner one evening when he said he didn't feel very well, then sat down on the couch and died of a stroke five minutes later,' Alfons told us.

In any case, he'd already inherited his father's wanderlust, travelling all over the Far East, until he arrived in Sri Lanka in 2000, fell in love with the country and a local woman in that order, and stayed.

'Although she did present me with a few surprises along the way,' he said as he hailed a passing tuk-tuk. 'When I met her, she had a six-year-old daughter, then after we got married two older ones appeared, and now I have six kids I didn't have before.'

He bargained the tuk-tuk driver down from a price that was Absolutely Ridiculous to Only Slightly Ridiculous for Foreigners, then jumped on his Bajaj 125 and led the way through streets which were like a more relaxed and less crowded and chaotic version of India.

Alfons had offered to lend Gary his spare Bajaj, so we made our way to his house, then to a bike shop to rent another one for me, then to a pleasant guest house a short walk from the beach in Negombo, a seaside resort about twenty-five miles north of Colombo.

All in all, we'd done slightly better than Clancy, who had stepped ashore in Colombo with scarcely a penny to his name, since his letters to the *Motorcycle Review* asking for payment for his articles had either disappeared in transit or vanished into the bowels of the magazine's accountancy department. He was then confronted by customs officials demanding to know if he had any liquor, tobacco or firearms in his suitcase.

Since his Savage automatic was in his hip pocket, he was honestly able to tell them that he had not, and stepping into a rickshaw, was borne to the Globe, a favourite watering hole of expats and the cheapest hotel in town, at which he arranged a line of credit for a room at $1.65 a day, including meals.

That night, sitting on the hotel verandah with the palm trees swaying in the warm, aromatic air, the sun sinking to the ocean and with a large lizard at his feet eating a moth in instalments, Clancy fell in love with the tropics. Even when he almost tripped over a beetle the size of a baby elephant, it was not enough to darken his mood, and after dispatching it with a well-aimed shoe, he retired happily to bed.

And if he had dined like a pauper on board the *Lutzow*, he feasted like a prince in the Globe, for he was woken at 6.30 a.m. by a boy with 'early tea for master', followed by breakfast at 10.30, tiffin at 1.30, afternoon tea at 4.30, dinner at 7.30 and supper from 9 to 12. Except for afternoon tea and supper, all were seven-course meals, most of which involved heaps of curry so hot he thought it would have been more appropriate to Iceland, washed down with lashings of lemonade or lime and soda.

Since the Globe is long gone, possibly as a result of feeding its customers six meals a day for $1.65, that evening we met Alfons and a couple of Dutch friends, Hans and Henk, at a little restaurant by the beach for lashings of beer and that well-known Sri Lankan delicacy, lasagne.

'I thought something Italian might make up for your disappointment in not meeting the Pope,' said Alfons by way of explanation.

As we sat down to eat on the patio, thunder rolled across the city and great, warm drops of rain came plummeting onto the courtyard with such ferocity that it was difficult to tell where they ended and their splashes began.

'Here,' said Gary, 'whose stupid idea was it to come to Sri Lanka at the start of the monsoon season?'

'Possibly the same person whose idea it was to leave Belfast in the worst snow in living memory,' I said, catching sight of the culprit reflected in the restaurant window.

'So how did you get into biking, Alfons?' said Gary, changing the subject in the nick of time.

'It's a weird story,' said Alfons. 'When I was at university in Antwerp, I got a scholarship to Santa Cruz in California, so I flew to LA, got a car for $20 on one of those one-way delivery schemes, then got lost in the worst part of LA after dark and ended up in a street where all the lights were broken and all the shops boarded up.

'Suddenly I saw lights about a mile away, and when I got closer I saw it was a pub. I pulled up to ask for directions, all these Hell's Angels piled out and swarmed around the car, and I thought they were going to kill me.

'Instead, they led me to the freeway, invited me back for a rideout the following week, lent me a Harley Sportster, then let me keep it for the three months I was there, so the moment I got home, I bought one, and I've been a biker ever since.'

To celebrate such a story, the least we could do was drink more beer as the lightning scorched the ocean, leaving a faint whiff of sulphur, the rain poured down and a large green frog sat in a puddle beside the table, regarding us with a mournful air.

With Clancy's stomach as full as ours, if not with lasagne, his wallet followed suit two days later with a cablegram bearing the news that he was back in funds.

'It was wonderful what a store of inspiration and courage came with the feeling of money in my pocket again, and the knowledge that the confidence of the powers at home continued,' he wrote in his diary, then took a rickshaw to the docks to get his Henderson.

Only to find that the Lloyd's office in Naples had charged him $30 for shipping the bike rather than the $14 agreed, and the only way he could get the machine released was to pay up. The manager of the Colombo Lloyd's office agreed that this was absolutely outrageous, but there was nothing he could do – then charged him another $3 for unloading it.

He was then directed to the customs office, where he was greeted by a lanky Englishman with the words, 'Are you in the habit of keeping your hat on in a gentleman's office?'

'Yes, sometimes,' said Clancy, annoyed at the man's insolence on top of Lloyd's endless greed.

After a stony silence, Clancy told the Englishman, who turned out to be the Chief of Customs, that he was there to get his Henderson cleared, after which the Chief thawed enough to waive duty on the bike.

Although Clancy was later told, during a visit to the American Vice-Consul, that British feeling against American products on the island, especially motors, was downright hostile, he was delighted to find such a healthy motorbike culture there. A dozen makes were sold in Colombo, and everywhere he rode, he was stopped and asked: 'Isn't this the Round-the-World Henderson?'

The president of the city's motorcycle club helped him sign a deal to sell Hendersons in the biggest car showroom on the island, and he celebrated by fitting his own with a new pair of Goodyear tyres and bidding a genuinely sad farewell to the ones which had carried him through seven European and two African countries with only three punctures.

I knew how he felt. Your head tells you that things like motorbikes and tyres are inanimate objects, and yet I'd been almost in tears when I walked away from Tony the Tiger, the Triumph that had got me all the way from Chile to Alaska in 2006. Never mind the state I was in when I finally threw out my Timberland deck shoes after thirty-one years. I'd had the soles replaced four times and the uppers twice, but they were the best pair of shoes I ever owned.

Having got his tyres sorted, Clancy was free to pass judgement on the high caste Sinhalese. With 'a queer pointed circular comb' in their long hair and their skirts and bare legs, it was very difficult to tell the men from the women, he decided, before concluding: 'Their manners are very effeminate and childish, too, but they often have attractive faces, appear far more intelligent than the Arab, but are almost as lazy.'

The lower class and darker-skinned Tamils, by contrast, were much stronger and more industrious, with girls often seen carrying bricks to and from building sites through an assorted populace of Muslim jewellery dealers, Hindus, Moors, Buddhist priests and other classes who painted their faces red, white and black.

Following Sri Lankan independence in 1948, the Tamils experienced decades of institutionalised discrimination. When their anger finally erupted, the country was plunged into a civil war that lasted for over twenty-seven years. But while the war may be over, you can still see the tension on many Tamil faces and their looks of vague disgruntlement. Perhaps they agree with Clancy's summary of a century before: that the Sinhalese, who are mostly traders or civil servants, are lazy and effete, while the Sinhalese believe in turn that the Tamils are little more than coolies.

Clancy, having praised and damned an entire population in a few lines, climbed on his Henderson and motored through the 'fascinating but odorous' Pettah bazaar district, across the great Victorian bridge and off on the jungle road, dodging naked children, small alligators and large bullock carts.

All around him was a new world: he passed native huts of bamboo and plaited palm almost indistinguishable from their surroundings and paddy fields being ploughed by water buffalo. He rode through Veyangoda – then a busy coconut and plumgado centre of five thousand people – and on to Kegalla, where he was forced to buy a gallon of fuel for 85 cents, evaporation from the furnace-like heat having put paid to his normal consumption of 60 miles to the gallon.

By comparison, the BMWs had settled down to a nice steady 48mpg, at an average speed of just over 50mph for the trip so far, including both that short stretch in Palermo of 0.0000000001mph and Gary's one attempt to find the top speed of the GS, topping out at over 120mph, although he would like me to point out to BMW and any traffic policemen who might be reading this that it was on a closed road.

In any event, we were going a lot slower the next morning when we rode south to Colombo, which rated about 8 out of 10 on the Naples scale of traffic chaos, but had the added twist of taking place in what felt like a Turkish bath.

As we were carefully dodging assorted tuk-tuks, bicycles, about four billion scooters, give or take a few, taxis and huge gaudy Tata trucks emblazoned with comforting slogans like God is Great, Praise Allah, Buddha is a Jolly Fat Fellow and, possibly most comforting of all, Fully Insured, a man on a Honda 250 pulled alongside me.

'Pardon me, sir, would you like to rent a motorcycle?' he asked.

'Er, I already have one,' I said hesitantly, not wanting to state the obvious.

'No, no, I can rent you a much better one for Colombo traffic, only 10 dollars a day.'

'You're okay, thanks.'

'Oh well, never mind. Tell me, what is your name, your profession and your home?'

'Mohammed Singh, clothing exporter, Amritsar,' I said.

'Oh, you are jesting me, sir. You look more like Hindu to me,' he laughed, and sped on.

Shortly after, I paid the price for jesting him when I almost ran into a young scooterist in a well-pressed white shirt.

'But sir, you were indicating right and you turned left,' I said.

'I am so sorry, but I was not intending to,' he said, and we went our separate ways.

Shortly after, the road was blocked by truck drivers protesting about a planned increase in fuel prices, but since no one noticed the difference between the road being blocked and the normal situation, they gave up after a while and went back to work.

We found Victoria Bridge, but it was a modern concrete replacement rather than the ornate wrought iron structure Clancy rode over, although the slum dwellers of Ferguson Road, washing their clothes in the sluggish brown waters of the river below, were probably in much the same state of optimistic penury as a century ago.

The Pettah bazaar was just as fascinating as when Clancy was there, give or take a mobile phone shop and internet café or two, and possibly less odorous, but the tall neoclassical building which once housed the Globe was now an empty shell inside a complex housing a naval barracks.

Since the president was paying a visit when we arrived, it was sealed even tighter than the Algerian border, so we drove to the Automobile Association to get our Sri Lankan licences.

Inside, the billiards room was in full swing, and a pleasant lady in a pink smock sitting at a desk surrounded by bound ledgers relieved us of 5,400 rupees, or about 35 quid, then made out our licences on a manual typewriter.

Since the licence was for a year and we only needed it for four days, it was a bit of a rip-off, but then Clancy would have empathised, having been ripped off in not only Colombo, but pretty much everywhere else so far.

Still, satisfied that we could now have accidents with impunity, we took the old road out of town that Clancy would have ridden, along the canal and past venerable colonial mansions, their pastel facades dappled by the shade of jacarandas and bougainvilleas.

The next morning, we had planned to set off with Alfons on

the Clancy trail around the island, but were awakened by a clap of thunder so alarming I feared the windows would break.

As we were sitting in our room after a hearty breakfast of white toast washed down by Nescafe with powdered milk, Alfons arrived with his wife Shama and their impossibly beautiful daughter Asha, who looked sixteen but was, in fact, thirty-four.

'Here,' said Gary, 'I can't get my adaptor to work in this socket.'

'Did you buy a worldwide one?' I said.

'What's that?'

'It's one that you'd use for going around the world, dickhead.'

'Well, how would I know? I've never been around the world before.'

He had a point, and shortly after, the universe got its own back on me when my adaptor disintegrated and Alfons had to give me a spare one he had with him.

We sat and waited, with the rain hammering so loudly on the roof that we were reduced to miming conversations, as if we were characters in a production of *The Undersea World of Jacques Cousteau* directed by Marcel Marceau.

At noon, it cleared slightly, if only to the extent that we could now hear each other, and we set off.

Before long, the road climbed out of the suburbs and wound up into dank, dripping jungle interspersed with paddy fields, although the road was so flooded in places that it was impossible to tell where it ended and the fields began.

In some of the fields, a bedraggled and sodden rice farmer could be seen working away, watched over by a squadron of white egrets, the raindrops hanging from the end of their beaks exactly in the shape of their country.

At half past one, the rain dithered and then stopped, and with appropriate serendipity we found a little roadside café serving delicious rice, dhal, breadfruit, chicken curry and a salad in which lurked hidden and deadly green chillies.

And then, as we tucked in, we caught sight of our first elephants; though admittedly they were only pink plastic ones which were hanging from a stall across the road that was doing a roaring trade in boiled maize for tuk-tuk drivers.

A little further on, gangs were rebuilding the road, so we sat patiently waiting for the tailback to clear, like the good Buddhists we were. When it finally did, the ecumenical scene was made complete when a Hindu cow came wandering at leisure across the road, and the Christians and Muslims were forced to wait for it as well.

'What to do?' said Alfons, in that catch-all Sri Lankan expression that can mean everything from 'There is nothing we can do' through 'We are all doomed' to 'It's time for a beer', although the last two are interchangeable.

Naturally, just as we continued, the rain started again, and got heavier. At the sides of the road women dressed as brightly as birds of paradise sheltered under umbrellas, waiting for the ancient rattling bus that plied this route.

Above their heads at one stop, a row of fruit bats hung from the telephone wire, waiting for an urgent call from Colombo on when the mangos were due to ripen.

As the road twisted and turned up the Kadugannawa Pass towards Kandy, from time to time we passed hamlets clinging to the mountainside, each of them specialising in pottery, jewellery or rattan chairs, and each one with its tea shop, one wittily named Thirst Aid Station.

In one, the entire stock of the village store seemed to consist of Munchee biscuits, faded boxes of 35mm film and, if the even more faded sign outside was to be believed, American Express travellers' cheques.

Climbing the same switchbacks, Clancy was rewarded with a view of the rugged mountains behind him, and across the valley a great waterfall thundering into space. It thundered still, and I wasn't a bit surprised, on its current diet of torrential showers.

As we climbed and climbed, I was yet again filled with admiration for how Clancy had ridden these roads when they were nothing more than rutted dirt and mud, on a heavy, underpowered machine with one gear, no front brake and only a handful of horses to fling at the hills.

At a fork in the road about twenty miles from Kandy, we asked an old man selling cinnamon if we were on the right road.

'I do not know, sirs. I have never been there,' he said.

When Clancy finally reached it, he found a picturesque lake bordered by restful hotels and luxuriant foliage, and checked into a small native hotel called the Kings, where a travelling English circus troupe tried to steal his US flag for a laugh.

As we reached the outskirts of town, the sun came out, and we celebrated with a stand-up lunch in a bakery whose delights included, 'buddy bread, colour bread, fancy loaf, milk bread, short bread, soft bread, special bread, spinach bread and carrot bread', or if your tastes ran to something more exotic, a choice of 'chocolate, butter, fruit, French café, eggless, fondent (sic), ribbon, banana or Nescafe cake'.

Across the street, one shop advertised pantry furniture and the one next door, quality beds from the Sheraton Hotel in Dubai, which must rank pretty close to genuine fake watches as a selling point.

And Kandy may be Sri Lanka's second city, but there was still an elephant wandering down King Street carrying half a tree in his trunk. Even if he was being passed by a Hummer with tinted windows.

Although that is the street in which Clancy's native hotel stood, there is no indication today of where it was, so we motored on and rounded a corner to be greeted by the lake, cradled by terraces of graceful white buildings rising into the forested hills all around.

It was a stunning setting, blessed even more by the sight of families strolling or boating, chaps playing tennis on the lakeside courts, or couples courting on park benches under giant umbrellas bought specifically for that purpose.

After a change of clothes and a spot of tiffin, in the cool of the afternoon Clancy backtracked to Peradeniya, the gardens of a royal palace dating back to the fourteenth century transformed into 150 acres of botanical garden in 1821 by the enterprising Governor Edward Barnes, who also planted the island's first tea trees three years later.

Giddy with the variety of trees, plants, bamboo and water lilies, Clancy was most impressed by the giant fruit bats, either flapping languidly overhead in scores, or hanging like shrouds from the trees, filling the air with the deep hum of their constant cries.

However, those could have just been the moans of hangovers, since as he noted in his diary, they were partial to a diet of palm wine from the vessels set to catch the flowing sap, as a result of which they were almost permanently bat-arsed.

Today, the bats were recovering from a Saturday night binge, the gardens were full of Sunday crowds, and the range of trees, flowers and shrubs was every bit as remarkable as Clancy found it.

As he was admiring the world's most alcoholic bats, he was approached by an English rubber planter who had spotted the Henderson parked near the entrance. The planter, who was in the city recovering from malaria caught in Malaya, was a keen motorcyclist, so early the next morning the two men set off on the Henderson heading for the Dalada Maligawa, or Temple of the Tooth.

This temple is allegedly the last resting place of one of the Buddha's molars, rescued from his cremated remains in 543 BC. Stolen by the Portuguese in the sixteenth century, pounded to dust and scattered to the sea, it then magically reassembled itself and flew to Kandy, where it has remained since 1592.

Listen, if you have to ask, you don't get it, okay? Next you'll be telling me Santa doesn't exist.

Since the tooth is only on show every five or ten years, Clancy had to take the word of the locals that it was at least seven inches long, although Bella Sidney Woolf, who saw it in 1914, described it as 'discoloured ivory at least three inches long', which suggests that for the forty-nine days the Buddha sat under the Bo tree he was waiting, not for enlightenment, but a dental appointment.

It may well be as much a fake as the four and a half billion genuine pieces of the cross from Calvary in circulation, and Mohammed's genuine beard clippings in Topkapi in Istanbul, but that didn't stop Clancy finding hundreds of penitents prostrate before the altar in which it was kept; a process possibly almost as pointless as the woman he found downstairs devoutly praying to a rude sketch of a rabbit on an outside wall.

Sadly, in spite of some dedicated searching in the dripping heat, I am sorry to report that I completely failed to find the rude rabbit.

Pausing briefly to admire an eight-inch statue of the Buddha carved from a single crystal, and fighting off the hordes of 'prosperous beggars' at the gate, Clancy and the planter motored on to Katugastota to see the tame elephants which were all that remained of the vast war hordes once kept by the Kandyan kings.

Clancy signed up for a ride on one and, as it began to move, soon began to slide back and forth in an alarming fashion which he described brilliantly as like 'trying to straddle a young earthquake'.

Once he relaxed and got used to it, he started to enjoy the experience of trundling through the jungle on a beast of ponderous but endless power, and as he climbed down at the end, was sure that the elephant winked at him, although whether it was an expression of indulgence or disdain, he could not tell.

'Yet I am sure this great beast felt very magnanimous in condescending to amuse such insignificant creatures as we,' he noted in his journal before they followed the narrow mountain road, the Englishman dumbfounded at how easily the Henderson conquered steep slopes with two on board. They arrived at Matale, a bustling town famous for its lacquerware, in time for elevenses at one of the many government rest houses set up around the country and in India for unpretentious but affordable accommodation.

As they enjoyed huge glasses of lime and soda under the cool breeze created by the punkah wallah, an American globetrotter that Clancy had met in Colombo waltzed in with a native in European dress. In a flash the Englishman was on his feet and out of the room, and when a baffled Clancy followed him out to see what on earth was wrong, the reply, 'Isn't your friend a bit weird to hang around with natives like that, and especially to bring them into a room with gentlemen?' instantly summed up for Clancy the English attitude to colonials: that they had to be kept in their place, and that education only spoiled them.

'In all of Ceylon I came across but one school, and was not a little disgusted at the way the heavy-drinking English "planters" aristocracy conducted themselves – ordering around as if they were dirt under their feet the descendants of a race who had ruled royally before England had been discovered,' he wrote.

In Matale today, the government was widening the main street by the simple expedient of chopping the front halves off the houses lining it, and up a side street to the right then up a steep lane through well-kept gardens, we found the rest house where Clancy had stopped, a handsome white three-storey building in which, Clancy would be pleased to hear, several locals were tucking into Sunday lunch washed down by pitchers of beer without a snotty Englishman in sight.

Clancy's next stop in an action-packed day were the Dambulla Caves in which King Valagamba sheltered for fourteen years from marauding Tamils in the first century BC before regaining his throne and turning the caves into temples in gratitude.

Led into the largest of the five caves by a guide, Clancy found himself surrounded by fifty-four Buddhas, their gold and enamel paint flickering in the candlelight, a sight so astounding that he was staring at one when he found he was leaning against the nose of another.

Frescoes over two thousand years old covered the walls, and from the roof into a jar dripped water, its source so mysterious, its rhythm so unvarying through the passing seasons and years, and its purity so exquisite, that no human was allowed to drink it.

At the foot of the steps leading up to the caves today is a sprawling complex dominated by the Golden Temple, a perfect symbol of the ornate kitschness which prevails in so much of the Orient, and which is so much at odds with the Zen minimalism of Japan.

Imagine, if you will, a florid wedding cake of a building, the entrance of which is a gold staring lion flanked by rows of giant pink rose petals then two ornate pergolas with conical blue and gold roofs, the entire edifice topped by a 90ft tall golden Buddha which, until recently, was topped in turn by a radio aerial.

You can stop imagining now, since you've probably suffered enough for one day, particularly if you step over the marmalade kitten snoozing on the doormat of the caves' ticket office, and climb the steps to find there the stiff, formal frescoes and the rows of stiff, formal Buddhas, like anorexic versions of their big brother downstairs. After all that, the drip of water from the cave ceiling, as pure as ever, is like the distant chime of a temple bell.

Clancy tarried so long in the caves that by the time he got back to the Henderson it was 6.30 p.m., and darkness was only minutes away. He prepared to ride through the jungle to the rest house at Sigiri, only for the locals to tell him that the rogue elephants, cheetahs, bears and wild buffalo that came out at night made the road so dangerous that they wouldn't dream of doing it in a group, never mind alone.

'I'll chance it. I hate to give up what I've started,' said the indefatigable Clancy, hauling out his Savage automatic and setting off into the jungle night with a cry of 'Sigiri or bust!'

As did we, with a cry of 'Sigiri or drown!' after yet another monsoon downpour, which stopped as quickly as it had started, leaving us proceeding onwards steaming gently.

He had bought his fifth headlight of the trip in Colombo, but dared not light it for fear of attracting wild animals, and within seconds he was plunged into darkness, riding as fast as he dared along a sandy track until he dimly saw a huge shape appear in the road ahead. Blowing his horn like mad and opening wide the throttle, he charged the monster with wild yells, and as it snorted and crashed off into the jungle, he saw that it was a wild buffalo.

Had he been taking the same road today, he would have seen a large sign saying: 'Warning – elephants are roaming. Travel after 6 p.m. is dangerous. 'And probably ignored it.

Not much later, his way was blocked by another buffalo, and when he finally rolled up at the rest house, startling the two lady guests, they told him he was lucky to be alive.

We had a similar, if slightly less fraught, adventure on the way to our own guest house at Sigiri. We arrived in the vicinity at five, but in spite of half a dozen calls by Alfons to establish where the guest house was, we then spent two hours going around in circles on dirt tracks as the sun went down.

Finally, well after dark, we rattled into the grounds of an elegant establishment with fish ponds in the garden and comfortable chairs on the verandah.

'Good evening, gentlemen. How can I help you?' said the manager, a tall gentleman with a polite and mannerly air who came out immediately to greet us, followed by a servant bearing glasses of chilled papaya juice.

'You could start by putting a better sign outside,' said Alfons, whose patience had been tested somewhat. 'That one's impossible to read.'

'Of course. I see you are motorcyclists. It's good news that the law has just changed to allow larger machines.'

'The law has not changed,' said Alfons.

'Oh, I believe it has.'

'The law has not changed,' said Alfons, more loudly.

'As you wish. Now, how can I help you?'

'We have a reservation for a triple room in the name of van Hoof.'

'No, I don't believe you have.'

'But you must. I made it personally. Look, it says here: triple room at the Kumbukgas Mankada Lodge.'

'Ah, but this is the Lion's Rock, sir. You are in the wrong place.'

We sighed, and set off again, bouncing around under the stars for another hour until we finally gave up, stopped outside a shop, phoned the guest house again and they sent a man in a tuk-tuk to guide us there.

It was, in truth, miles from anywhere up a narrow, rutted track and the only sign of its existence was a small white board with four rows of multicoloured elephants painted on it, like a code that could only be deciphered by elephant whisperers.

Even worse, when we finally got there, they had no beer, but after we playfully strangled the manager for several minutes, he sent the man in the tuk-tuk to find some and calm our shattered nerves.

While the beer was cooling and dinner was being prepared, I typed up my notes for the day on a bed on which several small beasts were variously hopping and crawling. It took me three attempts to rescue a beetle from the loo, and Gary spent a good ten minutes, watched by an earnest frog, tracking down a large cricket and freeing it into the night before we finally sat down and had beer and curry on a verandah on which several ancient tin trunks bore witness to the spirit of Clancy.

As for his nerves, they were, if not quite shattered, certainly frayed slightly around the edges, but a wash-up, a change of clothes and a good dinner restored his spirits.

After reading for a bit, he blew out the candle and settled down to sleep with his gun under the pillow. Except that with only a thin window curtain and a wire fence between him and the jungle, the chorus of snarling panthers, roaring bears, trumpeting elephants, baying jackals, screeching owls, flapping bats and snorting buffalos kept him awake all night, and it was a weary man who set off next morning to climb the 750 steps to the 1500-year-old royal fortress of Sigiriya, or Lion Rock.

By way of revenge, we kept the beasts of the jungle awake all night by a carefully coordinated campaign of Gary farting and me and Alfons snoring, so that several elephants turned up in the morning complaining that they hadn't slept a wink, and had to be compensated with the guest house's entire supply of buns.

Still, at least Gary was back on form, since over the past few days he had eschewed farting and swearing so comprehensively that I'd become increasingly worried that he was ill. Not that his jokes were getting any better. Have you heard the one about the priest and the panties? No? Lucky you.

The next day, although many of the hundreds of rest houses in Sri Lanka have been abandoned, we found the one in Sigiri still spick and span, with its shady verandah, easy chairs, ceiling fans slowly stirring the warm, aromatic air and monastic rooms exactly the same as when he stayed there.

Standing beside the old red post box by the gatepost, we had a clear view (if you don't count the elephant carelessly parked on the other side of the road) of Lion Rock, only half a mile away. On top of the 1,000ft rock are the remains of the Sigiriya fortress, surrounded by gardens, moats and fountains which were so well designed by the Sinhalese irrigation engineers that, when they were rediscovered after 1500 years, it only took their water channels to be cleared of leaves and branches to get them flowing freely again.

The country's single most important attraction, both when Clancy visited and today, Sigiriya was built in the fifth century after King Dhatusena handed over the throne to his son Mogallana rather than his son Kassapa.

Taking it well in the circumstances, Kassapa drove his brother into exile, walled up their dad and left him to die, then built Sigiriya as a combination of pleasure palace and impregnable fortress in case Mogallana returned to claim his inheritance.

When he did, Kassapa promptly climbed on an elephant, left behind his impregnable fortress and led his troops out to face his brother on the open plains below. The elephant, showing more sense than its owner, took one look at Mogallana's vast army of Tamil mercenaries and bolted, followed by Kassapa's soldiers.

Realising all was lost, Kassapa killed himself, and his brother handed Sigiriya over to Buddhist monks who found peace and solitude there until they finally left in 1155, leaving it abandoned until the British rediscovered it in 1828.

When Clancy arrived, restoration work was going on all around him, and as he wandered around, he predicted that the sight would soon be one of the wonders of the world, and his prescience was validated in 1982 when it was made a World Heritage Site.

Claiming he hadn't seen a pretty girl for two months, he was feeling frisky enough to climb a precarious wire and bamboo ladder to see the so-called Sigiriya Damsels, frescoes of five hundred girls who were either Kassapa's consorts or celestial nymphs.

Staggering into the cave and dusting himself off, he was

delighted to find that the gals not only had fresh teenage complexions in spite of being almost fifteen centuries old, but were, to a woman, topless. Sadly, several of the frescoes were destroyed by vandals in 1967, and today, many are roped off to avoid further damage.

The culprits were never caught but it is generally believed that they were, most likely, Muslim fundamentalists who, ironically, were the kindred spirits of the Christian missionaries who, when they arrived here, as they did everywhere, forced the native women to cover their breasts. The idiots.

Today, after you've recovered from the £25 entrance fee, walked through the gardens and gazed in awe at the lion's paws which are all that is left of the great statue that once bestrode the entrance, you climb the same steps that Clancy did, make your way up an iron ladder slightly less precarious than the one he used, and find yourself in the company of the celestial nymphs.

The lovely thing about them is that, unlike the later and more formal frescoes at Dambulla, they are touchingly human; in their facial expressions, and in the small, everyday things they are doing, such as admiring a lotus blossom, holding a seashell up to the light, or offering up a bouquet or a meal.

'Great tits,' said Gary.

Climb higher still, and you finally come out on top of the rock to a scene of courtyards, terraces, bathing pools and halls where, like me, you'll probably take a deep breath, look out at the shimmering forests and plains beyond, and wonder why on earth Kassapa left this place and rode out to his doom.

On his way to Polonnaruwa, the twelfth century Sinhalese capital, Clancy admired myriads of bright birds and herds of spotted deer which scattered at his approach, and the lovely lake of Minneria reminded him of Killarney until he spotted the crocodiles basking on its sandy shores.

We stopped at Minneria for lunch, and saw not a single crocodile, although we did meet a man from Luton.

During the reign of the enlightened warrior king Parakramabahu the Great, Polunnaruwa grew to a lavish scale at the hands of imported Indian architects, only to be ruined irretrievably, along with the monasteries and the country's extensive irrigation system, by the notorious Tamil mercenary Magha in the thirteenth century.

The restoration of Polunnaruwa started in the middle of the twentieth century, and today you can see more of the glory that it once was, but when Clancy was there, the jungle had been at work for eight centuries, and a dilapidated sixty-foot statue of Buddha at the entrance left him so crestfallen that when he found a miniature stucco version leaning against the wall of a tiny alcove, he took it with him for safekeeping.

'Homesickness has now broken him all up, but I still cherish the remains,' he was to write much later in his diary.

Today, the dilapidated Buddha has been moved from the entrance of Polunnaruwa to the centre of the restored area, but for me, the most poignant ruins were the untouched ones you stumble on in a clearing, their flat red brick walls and limpid green pools sleeping in the sun exactly as Clancy would have found them, before he tucked the little Buddha in his pocket and rode on to Anuradhapura.

Until it was left in a bit of a mess by Indian invaders in 993, Anuradhapura had existed for a thousand years, and at its height was one of the greatest centres of political and spiritual power in the world, with palaces whose architecture rivalled anything in the Greek and Roman worlds and vast temples which housed up to ten thousand monks at a time.

Clancy may well have been coming down with cultural concussion by this stage, for after breezing through a perfunctory list of theatres, bathing halls, gardens, fountains, palaces whose splendour had never been excelled and public buildings glittering with doors, windows and roofs of gold, he came across a threatening troop of huge grey monkeys leaping through the trees and making faces at him.

Pulling out his Savage to fire a shot and scare them off, he was only stopped by his guide pointing out politely that if he hit one of them, its mates would tear them both to pieces.

Sheepishly, Clancy put his weapon away and, after another night at the Sigiri rest house, satisfied himself the next morning by taking pot shots at snipe and jungle fowl.

He made his way back to Colombo to catch the boat to Penang in Malaya, steeling himself for another round with Lloyd's who, two days before his departure, proved that they weren't finished tormenting him yet.

When he called into the office to confirm his third class ticket, they told him third class was full, refused to honour his ticket and charged him another $100 which he could ill afford. Furious, he sought the advice of the US consul, who told him Lloyd's were notorious for their arrogance, but who flung on his jacket, and accompanied Clancy to see the German manager of the office.

It was no use: the only answer they got was a shrug, and a suggestion that if Clancy wrote to the head office in Bremen, he might get some of his money back in six months. And as if that wasn't bad enough, when he boarded the ship, he discovered Lloyd's had been lying to him, and third class was not even half full.

It's a wonder that when he got home, that America didn't declare war on Germany without waiting for Gavrilo Princip.

As it was, he mollified himself during his last half hour in Ceylon by buying a fabulous moonstone necklace, pendant and pin, and a five-sapphire ring, for $13.25, a tenth of what they would have cost him in New York.

Bearing his prizes up the gangplank, he bade a fond farewell to Ceylon as the *Bulow* set sail for its four-day journey across the Bay of Bengal to Penang in Malaya.

His companions included several brides-to-be taking

advantage of the voyage to fit in a few last-minute shipboard romances, and two miserably unhappy European women whose tales of how they were treated by their Chinese husbands made him strike 'the horror of international marriages' off his future plans.

As we said a final thanks to Alfons for his invaluable help and shouldered our bags to board the midnight Sri Lankan Airlines flight to Malaysia to pick up Clancy's trail in Penang, I could just imagine his worst nightmare: marrying a feisty foreign girl, then a honeymoon with Lloyd's.

We were as sorry to leave Sri Lanka as he had been, and it was appropriate that our last act there before we left for the airport was one which mirrored the gentleness and love everyone we met there had shown us: as we were standing outside the gardens at Perediniya, an old man in a sarong whose face had collapsed under the weight of its own sadness came up with his hand outstretched, and we gave him the last of our rupees.

Chapter Eleven

A short history of Malaysia

200 – 1957 AD

Very similar to Sri Lanka, with local royalty supplanted over the centuries by Portuguese, Dutch and British, except that instead of coffee and tea, Henry Ridley, the director of Singapore's Botanic Gardens, creates catalyst for the entire Malayan rubber industry when he works out how to tap trees commercially in 1895.

1957

Independence.

1969

Race riots lead to imposition of emergency rule and clampdown on civil liberties which still lingers on.

In Penang, Clancy's plans for a spot of gentlemanly motorcycling down the peninsula were scuppered by the news that the road petered out into swampy jungle 150 miles north of Singapore, which left no alternative but to continue to there on the *Bulow*.

Before it sailed, he leapt into a rickshaw for a tour around

Penang's capital Georgetown, during which he managed to condemn the typical Malay as 'about the most unreliable person on earth'.

How he managed to glean this comprehensive insight from a brief rattle around town is a mystery, but immediately after damning an entire race, he hurtled into the squalid business district to be greeted by the sight of dozens of stuffed pigs, roasted turkeys and trays of sweetmeats being borne to the funeral of a rich Chinese lady to nourish her spirit in the afterlife.

He was much more impressed with the residential section, with luxurious bungalows surrounded by velvety lawns, flowering trees and a view through the palms of the sea lapping the shore that created an air of beauty and ease. His sightseeing was cut short, however, by a sudden downpour which left him soaked, so he paid off the rickshaw driver and reboarded the *Bulow* for the day and a half voyage south to Singapore.

He probably made the right decision, for the first thing we saw as we arrived in Georgetown was a sign on the side of a bus saying: Taking the bus is thirty-eight times safer than riding a motorbike.

Finding a cheap hotel which was not the cheap hotel we were looking for, we checked in anyway and went to the Tourist Information Office and the Penang Heritage Centre, neither of which was able to furnish us with a tour.

The only answer was to do a Clancy and jump into the nearest rickshaw, proceeding at a leisurely pace through a residential section in which the bungalows still slumbered behind flowering trees and velvety lawns.

The business section, by which I imagine Clancy meant the jetties on which the Chinese clans lived and traded, and the area just inland, was still a hiving, hawking maze of temples aromatic with joss smoke, and noisy with the roar of small furnaces, the clang of tinsmiths, the buzz of saws and hiss of the planes of the furniture makers, the cluck of justifiably concerned chickens in cages, the urgent tick of sewing machines, the slosh and steam of laundries and the silent, methodical labours of rattan weavers.

On the largest, the Chew Jetty, one of the stilt homes was available for rent, complete with air con, TV, wi-fi and a karaoke set, just in case you wanted to invite the neighbours around for a good old sing-song of an evening.

Nearby, a stall was possibly the world's only outlet for durian ice cream, flavoured with the fruit so foul-smelling that it is banned from many buildings in the Far East. Naturally, I bought one, and the best that can be said about it is that, like surströmming, the Swedish delicacy of herring crammed into a barrel, buried and left to ferment for a year, it is not quite as bad as you expect.

Much more pleasurable was Ben's Vintage Toy Museum, which we stumbled on by accident while walking around after eating our ice cream; basically Ben's house crammed with cap guns, roller skates and tin cars that anyone of a certain age will remember having as a child.

'This is a bit like my house, but with less stuff,' said Gary.

'Aye, except I bet you don't have the first edition of *Superman*,' I said, looking with a strange mixture of happiness and sadness at a stereoscopic Viewmaster of exactly the sort my parents had, with which I travelled the world in images long before I did it for real.

To celebrate finding Ben's, we could have had afternoon tea at the Eastern & Oriental Hotel, built in 1885 by the Armenian Sarkies brothers who also ran Raffles in Singapore, but we had tragically forgotten to pack our white linen tuxedos, so we ended up having coffee and buns at a Starbucks.

Anyway, it's important to support these small local enterprises. Mark my words: you'll see them everywhere one day.

'Nice one crossing the street there. Don't look now, whatever you do,' said Gary as we stood up to go.

'Here, I am capable of spotting attractive women by myself, you know,' I said.

'I know, but you wouldn't want to miss one,' he laughed.

Gary's trouble, you see, was that he was like a fourteen-year-old obsessed with sex, whereas I was like a much more mature sixteen-year-old who had realised that the other one per cent of life matters too.

Back at Hutton Lodge, the former family mansion turned cheap hotel where we staying, I was pleased to see that the laundry which we'd handed over that morning had been done, and at the hefty sum of a quid. It was a pleasant treat, since I'd long since run out of both soap and travel wash, and for the past two weeks had been washing both my clothes and myself with apple shampoo, leaving both smelling faintly like a small orchard.

And so, freshly pressed, we went out for dinner at a Kashmiri restaurant, had too many beers, and the next day took the road south to see what Clancy had missed.

Like the Cameron Highlands, where wealthy planters escaped the heat and, in the process, created an area which looked like 'Tarzan does Surrey'; mock-Tudor mansions peeping out from the jungle, and afternoon tea with scones, cream and strawberry jam.

Or Kuala Lumpur, with Petronas Towers rising out of the early morning mist like the love children of Angkor Wat and the Sagrada Familia.

Or the old Dutch houses of Melaka, modestly admiring their reflections in the river when they thought no one was looking. Or the rickshaws, draped with flowers and fairy lights, tinkling through the streets after dark knowing that everyone is looking.

And the roads themselves, from the glorious curves of the Cameron Highlands to the fast six-lane motorways on which we swept south to Singapore, arriving several days later just in time to see the ghost of Clancy disembarking from the *Bulow*.

Chapter Twelve

A short history of Singapore

1819
Sir Thomas Stamford Raffles of the East India Company sets up trading post to take advantage of superb natural deep water harbour and position on sea route between China and India.

1887
Raffles Hotel opened by the Armenia Sarkies brothers who also owned those other colonial icons the Eastern & Oriental in Georgetown and the Strand in Rangoon.

1942
Japanese take Singapore and capture 130,000 British, Australian and Indian troops, many of whom die in slave labour camps or building the Death Railway from Thailand to Burma.

1965
Independence from Malaysia. Undeterred by unemployment and housing crises, and having no natural resources, by the 1990s Prime Minister Lee Kuan Yew creates one of the world's most prosperous nations, making it the Switzerland of Asia. In every sense.

Even in 1913, Singapore was already the commercial hub of a region stretching all the way from Sumatra to Australia, and growing at a furious pace. On Clancy's three-mile journey from the wharf to the city centre – during which he noticed that, as he had in Penang, the many motorbikes he saw were invariably English makes – the creation of new piers, hotels, businesses and gas pipes had turned most of the city into a building site punctuated only by grassy parks where games of cricket and soccer were played constantly.

After dinner at a large hotel where he managed to sample almost all of the twenty-four numbered dishes on offer, he loosened his belt a notch and went for a stroll in the toasty air, then fell into bed and the next day sailed on to Hong Kong.

As we motored into town, it was both more spacious and greener than I expected, with as much parkland as skyscrapers, and the well-kept cricket and soccer pitches of Clancy's day still in full swing, although one has been set aside for a war memorial: a quartet of slender white stalks nicknamed The Four Chopsticks by locals, to commemorate the dead of 1942 when, with all the British defences facing out to sea, those cunning Japanese invaded from the land. Although Churchill called it 'the worst disaster and the largest capitulation in British history', I suspect the equally sneaky Raffles would have approved.

Another patch of green hosts Singapore's version of Speakers' Corner in Hyde Park, conveniently situated beside a police station where would-be radicals have to register first. Not surprisingly, there are few takers.

We dumped our bags in an expensive hotel with cheap rooms and went for a potter around the sights that Clancy saw and some that he missed.

Among the former, of course, is Raffles, the lovely old wedding cake of a hotel named after Sir Thomas Stamford Raffles, the man who stepped ashore here in 1819 and, conveniently ignoring the fact that it was Dutch territory under a deal with the local sultan, appointed the sultan's brother as chieftain instead, hoisted the Union Flag and proceeded to turn a tiger-infested swamp into a major duty-free trading post.

Not that it did him much good in the end: returning to England in 1824 with his wife Sophia, he founded London Zoo, established a farm in Hendon and settled down to what he hoped would be a nice comfortable retirement. Only for the bank holding his £16,000 pension fund to fold and the East India Company to demand £22,000 for overpayment, the ungrateful swines.

Three months later, the patriarch of Singapore died of a brain tumour and was buried with no memorial in Hendon, since the vicar had shares in the West Indian slave plantations and didn't take kindly to Sir Stamford's friendship with William Wilberforce, leader of the British movement to abolish the slave trade.

Raffles would be pleased to know that the hotel named after him is still going strong, and that the Singapore Sling was invented in the hotel's Long Bar by barman Ngiam Tong Boon in 1915 and is still available there, although at a price which means you have to drink it immediately to get over the shock.

As for the building next door, Raffles and Boon would probably be turning in their graves at the monstrosity known as the Swissotel which is as dull as the country from whence it sprang.

Another building Clancy should be glad he missed is the Buddha Tooth Relic Temple, built in 2007 and such a tribute to opulence that even the lifts have brocaded walls. You can just imagine Siddharta sitting up there in between games of chess and backgammon with Jesus, gazing down at this and St Peter's and muttering, 'So, mate, where did it all go wrong, eh?'

This temple of the tooth is not to be confused with the temple of the tooth in Sri Lanka, since the tooth which is probably not the Buddha's there is only on show every five to ten years, whereas the tooth which is probably not the Buddha's here can't be seen at all. Although to make up for your disappointment, a separate room contains the cremated remains of his nose, brain and liver.

Much more impressive was the Marina Bay Resort; three glittering skyscrapers topped by a structure which was part submarine, part banana and part roof garden. And if you can imagine that, you deserve the rest of the day off.

Oh, and it's not true what they say about there not being a speck of litter in the streets of Singapore: within an hour of arriving I spotted two bus tickets lying on the street. Thankfully I picked them up from where I'd dropped them immediately, since the punishment for littering is life in prison with hard labour and foot tickling on Fridays, the same as for jaywalking, not flushing the toilet, spitting, dropping gum and laughing for more than two seconds in a public place.

If you do them all simultaneously, the sentences are consecutive; although if Singapore jails are as clean and tidy as the rest of the place, it might actually be a pleasure, in a dull kind of way.

It is, as the natural historian William Hornaday said of it in 1885, like a big desk, full of drawers in which everything has its place, and can always be found in it.

Closing the drawers, we tiptoed carefully to the airport and joined the queue for the flight to Hong Kong with a family from there who were boisterous with excitement at the thought that in a few hours they could jaywalk to the toilet, spit their chewing gum into it and not flush it.

Chapter Thirteen

A short history of Hong Kong

1842

After sporadic attempts to seize Hong Kong by the Portuguese and Dutch, the British, already trading vast quantities of opium from Bengal to China, force through Treaty of Nanking, granting them Hong Kong in perpetuity and the right to trade in Shanghai and Canton.

1880

Hong Kong already firmly established as a trading, shipping and banking powerhouse.

1898

British sign ninety-nine-year-lease with Chinese, setting clock ticking on eventual handover. D'oh.

1980s

Hong Kong now one of the world's leading financial centres.

1989

Tiananmen Square massacre. Hong Kong residents, horrified that they're about to be handed over to a bunch of murderers, stage successful protests for democratic institutions to be in place before handover.

1997

Handover. Chinese disband democratic institutions and install puppet leader Tung, so bad that he's soon replaced with Tsang, who proceeds to demolish historic areas for huge shopping malls.

Hong Kong, with its modern natives and matching shops, came as a complete surprise to Clancy, as did the fact that his plans to ride the thousand miles north to Shanghai were thwarted by the small but significant fact that, apart from a few miles outside major cities, there were neither roads, railways nor wheelbarrow tracks in southern China, rendering his beloved Henderson 'as useless as an aeroplane in a coal mine'.

Naturally, the fact that he only spent a night in Hong Kong didn't stop him subjecting the Chinese to an immediate Clancyfication, although unlike the unfortunate Malays, this was a positive one.

The people were, he decided, 'quiet, respectful, courteous and neat', and the women, with their 'becoming silk pantaloons, long embroidered coats and neat slippers', were very nice indeed

There. After summing up an entire nation, he tucked his pen in his pocket and went sightseeing with a couple of Marines from the US gunboat *Wilmington* who showed him around town in between making his hair stand on end with horror stories from the 1911 revolution which ended two thousand years of imperial rule in China.

Thankfully, the only evidence in Hong Kong two years after the event was the number of men who had been forced to cut off their precious pigtails and now wore them pinned to their hair, whether walking in the streets, sleeping on the floor of shops with wooden blocks for pillows or, in the case of one poor boy, asleep on the pavement squatting on his heels.

Sighing at the lack of motorcycling he was getting, he

climbed back on board the *Bulow* and sailed north west up the coast to Shanghai into the teeth of weather which was getting uncomfortably like that of the Ireland where he had started – cold and wet.

On our Cathay Pacific flight from Singapore, the two-hundred page shopping catalogue contained everything from a full set of golf clubs in case you needed to practise your putting up and down the aisle, to a case of Château Smith Haut Lafitte which was described in the tasting notes as 'approachable in its youth'.

Although that implied it got increasingly grumpy as it matured, I was almost tempted to splash out, since I've had a few wines that were unapproachable at any age.

Having read too many James Clavell novels, I fully expected to arrive in Hong Kong, spend three days negotiating a fiendishly complex business deal in fluent vernacular Cantonese, sign it with my personal chop, seal it with a bottle of fifty-year-old Macallan, then go out for dinner with my Chinese mistress, having left several ex-wives at home in New York, Honolulu and Skegness.

Sadly, none of the above happened, but it was just as hectic, thanks to Northern Ireland expat Peter Rolston, the former ITN and CNN presenter who'd forged a TV and media training career in Hong Kong and who'd lined up several speaking engagements and nights out for us during our three days there.

The brother of slightly bonkers TV superbabe Pamela Ballantine, Peter was even more bonkers, as evidenced by the fact that he'd been reading my newspaper columns and books for years since his wife Angela had bought him a copy of *Way to Go*.

When I'd written in one column before leaving for the Chile to Alaska ride how afraid I was that the moment I rode into Colombia, I'd be kidnapped and strung up by the dongles, his response was:

Dear Hill,

Have just read your latest dispatch; fear you may be going soft. Stop blubbing, man, and pull yourself together. After 6,000 miles in the saddle, your dongles will be useless anyway.

Dib dib,

The Major.

A few days before our arrival, I'd got an email from him saying:

Broadsword calling Danny Boy. Your imminent arrival noted. Kerb stones being painted and bunting unfurled. The third Wanchai District Accordion and Pipe Band mustered and in fine fettle.

Would be good if you could find a window for one of the good lady wife's candlelit dinners down our beachside gaff (behind the municipal shower block).

Peter had also put us in touch with Simon Large, the head of marketing at Cathay Pacific, who had come through with several flights for us, and Martin Cubbon, the Manxman and Chief Executive Officer of Swire Properties, who'd put us up at their East Hotel while we were there, helped out with flights and in return only asked, 'Be great if you could give a talk on your adventures at our conference facilities one evening followed by a bit of mingling with the crowd over drinks followed by slap-up feed with myself, Pete and some hairy-arsed types, although on reflection I sense this beast is now extinct in HK.'

Fortunately, Gary and I had brought our own hairy arses just in case, planting them on the airport bus on the ride into town for one of the most jaw-dropping skylines on earth: a vista of vertiginous skyscrapers, rugged mountains and billowing clouds for which no amount of gazing at photographs or films could prepare you.

Even the scale of the docks, with scores of ships, hundreds of cranes and thousands of containers, is astonishing. It is as if all the commercial energy of the world has been distilled into one drop of pure, unadulterated capitalism. You imagine it's the sort of place where they buy shirts with the sleeves already rolled up.

That evening, I gave a talk and slide show on the Clancy trip and previous bike adventures to the Royal Geographical Society, and afterwards, its director in Hong Kong, Rupert McCowan, took us out for dinner to the China Club, based in the old Bank of China.

As we walked up the stairs, past owner Sir David Tang's private and priceless collection of art deco paintings and ceramics, Rupert suddenly stopped and glanced down at Gary's training shoes.

'Ah, we might have a problem getting in with those,' he said.

We stood, scratching our heads and looking at each other, as blokes do.

'I know. Clancy's boots,' said Gary, pulling them out of the bag in which we had brought them for the talk.

Suitably attired, we entered a scene straight from the China of the 1930s, with white-jacketed servants, whispering fans and a string quartet playing Bach in the corner.

'They have several restaurants here, but I thought you might be getting homesick for Europe, so we're eating in Cipriani,' said Rupert.

It was no use, I thought; we were destined to end up eating Italian all the way through the Far East.

The next day, we made our way to Cathay Pacific HQ, outside which sat one of the two original DC-3s with which the company was founded in 1946, to give the talk again, and got back to the hotel just in time to make our way to do the same at the towering HQ of Swires.

Started in the early nineteenth century by Liverpool wool trader John Swire, it established an office in Shanghai in 1866 and four years later in Hong Kong, where it now owned half the city and had just been named by the Wall Street Journal as the most important company in Hong Kong, the other one being Cathay Pacific; which is, er, owned by Swires as well.

Ironically, considering the fact that my previous knowledge of the place had been based on James Clavell's blockbuster novel *Noble House*, I discovered that it was a thinly disguised fictional account of the rivalry between Swires and rivals Jardine Matheson.

Hurtling to the top of Swires HQ in the executive lift, we found Martin in an office with possibly the finest and most expensive view in the world; although bearing in mind that he was a multi-millionaire executive of a multi-billion pound company, he was the most down to earth and decent bloke imaginable. Not to mention being the owner of a nice little collection of bikes, including a Ducati 848 and an MV Agusta F4.

'Right,' he said after I'd finished talking nonsense to a large group of people for the third time in a row in two days, 'let's head down to the old red light district in Wan Chai for some grub. I know a nice little restaurant there called La Fleur.'

'It's not Italian, is it?' I said.

'Don't be silly. It's French,' he said.

We staggered home at about three in the morning, and six hours later, feeling somewhat green around the gills and clutching hangovers the size of mainland China, we presented ourselves to Martin's driver Kenneth for a tour of Hong Kong island, motoring along the wooded bays and inlets of the south coast to the beach at Shek O, where families were picnicking or splashing in the surf.

At Stanley, among the plush apartments and designer shops, we found the skin of the last tiger shot in Hong Kong where it has lain since its owner met his demise in 1942.

In Aberdeen harbour, the sampans on which entire families once lived were jammed like sardines, while the actual sardines were in the teeming, aromatic chaos of the fish market, since the fleet had just come in.

Back in Central Hong Kong, the old trams still rattled through the streets, their reflections bright on the steel and glass skyscrapers above which the kites once soared on the thermals rising from the wooded slopes, and today do so on the sheer heat of the energy resulting from the endless making and spending of money below.

That night we had a beautiful, civilised dinner on the rooftop terrace of the home of Peter and Angela overlooking the beach at Shek O, and as we took the bus to the airport the next day, we left Hong Kong both sorry and glad: sorry because of the astonishing hospitality we had received, and glad because our livers couldn't have taken much more of it.

Chapter Fourteen

A short history of Shanghai

1842
Treaty of Nanking starts similar process to the one in Hong Kong, turning Shanghai into major British trading port. By the time Clancy arrives, it boasts gas lighting, electricity, tarmac roads and a tramline.

1920s
City's glorious decadence earns it the title of the Paris of the East; or, as one visiting missionary put it, 'If God allows Shanghai to endure, he owes Sodom and Gomorrah an apology.'

1966
Communists succeed where God failed. Mao launches Cultural Revolution in Shanghai, and the party ends.

1990
New leader Deng Xiaoping declares that to get rich is glorious. Party back on.

2013
Responsible for a third of China's imports, Shanghai has more

skyscrapers than New York and is filthy rich in every sense, with five million tons of raw sewage and untreated waste dumped into the Yangtse every day.

As the *Bulow* slowly made its way up the Wusong River towards Shanghai, Clancy stood on deck, his jacket buttoned against the cold, admiring the picturesque Oriental architecture and spick and span gardens of the farmhouses lining the banks, behind them fertile farmland stretching to the horizon.

This was the China he had expected, he decided happily, even though the farmhouses soon gave way to giant oil tanks, cotton mills, shipyards and endless wharves lined with battleships from America, France, England, Japan, Germany and China, and huge junks piled high with merchandise.

Hailing two rickshaws, he and an English missionary on his way to Japan trundled down Nanking Road, through hundreds of wheelbarrows carrying everything from people to pigs, one motorcycle, a handful of cars and several carriages filled with aristocratic Chinese who gazed at him with haughty languor.

They clattered on, past the race course, cricket and golf clubs and swimming baths where homesick expats distracted themselves, and on down Bubbling Well Road, lined with the exquisite mansions of the city's great and good, until they came to the famous Bubbling Well itself; only to find it a dirty tank surrounded by a low stone wall and emitting an occasional dyspeptic burb.

They rickshawed on to Foochow Road, the so-called Paris of China, with its fabulous restaurants, theatres, tea houses and shops. Sadly, none of them sold the suit of heavy cloth Clancy wanted to ward off the cold, and even worse, when he and the missionary gave up and went to the nearest tea house hoping for an authentic Chinese experience, what they got was a cheap imitation of European style.

Still, as they sipped their tea, the scene on the street below was like one of the film sets which would become home to Clancy in his later life as a Hollywood scriptwriter and producer, with the faces of the locals milling about as diverse as the twenty-eight dialects they were chattering in.

The lack of a unified language, Clancy mused, was one reason why the country had so little development and commerce, but it was a fault the new republican government was already addressing.

After six o'clock service at the Church of England cathedral, they dined royally at the Carlton Grill, 'the only good restaurant in the East', to a background of ragtime played by a Hawaiian orchestra.

Today, the Carlton has disappeared without trace into the plush acres of the Ritz-Carlton Hotel, the sort of place where you can feel your credit card trembling with a combination of dread and excitement as you walk up to the door.

The next morning, he arrived in a downpour at the American Consulate, only for the consul to dash his hopes of motorcycling north along the Chinese coast due to a small but significant lack of roads.

Biting his lip to avoid a stream of curses, Clancy accepted his fate philosophically and, as he made his way to the docks to book the morning sailing to Nagasaki, he mused: 'Give China a little time, and she'll not only have plenty of trunk roads, but be one of the richest countries on the globe. Nothing can stop her.'

His prescience was spot on: by the Roaring Twenties, Shanghai was the most stylish and decadent city in Asia and, after years in the communist doldrums, now has three thousand skyscrapers (more than New York), with another two thousand planned, not to mention the only magnetic levitation train on the planet.

By 2020, it's expected to be the richest city in the world.

With Clancy's sailing booked once again on the *Bulow*, he

looked at his pocket watch, realised he still had most of the day left, hired a trilingual guide for 50 cents, and set off to explore the Chinese Quarter, which even then was being rapidly torn down to make way for progress, but was still walled to keep the Chinese away from the French and International Quarters.

Here, at last, he found the authentic China he had been seeking, as they threaded their way down narrow streets lined with the booths of ivory and sandalwood carvers, fan makers, silk weavers and embroiderers. The only machinery in evidence was the Singer sewing machines which were, Clancy hinted in a brace-twanging frisson of Yankee pride, 'along with Ford automobiles, Waterman pens, Eastman Kodaks [cameras] and Gillette razors … to be found in every city in the civilised world'.

Subtract Kodak, and just add Coca-Cola and McDonald's, and he's still more or less right.

His expedition then lurched from the sublime to the ridiculous: after finding the four-hundred-year-old Confucius Temple so full of filthy tea drinkers that it looked like a Wild West Saloon without the booze, he and the guide came to a great iron door in a high wall, and creaked it open to find themselves in the magical Yu Gardens, created in 1559 as the private garden of the provincial administrator.

Passing the old orchestra pavilion in a glade of peaches, the opium house and a dragon's pool of goldfish, they climbed a knoll to a summer house overlooking the gardens, and turned to gaze down in wonder on a scene so absolutely unique in every detail that it would have been inconceivable for a western mind to conceive of it, never mind create it.

After inspecting a gaudy cemetery veiled with joss smoke, Clancy was taken to the French Quarter, which is still shaded by elegant plain trees today, to see a shopkeeper who the guide claimed was the last opium smoker in town because tobacco had recently taken over as the carcinogenic of choice for the

162

upwardly mobile; although in truth opium stayed popular right up to the Cultural Revolution of 1949, when the Communists clamped down on it big time.

Finding him reclining on a suitably low couch puffing away, Clancy declined his offer of a smoke for 20 cents, declared that he liked the Chinese and their country, and went to bed, wondering as he fell asleep if he would finally find some roads in Japan.

Our contact in Shanghai was Roger Owens, or Junior as he was called back in the days when he was the youngest member of the Northern Ireland volleyball team I captained at the Commonwealth championships in 1981. Or was it 1881? I can never remember.

After graduating in engineering from Cambridge, he became a Captain in the Royal Engineers, then the Gurkha Engineers in Hong Kong, where he met his wife Daisy. He had been in business in Hong Kong and Shanghai for the past twenty years.

He was now General Manager of the Drennan Group, which provided large, noisy machines for building sites, and since Shanghai had been one large building site for the past three decades, had done so well for himself that he sent his driver, Li Jia Ming, in the company limo, a blue London cab, to pick us up at the airport.

'It'll be a pleasure to drag you and Gary around the fleshpots of Shanghai, and we have a fantastic array of flesh – floating pig, mink masquerading as mutton and rat replacing roast beef,' said Roger.

And about time too, since we seemed to have been eating nothing but Italian and French as we made our way through the Orient.

As our blue cab hurtled along the superhighway from the airport into Shanghai with Li at the wheel, it was like entering the set of *Bladerunner* on drugs, with the rivers of headlights and tail lights streaming constantly between some of the most exquisitely designed skyscrapers on earth.

One was covered in lights which changed colour constantly as we drove past, like an attenuated chameleon, while others, although they had been mostly designed by European architects such as Sir Norman Foster and his mates, paid homage to the Orient with their Chinese hats and pagodas on top, all of them beautifully lit and draped with lights, as if they were all on their way to a skyscraper party.

And yet, as we turned into the street where our hotel was, there was a tiny bicycle repair shop on the corner, with an old man squatting on the floor fixing a puncture, just as in Clancy's day.

We checked into our hotel, had dinner at a little hot pot and beer place that we found a few streets away and later that night fell into bed, contented and happy.

Perhaps it was because we had got into Shanghai without any hassles over the new seventy-two-hour visa waiver rule, or perhaps it was because after occasionally getting on each other's nerves in the early days of the trip, because we were quite different people, we had now settled into each others' company.

I had stopped getting annoyed at the fact that I had to organise everything, and at Gary's lack of computer literacy, and come to terms with the fact that while this was my fifth major bike adventure, it was all new to him, never mind the fact that he had never used a laptop before he bought one for this trip.

As for him, he had not only started helping out with day to day organisation, but had found his way around the laptop, was still taking great photos for the newspaper articles and blogs and, I imagine, had got used to the fact that no matter how much I tried to be a Zen Buddhist, I still turned into a grumpy bastard when things weren't perfect.

Like when we discovered the next morning that we couldn't get onto the internet because the Chinese government had banned free speech – again. Still, never mind, for it was time to go out on the Clancy trail with our guide, Kent Kedl.

Kent, who had been recommended by Peter Rolston's friend in Shanghai, Neal Beatty, the reigning Grand Wizard of the British Chamber of Commerce, was Neal's boss at a company called Control Risks.

He'd originally dropped out of high school and gone travelling, arrived in China, fell in love with it, went back to college and got a Masters in Chinese Philosophy, came back to teach with his wife Ann, and had now been here for twenty-five years, with his life spent flitting between homes in Shanghai and Hawaii.

'Kent, with a name like that, you've got to be either a Californian surf dude or one of Superman's mates,' I said as we met him.

'Neither,' he laughed. 'I'm from Minnesota but have residency in Hawaii and live in Shanghai, so I'm just another messed up expat,' he laughed.

'Fair enough. What does Control Risks do, by the way?'

'We control risks,' he said, which will teach me to stop asking stupid questions. Or possibly not.

'Actually, we're mostly involved in fraud investigation, kidnapping management and hostage negotiation. Most of that's in Nigeria and Mexico now, but unless there's a sudden outbreak of ethics here, I'll still be pretty busy for a while,' he said as we walked off a main street straight into the heart of old Shanghai, its narrow streets pungent with the aromatic smoke of assorted creatures being fried, boiled or roasted and noisy with the clack of old men playing mah-jong and traders advertising their wares.

In narrow windows hung bolts of silk, wool and cashmere which tailors would transform into fine suits and shirts in a matter of days for a song, while the cobbler next door would furnish you with a pair of bespoke handmade shoes in only a few days more.

Even better, the Bubbling Well was bubbling once more.

Emerging into the parkland of People's Square, we climbed the steps inside the old library for a panoramic view of Sunday strollers wandering around what in Clancy's day would have been the race course.

'It stayed that way until the Second World War, then fell into disrepair, although when I got here in the early eighties, you could still see the outline of the track,' said Kent. 'Then after Tiananmen Square, the Communists developed a dislike of wide open spaces for some curious reason, so they planted trees all over it, which has actually made it quite beautiful,' said Kent.

In the dappled shade, hundreds of middle-aged parents were waving printouts of the height, education and income of their children in a bid to get them married off before it was too late, since any woman not wed here at twenty-eight is considered past it, and men aren't far behind.

'You'll notice that hardly any of them have photos, since looks aren't considered as important as prospects,' said Kent.

On our left was Nanjing Road, called Nanking in Clancy's Day. When Kent came here, it was home to the Number One Department Store, with the imaginatively named Number Two nearby, but today Clancy's wheelbarrows and the Number One have been replaced by the glittering emporia of Hugo Boss, Cartier and Omega, making Nanjing the modern equivalent of Clancy's Foochow Road, which has long since been bulldozed in the scrabble to modernise.

'It was incredible in the nineties. The local politicians made it to national level and the money just started pouring in. I'd go away for three weeks and come back to find entire streets gone and buildings going up,' said Kent.

Thankfully, that process stopped when they realised the Chinese Quarter and Yuyuan Bazaar would be much more attractive to tourists if it was preserved, and today there were thousands milling around pagodas either prettified or rebuilt in classical style.

The Confucius Temple is still there, past a pond crossed by a zig-zag bridge so that ghosts can't find their way to the Starbucks opposite and are forced instead to queue for a pricey tea ceremony, although I doubt if Bill Clinton and the Queen coughed up a fiver for a cuppa when they visited.

And beyond, the Yu Gardens are exactly as Clancy found them: a haven of goldfish ponds, elegant trees, bamboo groves, cobbled walkways and temples for calligraphy, meditation or prayer.

As we emerged, Gary spotted a stall selling Mao hats and badges, and a white Chinese fighter pilot's helmet with a red star on the front for which the stallholder was asking 320 yuan, or about £32.

'How much should I offer her?' he asked Kent.

'Same tactics as hostage negotiation. Offer her 30 per cent, then walk away,' laughed Kent.

He was right, of course, and two minutes later, Gary walked away 12 quid lighter and a helmet richer.

'If you need a jet to go with that, I know a good arms dealer,' said Kent, and to celebrate Gary taking the first steps to having his own air force, we went for a beer on a terrace overlooking the Bund, then met Roger and Daisy for dinner.

The next day, having seen what Clancy saw, we met Roger for the tour of what he hadn't.

'Here, why do the cyclists and scooters ride around at night with no lights on?' said Gary as we wandered in the general direction of the Huangpu River which splits the old town from the new.

'They're not allowed,' said Roger. 'A mate of mine was stopped by a policeman and told to turn them off in case he dazzled someone.

'Right, follow me. The river's down this way. At least I think it is. One of the things the Army taught me was a complete lack of confidence in my innate sense of direction.'

He was being too modest, for in a few minutes we emerged on the riverbank boulevard called the Bund, home to the grand buildings of the banks and trading houses, and in Clancy's day a hectic working harbour at which vessels docked carrying silk, tea, machinery, round-the-world motorcyclists and wealthy tourists looking for rickshaws to take them to their hotels.

'That was the Shanghai HQ of Swires,' said Roger, pointing to a venerable five-storey red brick building to the right. 'I remember JB Rae-Smith, who's on the board, telling me about his dad Christopher watching the Japanese invasion from his office window there, flanked by the Sikh guards all the big companies used to guard their offices and ships,' he said.

'The Sikhs were fabulous. If they caught a pirate, they'd chop off his head and stick it on the front of the boat as a warning to others, right up to 1939. Bloody right, too.

'It's hard to believe, looking over at the skyscrapers in Pudong, that until a few years ago, the average living space for someone in Shanghai was six square metres, and most houses had shared kitchens and bathrooms.

'By contrast, a friend of mine urged me to buy an apartment over there ten years ago for half a million dollars, but I thought it was too much, and now they're worth about fourteen times that. Excuse me while I just cry a little.'

We took the ferry across the river into another world, of wide boulevards, countless skyscrapers soaring into the clouds, and the only sound the quiet whisper of money being counted.

Still, at least thanks to feng shui, the buildings are separated by parks and ponds, allowing you to get a good view of the most quixotic and elegant tall buildings on earth.

The first to go up in the Pudong area was the Oriental Pearl Tower in 1992, which looks, with its tubes and balls, as if at any minute Flash Gordon will stride towards it, disappear inside, press a large red button, and disappear into the heavens.

At the other end of the elegance scale is the tapering postmodern Jin Mao Tower, which when it opened was scaled by the French free climber Alain Robert.

'One of the peasants who'd worked on the building was so disgusted with all the fuss in the papers over the stunt that he turned up one morning in his brown polyester suit and ordinary shoes, and climbed to the top just to show how easy it was,' said Roger as we walked past the Jaguar showroom on the ground floor.

'I was actually talking to the manager in there last month, and asked him if anyone ever just walked in off the street and bought a car. Funny enough, he said, a man had walked in the morning before with a beautiful girl and bought her a brand new Jag. Then in the afternoon he came in with a different beautiful girl and bought her one. The two mistresses had obviously been talking to each other.'

Next door to the Jin Mao is the Shanghai World Financial Centre, the tallest building in China and the third tallest in the world, with an idiosyncratic hole in the top which immediately earned it the sobriquet the Bottle Opener.

'The lobby of the hotel inside is on the fifty-fifth floor, and the hollow atrium goes all the way up to the eightieth. Great place for a spectacular suicide if you managed to hit the grand piano in the lobby,' said Roger, cheerfully.

Even that building is just about to be surpassed by the Shanghai Tower, a spiralling cylinder due to open in 2014 which will be almost 2000 feet tall and with its hotel lobby on the sixtieth floor.

'That's the HSBC building over there with its rooftop bar,' said Roger. 'Although they're a bit snotty. I popped up for a drink once, and they told me the minimum charge was £150. I bought shares in them afterwards, because I thought if they treat their customers that badly, they must be making a fortune.

'And that curved building is owned by the Taiwanese company Aurora, who turn the whole building into a giant TV screen after dark, although with the Chinese, they have to be careful what channel they tune to.'

Having taken the traditional ferry across the river, we took the slightly less traditional psychedelic tunnel under it on the way back, and if entering Shanghai had been like stumbling on the set of *Bladerunner*, the tunnel was like the Tube on acid.

However, a much more civilised way to toast Clancy was to walk into the lobby of the Peace Hotel, with the late afternoon light streaming through the art deco stained glass of the atrium, and order dry martinis in the Long Bar, where Douglas Fairbanks and Charlie Chaplin once dallied, and where Noel Coward dreamed up *Private Lives* while laid up with flu.

In the corner, the hotel's legendary Old Jazz Band played just as they had as young men before the Communists disbanded them after the Revolution in 1949. With the city now buzzing again, they had been hauled out, dusted off and told they could start playing their decadent capitalist tunes again, even though they were now all in their eighties.

Far above us as we sipped our martinis and they launched into 'What a Wonderful World' was the penthouse which was once the home of the hotel's owner, the Sephardic Jew Victor Sassoon.

Sassoon, whose family were Iraqi refugees turned millionaire opium traders in India, moved the family fortune to Shanghai in the 1920s and almost singlehandedly started the decade of decadence there. His parties are still talked about: at one with a shipwreck theme, the prize for best costume went to a couple who turned up naked wrapped in a shower curtain.

'Well,' said Roger, raising his glass, 'who would have thought when we played at the Commonwealths that in thirty-two years we'd be drinking Martinis in the Long Bar of the Peace Hotel in Shanghai?'

'I always did,' I said, and we laughed.

Chapter Fifteen

A short history of Japan

1639

Annoyed by pesky missionaries, Shogun bans all foreigners,
leading to over two centuries of seclusion, stability and a
flourishing of the arts.

1853

Pesky foreigners return in the shape of the US Navy. Japanese
take one look at its firepower and mutter: 'Please, come in.
And don't forget to wipe your feet', then abolish feudal
and class systems and launch into enthusiastic
modernisation.

1930s

Military seize power and slowly lead nation towards attack on
Pearl Harbor in 1941 and war in the Pacific.

1945

After Hiroshima and Nagasaki, Emperor Hirohito goes on
national radio to announce that 'the war situation
has developed not necessarily to Japan's advantage',
which wins world understatement of the year award.
Or possibly ever.

1945 and a half

US occupy country and instigate political and social reform which eventually leads to 1960s economic boom and 1980s bubble economy.

1990s

Bubble bursts, creating years of gloom capped by devastating tsunami in 2011.

As the *Bulow* docked in Nagasaki, Clancy emerged on deck, breathed in the salt sea air, and almost certainly grinned with pleasure to see, as his Henderson was lowered onto the dockside, a sight he had not seen for some time: roads.

Indeed, as he cranked the engine into life for the first time in weeks and motored north, the roads were so good that not even being restricted to 15mph by culverts, mysterious 90-degree bends, rickshaws and pony carts dampened his spirits.

Around him was a country more delightful, beautiful, peculiar and above all different to anything he had ever seen, particularly the quaint habit of locals to dash out of their homes and into the road when they heard his horn, thinking it meant the arrival of the fried fish salesman, the pipe cleaner or the clog mender.

Still, apart from kamikaze pedestrians, rickshaws and carts, he had the roads to himself, since he saw no motorcycles and only a single car in his whole time in Japan. It is, as you can imagine, much the same today.

Even eight years after Clancy was there, motorised vehicles were such a novelty that the following official guidelines were published for foreigners driving in the country:

1. At the rise of the hand of the policeman stop rapidly. Do not pass him or otherwise disrespect him.
2. When a passenger of foot hove in sight tootle the horn.

Trumpet him melodiously at first, but if he still obstacles your passage tootle with vigor and express by word of mouth 'Hi! Hi!'

3. Beware of the wandering horse that he shall not take fright as you pass him. Do not explosion the exhaust box at him. Go soothingly by, or stop by the roadside till he pass away.

4. Give big space to the festive dog that make sport in the roadway. Avoid entanglement of the dog with your wheelspokes.

5. Go soothingly on the grease mud as there lurk the skid devil.

6. Press the brake of the foot as you roll around the corners to save the collapse and tie-up.

I'm sure they would have done Clancy no end of good as he followed the coast north from Nagasaki through Saga to Kobe, Kyoto, Nagoya, Mount Fuji, Lake Hakone, Kamakura, Yokohama, Tokyo and Nikko.

Although it was cold and so cloudy that only the base of Mount Fuji was visible and that, apart from a few hardy trees, the cherry blossom season was past its best, he was charmed by countryside which was like one huge market garden, with each weathered wood and tissue paper house surrounded by a dainty garden and hedge, and was delighted by the temples, palaces and tea houses half hidden in shady nooks.

The cities and the people didn't get off so lightly.

While he praised Kamakura for its wonderful temples, rare works of art and gigantic bronze statue of Buddha, Nagoya for its cloisonné, porcelain, castle and pair of priceless golden dolphins, Nara, Kyoto and Nikko for their temples and Yokohama for a nice line in bargain silk shirts and embroidery, he was just softening up the Japanese for a full-scale Clancyfication.

Tokyo, the first victim, was dismissed as flat, uninteresting and having no public buildings of interest apart from the

Imperial Palace. Apart from the few examples he picked out, he condemned the rest of the country's architecture as just 'a bunch of temples and shanties'.

And just as the country's architects were picking themselves up and brushing themselves off after that one, Clancy rolled his sleeves up and got stuck into the people. They were, he stated, 'nothing to write home about'. He complained that the men wore either slovenly kimonos or European dress which made them look ridiculous, and although they seemed 'pleasant and jolly enough', he didn't trust the look in their eyes or their mysterious manner, and 'wouldn't trust them around the corner with a sou'.

The women got off slightly better.

'Many were plump and rosy, but seldom graceful', and although their 'richly designed kimonos … lovely sashes and tasteful jewellery' made some into life-size dolls he could almost like, their efforts to beautify themselves were confined to 'grotesque' hair arrangements so complex that they slept on narrow wooden pillows to avoid ruining them. When they weren't wandering around smoking pipes or cigarettes, that is.

The Japanese people, he concluded, were 'a bunch of raw barbarians', and the country as a whole was bankrupt because of huge taxes to support the huge army.

Heavens. A festive dog making sport in the roadway must have become entangled in his wheelspokes that day.

There. Having left yet another nation smoking in his wake, he treated himself to a stock of fine silk shirts in the bazaars of Yokohama for $1.50 each and, feeling like a well-laden Christmas tree, boarded the last launch to the P&O steam yacht *Persia* which over the next three weeks would bear him home to the good old US of A, sharing with a 230lb, 6ft 6in Russian a cabin so tiny that they could only open the door if one of them stood up.

The food, meanwhile, was as bad as on the *Bulow*, but at least was conveniently served in the ship's hospital.

The *Persia*, built in 1900 on the Clyde, would go on to be sunk without warning off Crete, while the passengers were having lunch, on 30 December 1915, by a German U-Boat, killing 343 of the 519 aboard, and breaking both international naval law and the Imperial German Navy's own restriction on attacking passenger liners. She was carrying a large quantity of gold and jewels belonging to the Maharaja Jagatjit Singh, who had disembarked at Marseilles.

Among the passengers to survive was Baron Montagu of Beaulieu, although his secretary and mistress Eleanor Thornton, who was the model for the Rolls-Royce 'Spirit of Ecstasy' statuette by Charles Robinson Sykes, died.

As our plane touched down at Nagasaki, I felt that curious mixture of fear and excitement I had felt the previous time I had visited Japan, for three weeks in 1995: fear because it is the most alien place on the planet, and excitement because it is also the most fascinating.

Like Clancy, we arrived in Nagasaki just too late for cherry blossom season, that time of year when the petals come fluttering down to remind the Japanese of the fragile, temporary beauty of life.

But then, the city where we stepped ashore was an even greater reminder of that. On a summer day in 1945, almost four hundred years of relatively benign association with the West, which began when Portuguese traders sailed into Nagasaki harbour in 1570, came to a sudden, apocalyptic end when the second of the USA's atomic bombs fell.

Dumping our bags on the tatami matting of a traditional ryokan in the wooded hills on the edge of the city, we jumped on one of the trams which have been rattling through the city since 1911, so Clancy would have ridden past them on his way north.

Some of those original trams survived the bomb, and the city has not only been keeping them running, but buying scrapped ones from other cities and restoring them too, so that the one we stepped onto was immaculate – from the driver with his peaked cap and white cotton gloves to the brass pressure gauge above his head with the white dial.

Even if he did announce the stops in a voice so dreary that I suspected every evening he went down to the local karaoke bar and sang Country and Western hits until the owner threw him out before all the other customers committed seppuku.

The girl on the piped announcements couldn't have been more different, with a constant burble of what sounded like: 'Oh joy, oh bliss! Welcome aboard our humble tram, honourable customers. I am as happy as a bunny rabbit that you have honoured us with our presence this morning, and I hope from the bottom of my little white cotton socks that your journey is filled with happy, sparkly thoughts, tra la la la la, la la la la.'

I'm paraphrasing, but you get the picture. They were, I hope, engaged to be married so that she could save him from a fate worse than Hank Williams.

Leaving them to it, we pressed the little chrome button, which lit up red and gave a cheery ting, to get off at the stop for the Atomic Bomb Museum, which traces the events before and after that fateful summer day in 1945.

Although the US had warned the Japanese on 26 July to surrender or be destroyed, it had not mentioned the new atomic bomb and, in spite of sixty-nine leading American scientists signing a letter to US President Harry S. Truman asking him not to use the bomb without a specific warning, he signed the order to go ahead, and it was dropped on Hiroshima on 6 August, with Kokura planned as the second victim three days later.

On the morning of 9 August, the 240,000 citizens of Nagasaki woke to a warm but overcast day, and were glad when the clouds parted at 11 a.m. to reveal just enough blue sky to make a sailor suit.

They shouldn't have been, because at that moment the crew

of the B-29 Superfortress Bockscar returning from finding Kokura obscured by cloud, saw Nagasaki through the same gap and dropped their bomb on it from 30,000 feet. In three seconds, 70,000 people died and another 70,000 were fatally poisoned by radiation.

As in Auschwitz, with its locks of hair, its shoes and suitcases, it is the small human details in the museum that are the most poignant, like a schoolgirl's lunchbox, her name and class number still visible on the lid and the rice inside as charred as the bread from Pompeii which Clancy had seen in Naples.

In another bitter irony, the ones who died instantly were considered luckier than the ones who lived in what a local doctor described as concentric circles of death, so that the further you were from the blast, the longer it took for a slow, painful end by radiation poisoning.

Or a life in which you survived physically, but knowing that all your family and friends had been killed, enduring what survivor Sumako Fukuda described as a life of hopeless solitude until death.

The most moving epitaph of all, though, must be that of Dr Takashi Nagai, an assistant professor at Nagasaki Medical College who in spite of his burns worked all day tending to other victims.

That night, he walked home exhausted to find the ashes of his wife beside her rosary, and spent the rest of his life working for disarmament until his death six years later from leukaemia caused by the bomb.

'A person who prays for peace must not hide even a needle, for a person who possesses weapons is not qualified to pray for peace,' he said.

And yet the world still failed to listen. Witness the Cold War, the billions spent on weapons that could never be used, and the ridiculous posturing still going on in North Korea and Israel.

I stood there looking at the kind, suffering face of Dr Nagai, and wondered how on earth the murder of 140,000 civilians, most of them women, children and pensioners was necessary, after the warning of Hiroshima. Indeed, was it any more necessary than the mass murder of innocent civilians in Dresden or the Holocaust, or any of the other acts of collective lunacy we call war?

It is remarkable, I thought as I walked outside, that since Clancy rode through here we have come on in leaps and bounds technologically, but not moved an inch in terms of morality.

But then, there is little point in idly fretting about things we cannot control, and in the end, all we can do is to do good within our own sphere of influence with every small act of the passing day, whether it's giving a few coins to a beggar, or complimenting a girl in a shop on her hat.

Add up all the smiles and lightened hearts that creates, and you may well have a critical mass greater than that of any atomic bomb.

I was reminded of it that day in Nagasaki in the joyous laughter of the four billion or so schoolchildren at the museum to whom I said 'Ohayou Gozaimasu' or 'Konnichiwa, o-genki desu ka?' before they asked me at length how I was, where I was from and how I got to be so tall.

And when we emerged into glorious sunshine we bought two cones from an old ice cream seller, and in a few deft scoops she created what looked like two perfect roses almost too beautiful to eat. She handed them to us with a polite bow, and in that moment I was reminded again why I love Japan, for the infinitely loving care given to the beauty of detail in everything, from bathing and the tying of a kimono to the tea ceremony.

You may say, of course, that beauty is a shallow thing: but to me it goes much deeper than that: just think of how your heart lifts when you walk into a simple room, with a wooden floor, white walls and one beautiful thing in it, and how much it sinks when you walk into a space in which no care has been taken over its form or function; or when you see someone littering, or being rude, or spraying graffiti. They are all small things, but better small beautiful things than small ugly ones.

And so, with world peace in the balance but my love for Japan secure, I returned to our traditional ryokan and a struggle with the four thousand buttons on the slightly less traditional automated toilet.

At one stage I accidentally cranked the heated seat and hot air bottom drying fan up to maximum heat, leading to a few seconds of intense panic that my nether regions would burst into flames and I would be charged with arson.

Fortunately, I found the off button just in time, and we celebrated by going out to a little bar in town for sashimi.

'Chin-chin,' said Gary, raising his glass of Kirin as the food arrived.

'Er, I wouldn't say that too loudly in Japan if I was you, chum,' I said.

'Why not?

'Because it means penis. It's why Tintin's called Tantan here, although I think Snowy's safe enough.'

We wandered around Nagasaki in the sun the following morning, then climbed the hill overlooking the bay to the home of its most famous Western resident, the Scotsman Thomas Glover, who arrived in the city in 1859 at the age of twenty-two.

It was perfect timing for a man who wanted to make his fortune, with young revolutionaries keen to overthrow the Shogunate, embrace the West and modernise Japan. In between sheltering them and sending some abroad to study, including future Prime Minister Ito Hirobumi, Glover made a fortune in shipbuilding, coal mining and tea, although his most important contribution was introducing beer to Japan by founding the brewery which later became Kirin, whose logo is still adorned with his splendid moustache.

He lived in an elegant wooden clover-shaped bungalow on the hills above the town with his wife Tsuru, a former geisha, and son Tomisaburo. It was a shame, I thought, that Clancy had missed him, but Glover died at seventy-three just before Clancy arrived, and today, all that remains is the house, still with the best view in town, looking down over its elegant gardens to the bay.

Its wise design leaves every room open to light and the sea breeze, and in the gardens, between the other elegant houses of western merchants, are ponds full of koi carp so tame they let us tickle their noses while we fed them.

Leaving the ghost of the Glovers behind, we tilted north following the ghost of Clancy through Saga, which was unremarkable but appropriate, since Gary and I had now reached the age where we'd started getting kind offers of health insurance and discounted Zimmer frames from the organisation of the same name.

As we rolled through the ultra-modern skyscrapers of Osaka, I thought that, although there is much in Japan that would have baffled Clancy – like the shop sign we were just passing which said 'Go go funky singing monkey, I am being nice arrow OK', the giant TV screens on buildings, the pachinko parlours or the bullet train flashing through the countryside like a bolt of light – it is such a country of extreme contrasts between the futuristic and the ancient that today there are many things that have not changed in three centuries, never mind one.

Like the simple room with a single cherry blossom in a vase where I had taken tea in Kyoto.

Or the archers I had seen one moonlit evening by a lake in Yudanaka, standing on a cedar platform by a lake in plain white kimono and black overskirts, using unadorned bows almost seven feet long.

Or the geisha on her way to Gion Corner, with her snow-white face and cherry lips, timelessly immaculate, from her elaborately coiled hair held up by antique ivory pins and her kimono and obi in the most understated silks, to her simple white cotton *tabe* split socks and lacquered *geta* sandals.

Or the Temple of the Golden Pavilion in Kyoto, its perfection doubled by its reflection in a mirrored lake.

And Clancy's weathered wood and tissue paper houses may now have glass instead of paper in their shoji screens, but they are still surrounded by dainty gardens and hedge, and the temples, palaces and tea houses are still half hidden in their shady nooks.

As we passed Kobe, I could see grazing in the meadows the grandsons of Cecil, the prize bull I'd met the last time I was there, who had a life of free beer, free lodging and free massage, but with a price: becoming two thousand of the most expensive steaks in the world.

In Kyoto, we stood in the Zen garden of the temple of Daitoku-ji looking at the cherry tree that I had admired with the abbot the last time I was here.

'Yes, this tree is very famous,' he had said.

'Oh, why?' I said.

'No particular reason,' he said, and wandered off, his hands clasped behind his back.

As we were wandering by the lake in front of the Temple of the Golden Pavilion, I suddenly thought of Sei, the guide who had shown me around Kyoto when I was last here in 1996.

I had taken her out for teriyaki and beer at a little restaurant that evening, and we talked and laughed, and then she walked me back to the inn.

'You know, Geoff,' she said, as we stopped outside, standing close together in the dark, 'we have a saying in Japan that when we travel, we leave shame behind.'

I looked at her, knowing exactly what she meant. And then I thought of my girlfriend back home.

'Oh Sei, you are lovely, but I cannot,' I said, and watched her disappear into the night, with honour and desire wrestling in my heart, then went into the inn and slept the sleep of the just, but only just.

And walking through the same city now, just at that moment, I had a strange stab of regret. Perhaps it was because my then girlfriend had buggered off, leaving the noble ship of my fidelity foundering on the rocks of her indifference. Or perhaps it was because it was my fifty-seventh birthday, and all day I had been consumed by the niggling feeling that the years of fun and laughter were behind me, leaving only a long slide into decrepitude, tempered only by sagacity and acceptance.

Mark Twain was right when he said that in twenty years we always regret the things we didn't do, not the things we did, but since regretting the past and worrying about the future is the fastest road to misery, I put my little regret back where it belonged and went back to being a part-time Zen Buddhist living in the eternal now.

After all, as the inscription on the stone water basin of that most Zen of Kyoto's Zen gardens, Ryōan-ji, says, 'I learn only to be contented'.

Anyway, to cheer me up I got about ten squillion birthday greetings on Facebook, including one from biker Ron Ballard, who said, 'If you're in Kyoto, drop in to the Yamaha factory and see if they have any Mikuni VM34SS carbs knocking about for a 79 SR500. Mine is doing my head in trying to set the mixture right.'

And to cheer me up even more, Cate phoned that evening to wish me a happy birthday, and I told her about the page of the original score of Puccini's 'Madame Butterfly' I'd seen in Glover Garden in Nagasaki, since the humming chorus from that opera was the music she'd walked up the aisle to at our wedding.

'Aw,' she said. 'It was on the radio this afternoon. Sorry you're so far away on your birthday.'

'Don't worry. We'll have a grand belated birthday barbie

when I get back,' I said and hung up, thinking how lucky I was to have her.

At Lake Hakone, the burnt orange Shinto arches were still rising out of the dark waters, overlooked by the traditional pile of the Hakone Prince Hotel Annex, which the ferry stewardess had pointed out to me was perfectly asymmetrical, and in the distance, eternal and unchanging, was the perfect shape of Mount Fuji, so revered by the Japanese that it is home to the world's highest Coke vending machine.

But then, Japan is a country where you can buy almost anything out of a vending machine, including the cans of hot coffee to which I had become disturbingly addicted the last time I was here.

At Kamakura, hundreds of tiny grey statues of Jizo, the patron saint of children, stood on a hillside overlooking the sea, many of them had been draped with unused baby clothes by women who had lost a child and who had come here for solace or hope.

In Tokyo, the last time I had been there, I had stayed in a ryokan where, after a breakfast of spicy miso soup, glutinous rice, pickled this, that and the other, tiny strips of dried seaweed, cubes of tasty tofu and steaming bowls of o-cha, or green tea, I sat by the front door looking out at a white wall, a simple red lantern, a black wooden beam and the autumnal branch of a maple tree.

Suddenly into this rectangular poem had walked a passing salaryman, a Japanese white-collar worker, on his way to another brutal twelve-hour day at the office. As his footsteps receded, the scene began to slip back into the past, not stopping as it reached one hundred years ago, or two, or even three.

In Japan, life is art and the past is the present. Every day is filled with moments of the most extraordinary beauty, and you are often uncertain which century you are in.

Unless, of course, you do what we did this time, and stay in one of the capsule hotels originally designed for businessmen who had got so drunk after work that they had missed the last train home.

Fortunately, being a black belt in origami, it only took me half an hour to fold myself into my pod and fall asleep for a disturbed night in which I woke several times and thought for the first few seconds that I was in a spaceship on my way to another planet.

I would, I imagined, feel entirely at home.

Chapter Sixteen

A short history of the USA

12,000 BC – 1492
Natives live in relative peace and harmony, interrupted by spells of killing each other, and buffalo for snacks.

1492
Europeans arrive and show natives and buffalo how killing should really be done.

1773
Boston Tea Party. Yanks throw tea in harbour, forgetting that you need to warm harbour first. Impossible to get decent cup of tea in USA since.

1791
Second Amendment confirms the right to bear arms only because a well-regulated militia is necessary to the security of a free state. After a while, Americans conveniently forget the militia bit and stock up at Bob's Gun Store.

1920
Prohibition. American men ban alcohol, sober up long enough to give women the vote, then take to drink again.

1950s

Every household has a fridge the size of a house, and cars so long owners don't need to drive anywhere, but just climb in the back and walk to the front to get where they're going. Americans have never had it so good; unless they're black, gay or communist.

1980 – 2001

Reagan enters senility, Bush enters Kuwait, Clinton enters Lewinsky.

2012

After gunman kills twenty children and six adults at Sandy Hook elementary school, National Rifle Association declares that the answer is even more guns.

Let me tell you what happiness is.

Happiness is arriving at Tokyo Airport for our Cathay Pacific flight to Hong Kong then on to Los Angeles and discovering we'd got an upgrade.

Then stepping onto the plane and returning the stewardess' cheery, 'Good morning, sir' with an equally cheery, 'Good morning, *ohayou gozaimasu, ni hao* etc'.

'Heavens, we are multilingual. I'm impressed,' she said.

'Well, I am half Japanese and half Chinese,' I said.

'I could tell at a glance,' she said. 'Glass of champagne?'

It was the perfect James Bond flirtation haiku.

I settled into a seat the size of Texas with the glass of champagne, and opened my copy of *Motorcycle Adventurer* at the page where Clancy arrives in San Francisco and steps onto home soil for the first time in over eight months.

His first shock was that everyone was speaking English; for, while his head knew of course they would, in his heart it felt like sacrilege for Frenchmen, Italians and Chinese to be wantonly using his home language as their own.

However, he was in for an even bigger shock when he went to the docks to collect his Henderson to find that it had crossed the Pacific upside down, the Japanese for 'This Way Up' obviously having been lost in translation.

As he was rolling up his sleeves and preparing to laboriously clean the oil off it with kerosene, he heard the sound of another Henderson, and looked up to see a young man called Robert Allen rolling up on his brand new machine.

Bob, as everyone called him, immediately set to helping Clancy with the job, and by the time they'd finished, had agreed to scrap his plans for a holiday and join Clancy in riding across the States through Portland and Spokane to chart a route for a new northern transcontinental highway.

However, if Clancy had thought he was returning to civilisation, he was in for a shock, for it took him two days of hunting around San Francisco for information on the road north, before he finally tracked down the secretary of the American Automobile Association, who announced confidently that only 40 of the 900 miles between San Francisco and Portland were poor.

'If he had said there are only forty miles of good roads he would have come much closer to the truth,' Clancy later noted in his diary, since he and Allen had set off through Tracy and Stockton for Sacramento on dirt tracks that made the highways of Tunisia seem like ribbons of silk.

At least we arrived at the Virgin Atlantic freight depot in LA, clutching a wad of paper from the customs office around the corner that would have choked a whole family of donkeys, to find the BMWs the right way up in their crates.

We were lucky they were there at all: at one stage, trying to find someone to ship the bikes to the States had proved so difficult that Dr Gregory Frazier had offered to lend us a slightly used 1983 Suzuki 50cc chopper with less than 300 miles on it.

Perfect. Just my size. I'm sure Gary could have ridden pillion.

Thankfully, Roddy Warriner and Giles Ernsting at James Cargo had come to the rescue in the nick of time by offering to waive their profit.

Feeling like boys on Christmas morning, we freed the bikes from their bonds of wood, gaffer tape and bubble wrap, brought the engines coughing into life and rode through the dry, aromatic air of southern California to the hillside house of my cousin-in-law Rick and his partner Chris, who were putting us up for a couple of days.

We were just in time to drink wine and order pizza as the sun went down over the Hollywood sign across the valley, then we spent a couple of welcome days lounging around before riding north. We found a clean and tidy motel in Morro Bay, and that night I was checking emails when I suddenly sat bolt upright and a shiver ran down my spine.

Because the one I had just opened was from Liam O'Connor in Australia, who had sent me Clancy's boots. And although we had all thought Clancy left no surviving relatives, we were wrong.

'It turns out that Carl Stearns has a nephew, Dr Edward Philbrook Clancy, a retired physics professor who lives in Portland Maine and has his hundredth birthday in a few weeks, on 3 July,' wrote Liam.

'I have been in contact with three of his daughters: Cynthia Thompson, Lynda Clancy, a journalist in Rockport, Maine, Gwen Clancy, a filmmaker in Nevada, and Gwen's son John Clancy-Tone, who lives in San Francisco and has been working on a screenplay of Carl Stearns' adventure.

'John has expressed an interest in being present for the start of the US leg in San Francisco and Lynda for the finish.'

Brilliant, I thought. And even more wonderful that as writers, filmmakers and screenwriters, they're following in the grand Clancy tradition.

Sadly, the shiver going down my spine then met one coming the other way, for the next email I opened was from the *Sunday Times*, telling me they were dumping their weekly bike column, and with it two thirds of my income.

I sat there looking at the email, feeling faintly sick at heart with worry about the future. But then there was no point in worrying about it, since all worrying does is make you worried. I had enough in the bank to do us for a while, and I would find a solution when I got home, since I always do.

In the meantime, I had a motorbike sitting outside, a road to ride and a book to write, and the next night, after a glum day of glum thoughts, we checked into a glum motel in Monterey and I found, through the crackling ether of a dodgy internet connection, an email from Gwen Clancy:

Dear Geoff,

How exciting to be linked up with you intrepid motorcyclists and re-enactors of our Uncle Carl's grand adventure one hundred years ago! Thanks so much to Liam for connecting us.

As he correctly noted, our dad, Dr Edward Clancy, is just about to turn 100 and is Carl's closest living relative, as Carl had no children. Dad remembers his Uncle Carl telling many tales of his motorcycle ride around the globe.

In fact, my dad was pretty much the only offspring of his parent's generation, with one or two stray cousins who are no longer living. In the various family photos, you'll see Dad in shorts, surrounded by a whole raft of childless aunts and uncles, including Carl and his sister Agnes, both of whom lived in Alexandria, Virginia, in the later years of their lives, and where the young Liam O'Connor got to know them.

Ben Clancy is a captain in the Navy, living in Coronado, and we also have a brother Jon Clancy, in Pullman, an hour from Spokane. I see your motorcycle route goes from Portland, or to Spokane, so perhaps he too could meet you if times work out.

My son John Clancy-Tone is making plans to meet you on 2 June, and will hope to get some footage of your ride and get a few comments from you on tape. He has long been fascinated by his great-great-uncle Carl, whose photo graces our hall table. In the photo, Carl is sitting proudly on his motorcycle on a city street at the end of the globe-girdling adventure.

As you can imagine, he was quite a fascinating character to us kids as we grew up, and we always referred to him as Uncle Carl, and still do.

We look forward to meeting Dr Gregory Frazier, whose book we discovered a few years ago on Amazon and purchased and read with great interest. In fact, we were so excited to see the book on Uncle Carl that we left a couple of messages at a phone number for Dr Frazier we found somewhere on the internet, but the communication must have fallen through the cracks.

At any rate, we are now delighted to be linking up with all of you and looking forward to meeting you through John and Lynda, if she can make it to New York City. It would make a great photo, especially if the photo we have of Uncle Carl is indeed in NYC. How cool would that be, to find the same spot?'

It was such a cheery email that it took the edge of the glumness, and I drifted off to a decent night's sleep, interrupted only by a dream in which I was bankrupt and sitting on a street corner in Belfast in the rain clutching a cardboard sign saying Will work for final salary pension.

The next morning, we were sitting outside a nearby Starbucks having coffee and croissants in the sun, since our motel didn't run to breakfast, when a blonde woman of a certain age stopped to admire the bikes. She turned out to be from Rotterdam, and the owner of a little arts and crafts shop nearby.

'I only started it because I had to reinvent myself four years ago when my husband was jailed for ten years for carrying marijuana across the border from Mexico,' she said. 'It was so stupid. Top of his class PhD, university professor, successful business: all gone. But then, I think he always had a self-destruct button lurking in there somewhere. His mother hid him from both sides in the war because his father was a double agent for both the Nazis and the Dutch Resistance and was shot in 1945. I think he felt he never deserved to be happy.

'He'll be seventy-five when he gets out. If he does. He's an old grey-haired man, and everyone else in there is bald and covered in tattoos.'

And so, having treated us to a flake of her life, she shook our hands and wandered off to open her shop.

As we rode north through the cherry orchards and rolling vineyards, even the Californian sun blazing down couldn't penetrate the shroud of anxiety and gloom wrapped around me about the future.

Only the presence of Cate, invisible but tangible on the back seat, and giving me an occasional squeeze as if to say things would be all right, kept my hopes alive.

So I was not alone. As well as Cate, I had the ghost of Uncle Carl, who had fretted about money throughout his adventure, and I was sure had worried about his own uncertain future when he had ridden these same Californian roads in the closing weeks of his journey. And added to those two, I now had the good thoughts of the whole host of Clancys who had appeared in the past few days.

The next day, I woke to an email from one of them, Ben, saying:

I remember from my childhood that his round-the-world trip was legendary, at least in our family circles, but I don't specifically recall him talking about it. One of my memories of Uncle Carl was him showing us, while we were young kids, the *Headless Horseman* movie that he made.

I don't remember him being a motorcyclist in his later years, which is when I came along, but I do remember him always owning a Ford automobile, never a Chevrolet or a Buick.

Riding north that afternoon, I saw a University of San Francisco poster saying 'Become wildly successful without being a jerk no one likes. Change the world from here.'

Splendid. That would be my motto from now on.

And so, at last, it was time to meet Dr Gregory Frazier, or Dr G, as he had become dubbed in our email correspondence. Or indeed Sun Chaser, the Indian name his grandfather had given him when he was four after his habit of running around the reservation chasing the sun.

It was a habit he carried into adult life: after a motorcycle racing career, he'd ridden around the world five times, the last time with a sixty-three-year-old grandmother of six who had been diagnosed with Parkinson's disease.

Although she had never been on a motorcycle before meeting Dr G, she convinced him to take her around the world on the pillion in an adventure lasting fourteen months and covering nearly 30,000 miles.

In 2010, aged sixty-two, he announced that increasing costs, red tape and age had caught up with him, and he was giving up the gentle art of circumnavigation and was now going to spend the summers in the US and the winters in Thailand.

'It's likely I'll keep logging between 30,000 and 50,000 miles a year, but I simply plan on being more fiscally conservative and responsible during these lean economic times and less of a wastrel merely circling the globe,' he said.

Aye, right, as they say in Belfast, for there's no known cure for itchy feet, and now he was off again around the planet with his mate Richard Livermore, with a recreation of Clancy's last leg as a gentle warm-up.

They'd ridden up from Los Angeles that day to the hotel

where we were staying, so when we arrived in San Francisco at teatime we left a message with reception to ask them to let us know when they arrived.

Time passed. Nothing happened. At eight we went downstairs for dinner and a beer, but on the way spotted two immaculate thirty-year-old Honda GL650 Silverwings parked outside, and found from the receptionist that Dr G and Richard were in Room 212.

We phoned. And knocked. And went for dinner, then phoned and knocked again, to no avail.

Back in the room, there was a flurry of emails from John Clancy-Tone and Gwen Clancy asking where we were meeting in the morning, and a single reply from Dr G giving a link to a website.

We phoned and knocked again. There was no answer. Curiouser and curiouser, said Alice, and she was right.

Then, next morning, I was standing in the lobby when the lift doors slid open to reveal a figure I had never seen before, but who was all too familiar, with his ponytailed hair as black as the bird from which his Crow tribe ancestors took their name.

'Dr G! I was beginning to think I'd imagined you,' I said, shaking his hand warmly.

'Yeah, sorry about last night. We left LA at four in the morning, and by the time we got here we were so bushed we fell asleep,' he said, introducing Richard, his riding partner on this trip.

'Er, just out of interest, why are you guys wearing shirts and ties?' I said.

'Well, Clancy did, so we felt we ought to,' said Richard.

'You'd better sharpen up, Geoff, you scruffy bastard,' said Gary.

'You speak for yourself, dickhead,' I said cheerily as we walked out to the bikes.

'You guys got GPS?' said Dr G.

'Er, yes, but they don't have US maps,' I said.

'No problem. Richard has one, so he can lead. All those in favour say aye.'

'Aye,' we all said. Except Richard.

'Democracy. I love it,' said Dr G, and Richard duly led the way down to the docks where one hundred years ago to the day Clancy had stepped ashore.

There were several bikers there already, and two suitably Clancy-era boats in the harbour; a tall ship and a paddle steamer, and before long Dr G and Gary were engaged in conversation with the gathered throng as they compared their respective bike collections.

Gary won 20 to 15 in numbers, but lost out in exclusivity, since his Ural and sidecar, and the Enfield I'd ridden back from India which was on permanent loan to him, were no match for Dr G's trio of vintage Indian Chiefs and a 1931 Henderson.

By noon, all the photographs had been taken, all the bikes in the world had been discussed, and it was time to go, except for one small detail: the mysterious non-appearance of John Clancy-Tone.

'Weird. He knew where we were, but we gotta go,' said Dr G, and after a brief diversion to ride down the rollercoaster that is Lombard Street and buy a Macbook charger to replace the one Gary had left in the motel in Santa Cruz, we headed north to Tracy. Clancy had stopped for ice cream there, and we had planned to do the same at Johnny's, a genuine fifties diner.

'Nice one walking down the street there,' said Gary, nodding his head at a California blonde in a sundress swinging along the pavement.

'Already on it,' grinned Dr G, showing that he and Gary had more in common than bikes.

Like most bikers, though, he proved quickly to be a kindred spirit, giving me a tube of Goop to glue the sole of one my ancient Altberg gentleman's motorcycling boots which, after making it all the way from Chile to Alaska, around Australia and now most of the way around the world, had finally come unstuck.

Richard was just as kind: earlier, he'd phoned every Apple shop in San Francisco to find one that stocked a charger for Gary. A sixty-seven-year-old construction insurance specialist and ex-army man, his wife had died of cancer three years before, but happily, he'd just got engaged to a fifty-six-year-old called Bonnie.

'My son's just glad she's not younger than he is,' he laughed when we stopped in Sacramento, where Clancy and Allen were so delighted to find a hard driveway encircling the Capitol that they rode around it twice, then went around every motorcycle dealer in town trying in vain to interest them in stocking the Friel's backrests they'd fitted before leaving San Francisco.

' "Sacramento always has and always will be dead", they'll tell you in San Francisco, and they sure are right!' fumed Clancy, who at least got some solace when one of the dealers invited him to a hill-climb challenge on a nearby railway embankment.

When the dealer's well-known twin-cylinder machine, probably a Harley, got stuck, Clancy climbed on his machine whispered to the old boy to do his best, and the Henderson responded with pride, sailing past the dealer with ease in spite of the 14,000 miles on the clock.

Only for hubris to strike with a bang: heading north out of town, they ran straight into twenty miles of deep sand, and Clancy's bike took a fall which broke off its magneto distributor.

Wiring it back in place, they ploughed on through the choking dust of the horse-drawn wagons known as prairie schooners on roads which regularly took a wide berth around sheep ranches.

Covered in dust, they treated the bikes to fuel and themselves to ice creams in the mining town of Oroville, arrived in Chico just before dark, and after riding up and down the main street, found a local mechanic who spent the evening fixing the distributor bolts and giving them copious but erroneous information on the roads ahead.

However, he was right about one thing: bad as the roads had been, at least they were bad and flat, and they were about to get worse and mountainous.

The dirt track which Clancy and Allen had ridden to Sacramento is today a six-lane freeway, but Sacramento was as sleepy as they found it, with the only sign of life a solitary ice cream salesman and a handful of Sunday strollers.

But then, it's hardly surprising Sacramento is sleepy: it was founded by the Swiss John Sutter, who arrived in 1839 and worked hard for ten years to make it a busy trading centre and cattle ranch, only for all his workers to bugger off when gold was discovered nearby in 1848.

After that brief spell of excitement, it settled back into being one of those places where you see plaques on walls saying: On this spot in 1897, nothing happened.

Still, the hard driveway around the Capitol, a fine neoclassical building topped by a dome glittering white against the deep blue sky, was still worth riding around twice, although our plans to challenge the local Harley dealer were doubly foiled by the fact that he was closed, and that those twin spoilsports, health and safety, had fenced off the railway embankment.

Even so, that wasn't the worst discovery of the day. No, that was when we went out to dinner and discovered that Dr G had given up drinking.

'I'm just trying to lose some weight for a bit,' he said shamefacedly.

'You could always drink light beer,' said Richard helpfully.

In the end, we just had to drink more to make up for him. There is, as I said earlier, always a solution.

The next morning, we were loading up the bikes when Richard pointed to a rough dirt mound on the edge of the parking lot.

'There you go. There's the hill climb you missed,' he said.

Dr G needed no further encouragement, and within seconds he had his Honda firmly stuck halfway up with a wide grin on his face.

'We just never lose the child in all of us,' said Gary.

'Good grief, chum, that's your first complete sentence without swearing, farting or pointing out the obvious attributes of every girl we meet,' I said.

'I have my moments, mothaf**ka,' he said. 'That girl on reception last night was a bit of all right, wasn't she?'

I knew it was too good to last.

What a fine feeling it was to saddle up and ride north with our newfound friends in the cool of the morning through the orchards of northern California, past poplars planted by the French and Italian fruit farmers who like so many others had flocked to this golden land, and which gave the scene a delightfully European air.

In Marysville, the State Theater had come and gone since Clancy's day, its entrance boarded up and its dusty screen a palimpsest bearing only the ghostly trace of ten thousand Saturday matinees.

By late morning, we were riding through the rolling grassland of cattle country and the sun was so bright that I had to check that my dark visor was actually flipped down.

We rode for so long that my nether regions began to wonder if Richard and Dr G would ever stop for a break until, at last, we pulled up outside a café in Redding – chosen solely because the owner had an impressive collection of model aeroplanes hanging from the ceiling – and tucked into sandwiches that were the size of Belgium, but a lot more interesting.

Before long, we were riding through the foothills of the Sierras with Mount Shasta visible in the distance and covered in snow, even in June.

Which is where it all started to go horribly wrong for Clancy and Allen.

With the mountains looming, they stopped at the express office in Redding and shipped their 50lb panniers on to Portland, bought cheap blankets in the general merchandise store for camping, and got the owner of the harness shop to sew some canvas saddlebags so they could carry the kit they needed to get them over the mountains.

That sorted, they tanked up with more ice cream, fuel and oil, and set off late in the afternoon for the dreaded road that lay ahead.

They didn't have long to wait: within a few miles out of Redding, they were climbing an endless succession of rocky grades with hairpin bends, then sliding down the other side to be greeted by small but lethal lakes full of boulders.

Often the road got so steep that they had to dismount and run beside the machines and, as they were sliding down one hair-raising slope with their back wheels locked, they came upon a young couple in a Cadillac stuck fast on a tree stump.

They got the car free, but the hill was so steep the fuel couldn't make it up to the carburettor. Not to be beaten, the resourceful Bob blew into the top of the fuel tank, his face slowly turning the colour of a beetroot, while the driver cranked the starter handle until the engine spluttered then fired into life and settled down into a steady rhythm.

Before parting ways, the grateful couple gave the riders six eggs, a small can of baked beans, an even smaller can of condensed cream, a little bread, sugar and coffee, and a pail to cook it in, and since by now it was growing dark and they were still in the heart of the mountains, they found a grassy spot near a crystal stream, and set up camp. Clancy cooked up a feast in the pail, while Bob made a bed of weeds and leaves between the Hendersons then, having enjoyed their dinner, they wrapped themselves in their blankets and, with strange sounds from the woods all around and lightning crackling overhead, finally fell asleep just before the grey light of dawn woke them again.

At 5 a.m., tired and hungry, they fired up the Hendersons and set off on roads which, impossibly, were even worse than the day before.

A ferry carried them across the raging Pitt River, and halfway up the next mountain, Clancy's Henderson ground to a halt with a dry and slipping clutch.

He greased it with oil from his tank, but the clutch was so worn and the track so steep that he could only push the Henderson up it in the fierce sun, stopping when he was so exhausted he couldn't hold the bike upright and resting until he could try again.

It took him twenty attempts and two exhausting hours to get up that one hill, and there were a dozen more beyond.

'If ever a man was bitter against motorcycling, it was I and then,' he wept, so worn out with heat and exhaustion that he was close to flinging himself in despair onto the rocks below when a Good Samaritan with a two-horse team towed him up the last slope to find Bob, who had stormed ahead with his new 8hp machine, sitting cool and collected and full of wild strawberries.

Clancy, presumably too exhausted to strangle him, collapsed beside him instead and, when he had the strength to lift his head, realised for the first time the extraordinary beauty around them.

Silver waterfalls tinkled to the ravines far below, piney summits strode to the horizon, and in between, the so-called Pacific Highway threaded its way through the virgin wood. They were further cheered by six miles of fairly good road, but it was only playing with them, for it soon returned to water, rocks, mud and hairpins, and they were exhausted as they staggered into the lumber town and summer resort of Dunsmuir.

A busy railroad hub back then, today it is a village of sleepy clapboard houses whose residents are slowly getting older and popping their clogs, and a solitary café where we tucked into ice cream on the verandah.

'Bought this place on a whim years ago,' said the owner. 'Best way to get a minimum wage from maximum work.'

The next morning, too stiff to move without pain, Clancy and Allen limped outside to find a fellow adventurer who had just spent four months riding there from Chicago, although when he said riding, he confessed the truth was that the roads were so bad he had walked most of the way pushing his machine.

Still, as they crossed the border from California into Oregon, their spirits were lifted by the sylvan idyll that greeted them, with its farmlands and orchards, its snow-clad peaks and rushing torrents, and its woods teeming with 'all things alive that delight the sportsman's heart and invite him to slaughter'.

Best of all, good roads led them in matching heart to Medford.

Compared to that, we had it easy as we swooped along silky tarmac through a landscape of pine-clad mountains and rushing rivers and across the state border into the alpine glories of Oregon, filled yet again with respect and admiration for Clancy and Allen getting through this landscape on what were basically mule trails.

Even worse for our reputation as real men, Richard and Dr G had organised, not a grassy spot near a crystal stream, but rooms at the Hampton Inn in Medford, where a girl with bright red hair swiped my credit card and pointed out the details of the fitness suite, pool, spa and free wi-fi.

Though, when we got the bill the next morning, I couldn't help thinking that Clancy and Allen had got the better deal. Particularly since we had been so busy writing up the day's events, blogging, organising photos and planning the next day that we had used none of the facilities we had paid so handsomely for.

As for Clancy and Allen, the good road to Medford was only building up their hopes to dash them again, for it disappeared immediately, with the seventy-seven miles from Grant's Pass to Roseburg taking them an entire day and leaving Clancy's long-suffering Henderson with the handlebars and back wheel jammed, and Bob's with a broken fork.

Shortly after passing a prairie schooner with a prospector, his wife, small son and dog aboard, they had encountered the worst section yet: the twelve miles of Cow Creek Canyon which Clancy described grimly as like an endless frozen pig pen as steep as a roof and littered with logs, rocks and ruts.

Arriving in Roseburg as darkness fell, they collapsed into the first inn they could find, and emerged to find that someone had stolen Clancy's gloves.

Still, at least the local hardware dealer was so impressed by the fact that the Hendersons had made it up that road that he signed up to be a dealer on the spot.

The next day, the road was so bad, and the scenery so glorious, that as Clancy put it perfectly, a poet would have been in heaven, and a motorcyclist in hell.

At one stage, a surprised Bob found himself and his Henderson leaving the road entirely and plummeting into the canyon below until his progress was arrested by a stout bush.

They spent the night in the pleasant town of Eugene, but throughout all of the next day and night it rained so hard they gave up the thought of riding and went to the movies instead. The next day they sped on dry and improving roads to the neat little town of Albany which, with its asphalt streets and electric lights, built up their hopes that they had rediscovered civilisation as they rode through Salem and struck north for Portland.

Yet again, they were wrong: as darkness fell, they hit a five-mile stretch of deep, slimy mud and ruts which caused them four hours of 'falls, bruises, sweat, exhaustion, pounding hearts and misery'.

When they finally rolled into Portland at 11.30 that night, their misery was compounded by the sight of the crowds going home from the last night of the annual Rose Festival, which they had been looking forward to all the way from San Francisco.

Disappointed, fed up, and tired beyond measure, they spent the next five days in Portland getting men and machines back in order and waiting for the swollen Columbia River to recede. During this time they encountered many astonished locals who told them that they were the first motorcyclists to have made the journey from San Francisco, a fact that Clancy absorbed with no small sense of pride.

As we checked out of our hotel in Medford next morning, we met our own friendly local, a man called Dave Bosworth, who was seventy-five but looked about fifty, and who came over to ask where we were from.

'That's a great adventure you guys are having,' he said. 'In 1959 a buddy and I drove a VW Bug all the way down to Panama. We floated it across rivers and tossed a coin to see who'd drive it over the rickety bridges, and then after all that got to Panama to find we couldn't get through the Darién Gap to Colombia.

'Tell me about it,' I laughed. 'I had the same problem coming the other way.'

Outside, I found Dr G arriving back from a meeting at the nearby offices of *Motorcycle USA* with one of the magazine's writers, Bart Madson, who was riding with us for the morning.

'Geoff!' said Bart. 'Haven't seen you since the GS launch in South Africa. Did they ever find out why Kevin crashed?'

'Still a mystery, Bart,' I said.

As we were riding away, the conversation with Dave reminded me that I hadn't seen a single VW the day before, since the vehicles driven by the locals had changed from the Beetle convertibles, classic Porsches and hot rods of California to monstrous pick-ups with sweet, romantic names like Dodge Ram and Ford

Asskicker, which trundled past with a subterranean growl from V8 engines doing about a mile to the gallon.

The houses had changed too, from beach villas and cool duplex condos to log cabins peeking out from the woods, some of them looking as if they had been put up yesterday and others looking as if they had been falling down since Clancy was here.

Even the air had changed: rather than the salt smack of the ocean, here it was sharp and sweet with the tang of resin from countless lumberyards.

As for Cow Creek Canyon, Clancy's endless frozen pig pen, it was now a perfect motorcycling road, twisting and turning under the dappled trees, over the railroad tracks and past a river sparkling in the sun.

Gary raced ahead as usual, and Dr G showed he still had it to go in spite of his claim that he was an old fart who was now the slowest biker on the planet – a title I've proudly held for years – but all of us gloried in every curve, then said farewell to Bart and rode on through a state which is still the sylvan idyll it was in Clancy's day.

On wooded hills and dales here and there, little communities of pastel wooden houses gathered, close enough for company but far enough apart for breathing space with, more often than not, a handsome horse grazing in a meadow behind each home.

In Roseburg, where Clancy had had his gloves stolen, we locked ours in the panniers just in case, but the locals couldn't have been friendlier.

'Don't cost a dime to be pleasant to folks,' said the man who filled our tanks at the gas station. Then, like Clancy, we decamped to the nearest inn, in our case the appropriately Irish McMenamin's which was housed in the 1907 railway station with a faded sign of the same vintage on the wall warning cyclists not to practise their dark arts on the platform.

In the leafy student and hippy enclave of Eugene, there was no sign of the cinema Clancy and Allen had spent a wet afternoon in, although the most likely suspect was the Bijou, which had replaced the original of the same name.

The railway station, which had been there in Clancy's day, was still well-kept but filled with glum folk sitting around and bums sleeping on the floor, while across the tracks and up a wooded hill, the pale green turreted bulk of the Shelton McMurphey Johnson House, a local landmark since 1888, looked down in faint disapproval.

As we rode on in the golden light of late afternoon, I looked at my watch. We had just over a hundred miles to cover before we reached Portland, so I estimated that we would arrive there at about six.

And indeed that's what we were on track to do; until Richard's bike started to run out of fuel. And his relationship with the GPS proved to be as good as ours had been in Europe.

I will spare you the details of our several scenic tours of Portland. Suffice to say it was well after 8 p.m. when we finally got to the hotel where he and Dr G had booked a room. Only to find they had none left for us.

Still, two phone calls later by the friendly receptionist, and we were booked into a hotel up the freeway. We arrived in well after nine, and I got into the room and sat down to work; only for Gary to walk through the door.

'The good news is there's a bar and a restaurant,' he said. 'The bad news is they both close at half nine.'

Still, I thought, as we ordered a beer and some food with a minute to spare, at least there were two things to celebrate.

We had made it to Portland almost two hours before Clancy.

And the accommodation was much better than it had been the last time I was here, when I had stayed in the White Eagle, a former Polish hostel, and shared my room with the ghost of a prostitute called Sam.

As I went to bed that night, though, there was one thing troubling me. Richard's job in the US Army had been rescuing downed airmen at sea, and as I finally fell asleep I wondered just how many of them had been left floating out there in the waves, with their last words: 'Thank God, I'm saved. No, Richard, not that way! Over here …'

Not that we were the only ones who got lost in this part of the country: Clancy and Allen, having finally left Portland, were met by torrential rain and floods which swept away houses and roads alike, and separated the two men from each other.

By nightfall, Clancy was still lost, so he slept in a nearby barn and the next morning found Allen, who had taken shelter in a hayloft, breakfasting on sardines and ginger snaps from a crossroads grocery.

So bad were the roads by now that they scraped down John Day Hill, the steepest slope of the entire trip, using their feet as brakes, and when near Ione they came upon a stretch where the locals had laid straw to give some grip, they almost wept with joy.

Only the thought of ice cream sodas in Echo kept them going enough to get to Pendleton before dark, in spite of having to cadge petrol then oil after running out of both.

With the worst rain for forty years, they finally gave up the next day and flagged down a freight train to take them and the bikes to Walla Walla in Washington State, only to find it the dreariest town imaginable, with drunken cattlemen staggering out of the countless saloons.

Still, at least the grocery store was doing a good deal on cherries, so they stuffed themselves, waited two days for the rain to stop, and to their joy found the road to Spokane so good that they did a glorious 156 miles in a day to be greeted by skyscrapers rather than the log cabins they had expected.

Even better, when they got there, the manager of the city Henderson agency treated them to twelve days of parties, dinners and rideouts with local bikers.

As we set out the next morning to retrace their journey from

Portland to Spokane, and with Dr G away for the day at business meetings, Richard redeemed himself in spades from the GPS saga of the night before, leading us north out of town through an idyllic scene of sailing boats dancing on the river to our left, and little aeroplanes taking off from an airfield to our right.

Before long we had finally turned east, with the long road which would end in New York in front of us, and alongside us the railroad tracks and the telegraph poles which are the companions of any road trip in the American west. All around were the rugged mountains reaching up to the arcing dome of sky, and below us the vast sweep of the Columbia River, its banks piled high with logs of Oregon pine waiting to be shipped downriver to become the coffee tables and sideboards of America.

As I was riding along idly wondering why you never see a headline saying Fortune Teller Wins Lottery, it suddenly occurred to me that there were only two and a half weeks left of the trip, which filled me with a multitude of emotions.

Sadness that soon the days of getting up in the morning, putting a few belongings on a motorbike and riding off, not sure what the day would bring, would be over.

Gladness that the huge organisational headaches were, touch wood, over, and the adventure was finishing with us following Richard and Dr G on good roads in good weather in a country made for road trips.

Gladness, too, that I would soon be seeing Cate, for whom this was the third time her husband had buggered off for three months, which is always harder for the person left at home.

Sadness that I had these adventures without her, rather than being able to share them.

And in there, a little niggling worry about our financial future, but I would leave that aside for the moment.

In the meantime, John Day Hill was every bit as steep as Clancy had said, and by lunchtime we were barrelling across rolling downs stretching all the way to the horizon, as if the Yorkshire Dales had won the lottery and decided to show off.

Since the roads were straight and empty and the sky was blue, I dumped my jacket in the top box and rode in shirtsleeves, savouring the sun and feeling like a boy on summer holidays.

Absolutely disgraceful and irresponsible, of course. Don't tell the Institute of Advanced Motorists, or I'll be thrown out; and whatever you do, don't tell Adelaide and BMW, since they think I'm working.

By lunchtime we were rolling into Ione, which you'll be pleased to hear won the State volleyball championships three years running; and possibly surprised, since to call it a one-horse town would be a victory of marketing over reality.

The sole pub had long since closed, but the owner of the deli down the single street rustled us up some sandwiches and her husband rustled up a potted history of the town, which when Clancy passed through was a thriving railroad hub and wheat freighting town of several thousand souls served by six grocery stores, eight churches and three brothels.

Today the population was 340, and falling, because back then a grain farmer needed thirty or forty men to run his concern. These days he just needs a combine harvester and an iPad app.

On we rode, through endless plains of wheat, the wind caressing them as gently as a man's hand through his sleeping wife's hair.

In Echo, St Peter's Catholic Church would have been brand new and gleaming white when Clancy and Allen rode through, but today the paint is peeling, the windows are broken and the walls have not echoed to hymns for many a long day.

The town was founded in 1880 by businessman James Koontz as the first stop on the Oregon Trail, the route used by the pioneers making their way west in wagon trains. He named it after his three-year-old daughter Echo, who grew up to be a bit of a sweetie with a mischievous grin and a twinkle in her eye, if the photo of her hanging in the foyer of the locked town museum is anything to go by.

When Clancy passed through, the sparkling white, two-storey neoclassical building that now houses the museum was the town bank, which looked out over a town of three thousand people. Echo was a major shipping point for wool, cattle and sheep, with miles of stockyards above ground and miles of tunnels below in which the good townspeople kept the Chinese railroad workers out of sight and mind. But as we had seen in Shanghai, expected to be the richest city in the world by 2020, China's economy is booming – which seems to be a fitting sort of revenge.

Today, the old bank looks across the dusty street at the H&P Café, which dates back to 1904 and is the most likely spot where Clancy and Allen tucked into welcome ice cream sodas.

'I'll call the mayor and see if he'll open the museum for you. I just made his wedding cake, so he owes me a favour,' said the owner, a tall and friendly thirty-year-old blonde called Challis Buck.

She'd grown up in Echo and worked in the café as a teenager, then trained as a chef, and worked with her German husband Danny Besser running five-star restaurants in New Jersey. Tired of twelve-hour days and six-day weeks, they came back to Echo in 2011 and fulfilled a childhood dream of buying the café.

The first thing she and Danny did when they opened the café was nail a sign above the kitchen door saying, 'Bless this kitchen and the food that is prepared. May it be a gathering place of happy memories shared.' Which made it all the more poignant that not much later Danny shot himself, having, unbeknownst to her, attempted suicide three times before.

'But what can you do except keep going?' she said, and two minutes later produced three ice cream sodas which were every bit as good as the ones Clancy and Allen had tucked into.

She was well-named, I thought as we shook her hand, wished

her all the good luck in the world and rode away, since challis is a fabric made from silk and worsted, both gentle and tough.

Oh, and the mayor never got back to her, so the only sign of him that we saw was a white postcard in the café window saying: Hi, I'm Richard Winter. I'm standing for Mayor (again). I'd appreciate your vote. Thanks, Richard.

Richard, I suspect, had not quite had the budget of Barack Obama or Mitt Romney in his bid for global domination.

Pendleton, too, had its tunnels for Chinese workers, although the locals weren't above spending a pleasant hour in the opium dens down there while their laundry was being done. During Prohibition, the tunnels were put to use as saloons, card rooms and brothels, but ever since booze became legal, the town's main attractions are, in no particular order, the stadium where the annual rodeo is held, Burns Mortuary, which is presumably also available to anyone dying of natural causes, and Hamley & Co, established in 1883 as purveyors of fine food, fine saddles and fine whisky.

Not forgetting what is possibly the USA's narrowest shop, the seventeen-inch wide Rivoli Cigar Store and Soda Fountain Emporium founded by Frank Griggs and J. Tyson, who were presumably slimmer than the average American today. Earlier, I'd seen two teenage brothers who wouldn't have looked out of place on a Japanese whaler, and I don't mean as crew.

In Walla Walla, there was not a drunken cattleman to be seen, even though the town is famous for its winery and, from the special offer signs in every beer shop, they didn't sell anything less than eighteen-packs.

'How far is it to Spokane now?' I asked Richard as we filled up with fuel.

'Oh, about two hundred miles,' he said airily.

I looked at my watch. It was 6 p.m.

We had fallen into a gap in the space-time continuum for the second day in a row, and three hours later – by which time

I'd driven myself slowly mad by singing, 'Spokane, Spokane, running all around my brain' – it was three weary men who rode into Spokane after twelve hours on the road.

It was too late for dinner, and too late for anything other than to sit down and write up the events of the day then fall into bed without even the comfort of a sardine or ginger snap.

That'll teach me for having fun earlier.

In any case, I thought as I fell asleep, the most exciting news of the day was that my fuel consumption had reached a stunning 55.4mpg, giving me a range of almost four hundred miles to a tank which cost a piffling $25 to fill.

America may not be the land of the free any more, but at under $4 a gallon, it's pretty close.

As for Clancy and Allen, they paid the price for their twelve-day party in Spokane: on their first night after leaving there, they had a supper of stale bread, syrup and water, and fell asleep wrapped in their blankets with only mosquitoes and rats for company.

In the mining town of Kellogg the next day, they were interviewed in depth by the sole reporter on the sole newspaper and, after riding through the devastation caused by a recent forest fire to be greeted by the paved streets, electric lights and tuxedo-clad waiters of Wallace, Idaho, decided that the Wild West now only existed in movies.

Only to have their certainty overturned the very next night when they arrived in Missoula, Montana, to find a posse in hot pursuit of a gang of desperadoes who had shot at their landlady, stolen the sheriff's six-shooter and terrorised the town before heading for the hills.

Wincing at the outrageous bill the next morning, they rode off into a thunderstorm so bad that by dark they had only covered twenty miles and were forced to spend the night in the shack of prospector Isam Cox, who rustled up a feast of bacon, beans and coffee for the exhausted but grateful duo.

It seemed like paradise, particularly when the next night, after riding through Clark's Fork, Horse Plains and Palermo, they camped by a river and, all night long, were eaten alive by mosquitoes.

The next day, they found the land around Butte ravaged by copper mining and, in the town itself, hardly a soul who could speak English, every third man drunk, not a policeman in sight and the prices on a par with New York.

The reason, they soon discovered, was that the labour unions were so strong that plumbers wouldn't fix a leak for less than half a day's pay. Of course, the shopkeepers took advantage by hiking up their prices so much that everybody lost, particularly visitors like Clancy and Bob.

They had personal experience of it the next day when Bob tried to fix a leak in his fuel tank, only to be told by a mechanic that he couldn't fix his own tank without a union card.

When he remonstrated, the mechanic told him that a plumber had been fined $50 for fixing a leak in his own house one night rather than calling another plumber; who wouldn't have come anyway because union rules forbade working after hours.

'Butte's as bad today for drinking,' Bart Madson had said back in Medford. 'The first time I was there, I was walking up the street at 11 in the morning when a man was thrown out through the swing doors of a saloon for being too drunk.'

'And it's catching,' said Dr G. 'I've a house up in Montana, and it's so far out in the woods that there's no cell phone signal, so I had to get a land line in. Then the office phoned me so much on it that one night I got drunk and blasted the damn thing off the wall with a shotgun.

'Now that I think of it, Calamity Jane worked in a brothel up there, but these days Butte's better known for two things. It's the birthplace of Evel Knievel, and it's where the FBI sends all its crap agents. They sit there doing nothing for $120,000 a year, and whenever there's a big case, the FBI sends in some good guys.'

'Tell them to call me,' I said. 'I'd do nothing for half that.'

We set off from Spokane in glorious sunshine, and before long were rolling up the main street of Kellogg, where Clancy was interviewed by the local newspaper.

I wandered into Bitterroot Mercantile, the first shop we came to, and the owner, a pleasant grey-haired man, came out from the back and introduced himself as Gary Corbeil.

'You wouldn't happen to know what the local paper here was called back in 1913?' I said.

'Sure do. It was the *Kellogg Wardner News*, covering both towns. It finally closed in 1985 when the mine shut, taking a million-dollar payroll out of the local economy every month. Can't really survive after that sort of blow.

'For sure. How do you know all this, by the way?'

'I was the publisher,' he said.

In Wallace, the electric lights were still working and the streets still paved, but the waiters in Albi's Bar, Sweet's Café and the Jameson Inn had cast off their tuxedos, as a result of which all three were now closed and up for sale.

Quite right, too. You can't let your standards slip without paying the price.

Even worse, the town brothel had closed in 1988 and was now in a museum. The girls had left in such a hurry that they'd left their clothes behind, and by the looks of it they didn't have much to wear but a few skimpy underthings, poor dears.

Still, the town won our prize for the best railway station so far, a mock-Tudor turreted fantasy which looked like it was home to Stationmaster Hansel, with Gretel living down the other end of the street in the matching Insurance Building, which she'd painted a very fetching shade of powder blue.

The mines around Wallace took a billion dollars worth of silver out of the surrounding hills, and when they closed, the dying town came within an inch of being demolished to make way for the freeway before a concerted local effort to have the fine old historic heart of the town listed.

And while some bars and hotels and the brothel have closed, we met fellow GS rider Dan Clark and his business partner Tim Johnson, who showed us around the 1904 Ryan Hotel they were refurbishing to reopen as a biker-friendly base for tours on the glorious roads all around.

'There's a room down at the back where Mrs Montgomery, a local schoolteacher, lived for twenty-seven years with just a sink, not even a single ring stove,' said Dan as we walked around the corner to a former tyre shop which entrepreneur Nick Fluge had converted into his own private art gallery.

'Nick made a heap of money, although we're not quite sure how, and he has places like this in LA, Manhattan and Paris; and they're not even for selling the paintings, just for showing them,' said Dan. 'And upstairs he's got an original painting of Norma Jeane Baker before she became Marilyn Monroe which is probably worth more than the rest of the town put together.'

'So what does Nick do now?' I said as we stood on the polished hardwood floor looking around at the paintings on the brick walls, a Steinway grand piano, a Seeburg Select-o-Matic jukebox and a 1948 Indian Chief parked in the window.

'He just travels the world having adventures.'

'Lucky boy. Wish I could get a job like that.'

'You already have, you mug,' laughed Dr G, and we shook hands with the guys, wished them good luck, and walked back to the bikes for Richard to go off exploring on his own for the rest of the day and Dr G to lead the way to Butte, Montana.

'Greg, if I'm going to get to the hotel after you, you'd better phone them and tell them we have a reservation,' said Richard as we put on our helmets.

'No need. Dr G's from the Crow tribe, and they've already got a reservation,' I said.

Laugh? I thought they'd never start.

Ten minutes out of town, Dr G pulled into the mountaintop layby at Lookout Pass. 'Welcome to Montana. Fourth biggest state, size of Germany, only a million people, and you can see why they call it big sky country,' he said.

Indeed we could, for apart from the bit which was mountains and forest, it was entirely sky.

This was home to Dr G when he wasn't either adventuring or spending the winters in Thailand.

'For a couple of years during the seventies I lived in a converted 1958 school bus that I used as a race base. My wife at the time and I decided to change our lives and move to California, so we sold everything, put two motorbikes in the bus and a car on the trailer hitch and set out for San Diego,' he said.

'Only for a guy in Albuquerque to offer me a job and f**k everything up. Then in the divorce, my wife got the money and I got the bus. Tried to sell it for years, but nobody wanted the damned thing because it only did five miles to the gallon, so I finally had to give it away.'

Another ten miles down the road, he stopped again, this time at the 50,000 Silver Dollar Bar, so called because that's the number of silver dollar coins embedded in the bar counter and around the walls.

'They've had to laminate the bar because some of the old coins, like that 1921 one there, are worth twenty dollars, and folks kept getting drunk and prising them out,' said Dr G, looking at his watch. 'OK, we gotta go. I'll take a leak, and see you out at the bikes.'

A quarter of an hour later, he came wandering out with an apologetic grin. 'Sorry, guys. Met a real pretty girl as I was coming out, and got talking,' he said.

Further down the road, a series of billboards heralded the forthcoming week-long Rock Creek Lodge Testicle Festival, presumably culminating in a series of gala balls.

This, since you ask, is a celebration of the time of year when young bulls and rams are deprived of their family jewels, which are then fried and eaten as a delicacy known as prairie oysters. They are, by all accounts, delicious, but you'll have to take Rock Creek Lodge's word for it, since, although I've eaten everything from grasshopper to guinea pig, a chap has to draw the line somewhere.

In Butte, we were filling up with fuel when Dr G suddenly disappeared, and we spotted him checking out a 1982 Honda Goldwing at the dealers across the street.

'Nice bike. And he's only looking $2,500 for it,' he said, and then, as we were checking into the hotel, he leaned closer to the receptionist and said: 'My father Richard will be checking in later. He's a bit senile, and forgets sometimes that I'm his son, so just be gentle with him.'

As for the citizens of Butte, they were as disappointingly sober as in Walla Walla, so we were forced to go out and buy several million beers, and a bottle of vodka for Dr G, who had announced that he was giving up his diet temporarily to make up for the appalling and unexpected sobriety we had encountered.

Suitably supplied, we decamped that evening to a barbeque at the home of John and Linda Davis, fellow members with Dr G of the Airhead Club. This was not a reflection of their innate scattiness, but of their appreciation of air-cooled BMWs, several fine examples of which were parked in their garage.

On the workbench sat a manual for the lovely old R100 that John was currently working on, and for a moment I wished I had the talent of my father, to understand how things worked, then take them apart and make them work even better.

But then, my talents lay elsewhere, and whereas Dad had never travelled any further than Liverpool, I had been all over the world, and was now standing in the sun in John and Linda's back garden drinking delicious microbrewery stout, tucking into elk and potato salad and chatting to their daughter Gina, a fit, tanned brunette with a big outdoors smile.

'Mmm, this elk is lovely. Where did you get it?' I said.

'Shot it. Like another beer?'

In return for the beer, I gave her a perfect movie dialogue which had come into my head on the road that afternoon and had no home for, which went like this: a man is driving a car along a highway through the west when he sees a beautiful girl hitching. He pulls over, and she leans in the window.

'Where you heading?' he says.

'Does it matter?' she says.

'Not really,' he laughs, and she gets in.

'Love it,' said Gina. 'I hope they're still together.'

We staggered back to the hotel sometime around midnight, and found the receptionist still on duty.

'Has Dad checked in yet?' said Dr G.

'I won't even tell you what he said,' she laughed. 'He's in the room, and you owe him a beer.'

Clancy and Allen left Butte with no regrets, crossed the Continental Divide at 6,230ft that afternoon, and camped that night east of Whitehall, only to spend the entire sleepless night being tortured by the biggest and most voracious mosquitoes yet.

After a bleak breakfast of apricots and unripe bananas in the barren crossroads town of Warren Creek, they met a fellow biker who was on his way to Chicago. A keen reader of the *Bicycling World and Motorcycling Review*, he asked Clancy if he'd read about the bold youth riding around the world on a Henderson, then proceeded to regale Clancy with his own adventures until Bob spoiled the surprise by revealing the truth.

After getting separated from Bob in the dark, Clancy finally spotted a light and was glad to find his companion waiting on the steps of the Corwin Hot Springs Hotel, where after sixteen hours in the saddle they were glad of the eponymous springs around which the hotel had been built in 1909, boasting seventy-two rooms, a large swimming pool and hot showers fed from the springs.

Barred from riding into Yellowstone National Park the next morning, Clancy and Allen joined a coach party tour, then set off on a road so bad that they were forced to ride on the railroad sleepers, at which point Clancy's saddle broke, treating his nether regions to miles of painful bumping. By this stage, they were unable to leave the tracks, having been hemmed in by a 'stout fence and grass-grown field' and Clancy's progress was so slow that it was dark by the time they got back on the road.

With his light broken after ramming a cliff the day before, he then hit a stone wall head on and went sailing over it, and by the time they finally got to Livingston at midnight, they were amazed to be alive, and even more amazed to find a restaurant open.

Starving, they ordered the 70-cent special, fell to it with relish, and fell into bed.

Remarkably, none of his travails had sapped Clancy's boyish enthusiasm, for the next day he begged a ride on a locomotive, then regretted it when it sped into a tunnel and he almost suffocated on the sulphurous fumes while the fireman cheerily related how his predecessor had been asphyxiated in that very same tunnel the previous summer.

As we had breakfast before leaving Butte on the trail of Clancy and Allen, I could tell we were firmly in the Midwest, because all that the hotel had to offer was processed this, mushed that and multicoloured breakfast cereal consisting of 100 parts sugar to 0.0000000000000001 parts goodness. It was like a dietary plan for spoilt children who refused to eat proper food.

Even worse, the alleged library had only a computer and a wall of shelves lined with leather-bound copies of *War and Peace*, *Moby Dick*, *Jane Eyre* and so on, but closer inspection revealed that they were all fake.

And while I'm having a rant, rather than using the large refillable bottles of liquid soap, shampoo and conditioner common in Europe, and some of California, they still use individually wrapped little bars and plastic bottles. Not to mention the mountain of disposable plates, cutlery and cups, and tiny plastic containers for milk, butter and jam left behind after every breakfast.

Ironically, on top of the plastic containers of plastic cutlery, you will invariably find perched an example of a real metal knife, fork or spoon, either for the plastic ones to aspire to or to show diners what they're missing.

There. I feel better now.

And to be fair, although the breakfasts were nothing to write home about, I don't think we had a bad lunch or dinner the whole time we were in the States.

As for Dr G, he had disappeared again, and as we were packing the bikes, he appeared around the corner on the Goldwing he had been admiring the previous evening.

'Just bought it. All your fault, for making me drink that vodka last night and messing with my head,' he said. 'Now all I have to do is get him to deliver it.'

That organised, he returned on his original Honda, and we rode out of town and up the hill to the Continental Divide.

West of here, all rivers flow to the Pacific, and east, to the Atlantic, and by the roadside was a small puddle left from the overnight rain trying to make up its mind.

At Bozeman Pass, we stood right over the railway tunnel where Clancy had almost been asphyxiated, while beside us a wooden sign related the history of John Bozeman, the adventurous Georgian who led a wagon train through hostile Indian territory and across this pass in 1863.

'Hostile is right,' said Dr G. 'The Crow were such mean motherf**kers that when they stole horses and women from the Sioux, the Sioux would only come over in raiding parties of up to fifteen thousand to get them back. Then of course the Crow would steal the horses back.

'Why not the women?' said Gary.

'The women would come back by themselves because the Crow were such good lovers. Still are, of course,' he grinned. 'There was a movie back in the seventies called *Jeremiah Johnson*, starring Robert Redford as a cowboy being trained up by an old man. They're standing looking down at some Indians one day and the old man says: "Those are Crows, my boy. They're the best horsemen on the plains, and the best looking, but oh, they are adulterous."

'Then the preachers arrived and tried to stamp out men having more than one woman, even though it worked perfectly well. If a man was a good enough hunter to support five women and their kids, everybody was happy. If he wasn't, the women would go and find someone better.

'Some bright spark in Washington DC came up with an idea of presenting an award to any woman who had sexual relations with only one man for a year, so at the end of the year they got the whole tribe together for a grand ceremony to present the awards to the four women who said they'd qualified.

'Only for one guy after another to stand up and say: "She can't get the award; she's lying", so none of them got the award, and the bright idea was dumped.'

Mind you, Dr G did have a personal grudge against religion: his parents had sent him to a private Quaker school at which he was the only Indian among two hundred whites.

On the first day, an older boy walked up to him and said, 'You're from Montana, right?'

'Yip,' said Gregory.

'And you're Indian, right?'

'Yip.'

'I hate Indians.'

The next thing the young Dr G knew, he was lying flat on the floor after being felled by an uppercut.

'So I jumped up, got him in a headlock and kneed him in the head a few times to teach him a lesson,' Dr G told me when he related the story. 'Then the next day his room-mate, a German called Erich von Kaiserling III, came up and said he was going to beat the shit out of me. I got suspended for three days for fighting, and he got nothing. So that was my experience of the peace-loving Quakers, and I took to being an agnostic ever since.'

At Livingston, where Robert Redford returned to film his 1992 movie *A River Runs Through It*, we found part of the railroad line that Clancy had ridden along, and since there were no trains in sight, we had to follow suit and ride the tracks.

I wouldn't recommend it, and for Clancy to have chosen that option on a machine with no suspension other than the springs in his saddle, the road must have been bad indeed.

From there, a road forks right into the epic river valley that leads to Yellowstone National Park and, after taking a photo at the entrance where Clancy and Allen were turned back with their bikes, we went in search of Corwin Hot Springs.

The sumptuous hotel they were so glad to find after sixteen hours in the saddle that day was, according to contemporary photographs, a magnificent Gothic creation with a red-tiled roof with the mountains on one side and the Yellowstone River on the other.

It was destroyed by a fire in 1916, and an adobe construction looking somewhat like the Alamo, except without the dead Texas heroes, was built nearby in 1929 by Walter Hill, who added a tepee-shaped petrol station. That building became a game farm before it was bought by the Church Universal Triumphant, who had then failed to live up to their name and abandoned it.

Today all that is left on the site is that building, a restaurant, a post office, and a smattering of mobile homes and log cabins, but all that remained of the original clubhouse, according to my research, was the great stone fireplace.

Outside the deserted restaurant, the only sign of life we found was a truck with its engine running, guarded by a black Labrador, but at the mobile homes, log cabins and the Alamo, not a human was to be seen.

We had given up searching for the fireplace and were riding away when Richard, who had given up on GPS technology and was using his instinct to much better effect, suddenly swerved off the road, down a rutted path and into a grassy meadow by the river. And there we found the great fireplace.

As Richard and Gary wandered off to take some photos, I lay down in the warm grass at the spot where I imagined Clancy and Allen lounging in a leather club sofa and toasting their toes by a roaring fire.

All around were the faintest of sounds: the comings and goings of honey bees, the whisper of the river, the distant, haunting cry of a loon, and the luting warbles and clicks of jays in the riverbank cottonwoods and quaking aspen, so called because its delicate leaves shiver in the slightest breeze.

I closed my eyes, all the better to see the image of Clancy gazing into the firelight and looking back on an entire lifetime of hopes and dreams which had been condensed into his past few months. I imagined he felt as if Dublin trams, Paris traffic, Spanish brigands, German shipping companies, the burning sands of Africa, the exotic souks of Tunis, the topless damsels of Sigirya, the aromatic clamour of old Shanghai and even the trials of Oregon's trails, already seemed like something he had experienced as a young man a long time ago.

And in that moment I felt at one with him, and strangely content.

That night, we arrived in Billings to find Dr G, who had raced ahead of us earlier that day, already there, and we walked to dinner at Famous Dave's Barbeque, where we were served so many bits of dead cow that, had we had a manual, we could probably have rebuilt it.

'Oh, sold that Honda I bought this morning to a friend,' said Dr G as we ate.

'Already? How much?' said Gary.

'Thirty five hundred.'

'Give up the writing lark, Dr G. You'd make more money as a motorbike salesman,' I said.

Bidding the Rockies farewell at Billings, Clancy and Allen began to wind their way through the badlands of eastern Montana, 'a great stretch of useless country that looked as if it had never been finished', and into North Dakota, where the roads were good, grain fields stretched to the horizon in every direction, and the saloons had been replaced with banks, since the state was dry by law.

In Minnesota, they rode between a sea of wheat to the north and an ocean of corn to the south, and before long, trees, woods and lakes began to punctuate the monotony.

They found Minneapolis dull and dated, but were at least glad of eastern prices such as five cents instead of twelve for an egg.

As we left Billings on the same route, riding with us for the next two days was Ronnie Weinzapfel, a veteran of Dr G's annual Big Dog runs, a series of group on- and off-road tours held at various venues around the US.

'He's the best off-road rider I've ever seen,' said Dr G. 'He can ride up a tree then reverse back down it.'

'You can show us that trick later,' I said as we shook hands with Ronnie, a retired trucking company director whose ancestors had emigrated from Alsace-Lorraine in the nineteenth century.

'We still alternate family reunions between there and Texas,' he said as he climbed on his immaculate 1973 BMW R60 and hit the road with us.

Between his Texan drawl and Dr G's laidback Montana

cadences, it took them entire days to finish a single sentence at the rest stops as we rode through eastern Montana and North Dakota.

The Montana badlands still looked as if they hadn't been finished, like a giant golf course waiting for greens, flags and a good clubhouse serving a fine selection of single malts.

Talking of which, one of the great things about the USA this time around was not only that North Dakota was no longer dry, but that there'd been an explosion in the number of microbreweries, as a result of which you could walk into many bars and be greeted by twenty or more local beers on draught.

The only thing to do was not panic – just start at the tap on the left and calmly work your way to the right, although anarchists can reverse the process for the sake of variety.

In the morning, Ronnie managed to run out of fuel a mile from the gas station, but it was nothing an improvised tow rope from Gary, using the ferry tie-downs that he'd squirreled away, couldn't cure.

We reached the gas station without incident and Ronnie was able to fill up. Meanwhile, I was lying on the ground checking the rear tyre pressure when Dr G came wandering past.

'What you doing?' he said.

'Practising my Indian tracking skills,' I said. 'Three white men just passed this way on horses, one with three quarters and a dime in his left pocket.'

'Impossible. Horses don't have pockets,' he said, proving that I still had some work to do on my Indian tracking skills.

By the end of the day, when we had done over four hundred miles and were nearing the rural Minnesota home of Richard's brother Steve and his wife Colleen where we would spend the night, Richard led the way around a tight bend, only to skid on some gravel then tumble off into the grass ditch.

He and the bike were fine, but as Murphy's Law would have it, two cops in a patrol car came around the bend a minute later.

Still, after they'd checked his driving licence and were satisfied he was legally entitled to fall off, they let us go.

Lucky it hadn't happened in Singapore, or he would have got life for damaging the grass.

As we were tucking into a feast rustled up by Colleen at their palatial pad, the evening was enlivened by the arrival of a neighbour, Adolf, in a bright red Porsche 911 Carrera who had just popped in with his friend Kevin on their way out to dinner.

Adolf, whose shoes matched his car, was tall, black and humorous, and had obviously not been affected a bit by his father's mysterious choice of name for him after returning from serving in the US Air Force in Europe during the Second World War.

Or maybe his dad's knowledge of history was just as sketchy as his, since before finishing his beer and heading off to the local sushi restaurant, he announced confidently that Eisenhower had started the nation's road-building programme in 1910.

In fact, Dwight had launched the freeway building drive after seeing the autobahns in Germany during the same war started by a former Austrian corporal whose name will come to me in a moment.

'You know,' said Steve as we set off the next day, 'I've known Adolf for forty years, and I've never asked him the reason for his name.'

He'd taken the morning off to lead us south-east through the wooded hills of Minnesota along the eternal, unchanging Mississippi.

At Prairie du Chien, he said goodbye, and the road did the same to the river, turning east through the rich farmland of Wisconsin.

Half an hour later, we met an Amish couple driving a one-horse buggy; she in floral smock and headscarf and he in dungarees and straw hat. Passing them on a Harley Sportster was a girl in shades and a red sundress, who was taking advantage of the fact that helmets aren't compulsory in the state to let her blonde hair flow in the wind.

I waved, and all three waved back. If Gary had had his camera handy, it would have made the cover of *Time* magazine.

The next day, it was a lazy 150 miles to Anamosa, the home of former racer John Parham who, in 1975 with his wife Jill, opened a small shop which went on to become J&P Cycles, the USA's biggest motorcycle parts and accessories mail order business.

'He's taking it easy at the moment,' said Dr G, 'because he's just back from making a trip in his private jet to get a double lung transplant.'

However, we were not there just to celebrate John's commercial nous, or even to toast his health, but because to accommodate his growing collection of motorbikes, he'd bought a disused Walmart down the road in 2010 and turned it into the National Motorcycle Museum of America.

And that museum, at the end of this trip, would be the last resting place of Clancy's boots, pith helmet, original diaries and photographs, and Irish and French driving licences, which Liam O'Connor had posted to Dr G for passing on to the museum. Printed inside the faded red lining of the pith helmet in clear black letters were the words Real Sola Pith, specially made for Selecta, Port-Said. Made in India.

Inside the museum is an astonishing private collection of four hundred motorcycles, not to mention a fulsome tribute to the lunacy of Evel Knievel. I defy anyone to watch the videos of him jumping a Harley two hundred feet over a row of buses and not wince as he landed with only a few inches of suspension travel to absorb the impact.

In the British section are some fine examples of the Rudges my dear old dad raced in the fifties, the Norton International and Manx Norton he would have raced if he'd had the money, and Brough Superiors and Vincent Black Shadows we'd all own if we had the money.

One Brough, the SS100 Pendine, was named after the long, flat beach in South Wales where every model was tested to 110mph before being handed over to customers, and on which George Brough set a world record of 130.6mph in 1928.

More within my means was an NSU Quickly which was the first motorbike I ever rode, racing up and down the avenues of Termon in my teens in Tyrone.

In the US section, there was Peter Fonda's Captain America chopper and helmet from *Easy Rider*, and past all the Harleys and Indians, exquisite machines from companies such as Reading-Standard, Racycle, Emblem, Thor, Pierce, Royal Pioneer and Flying Merkel which failed to make it past the twenties and thirties.

And then, at last, the holy grail: the only original 1912 Henderson in the world.

Of the fifteen or so Hendersons made in that year, John Parham knew of only three in existence today, and the other two had been restored with later parts, making this the only unrestored one, down to the original paint and tyres.

And while Paddy Guerin's Henderson at the start of our trip had been a 1922 three-speed model, this was the real deal, with 7hp, one gear, a hand-crank starter and no front brakes.

I stood there looking at the motorcycle which would soon be joined by the effects of the man who had ridden one of them around the world a century ago, and as much as I had marvelled at Clancy's courage in making the journey we had followed, I now marvelled even more when I saw the machine he had done it on. To contemplate it was the act of a madman, and to complete it the act of a hero.

That night, as if to bless our gift, the rain came pouring down in torrents, while on the horizon, tornadoes wreaked havoc, but the next morning, the skies were blue, and only the gently steaming fields gave a clue to the downpour of the night before.

Riding with us for the next two days was the appropriately named Tim Henderson, a local man who'd gone to Alaska to fish for the summer, stayed fifteen years and was now back home working as a factory electrician and riding a Moto Guzzi California. He'd joined us after following Dr G's blogs on the Horizons Unlimited site.

'Tough work, commercial fishing: twenty hours a day for weeks on end, but good money. Best day I ever had, we caught 65,000 pounds of halibut and I made $35,000,' he said.

Richard, given the day off from leading the way with his GPS, dawdled at the back while Tim led us through the back roads of small town America, stopping for lunch at the Iron Horse Social Club in Savanna, a bikers' bar on which thousands descend every weekend, and treating us to the best ice cream of the trip so far in the deli on the square in Marilyn.

'Real pretty here in the winter, with the snow on the town hall and that big tree in front all lit up,' he said, as I polished off my buttery vanilla with pecan nuts.

That night in Janesville, we were sitting in a bar drinking Fat Tire beer, which in spite of being a disturbingly expensive $5 a bottle was having no discernible effect whatsoever. Gary was having his usual dinner of burger and chips with a side order of onion rings, as opposed to his usual lunch, of just burger and chips.

'I think you're winning the battle against anorexia, ballix. Here, let me help by eating one of those onion rings,' I said, ordering a different beer to see if that was any more effective.

'Good to see you guys bonding so well,' said Dr G. 'So, now that you're near the end of the trip, what are the two most annoying things about Gary?'

'Everything,' I said, then thought for a moment. 'And everything else.'

'You'll have to be more specific,' said Richard.

'OK, thinking that farting is incredibly witty. And thinking that he needs to point out the obvious attributes of every single woman within five hundred yards every minute of the day.'

'Fair enough. And what do you reckon annoys him most about you?'

'Probably being a grumpy bastard. And using the Adelaide business cards for emergency flossing.'

'Nah, it's wandering around naked. And doing your laundry in the sink every night,' said Gary.

'OK, I'll do it in the shower. But nudity is normal. You're talking to a man who used to have a sauna in his back yard, and every Saturday night, everyone in the house, and maybe a few friends, would get our kit off and pile in there with a few beers. It was brilliant.'

'What, girls as well?' said Gary.

'Absolutely.'

'Bastard.'

By now, Clancy was on the scent of home: visiting his brother in nearby Beloit, he made the front page lead in the local paper, then was brought down to earth yet again by a crash twenty miles from Chicago which bent his rear wheel.

Riding on carefully, he came upon two bikers repairing a puncture who regaled him with thrilling tales from their two-hundred-mile adventure, then guided him to the Henderson branch factory on Michigan Avenue.

We were now in the last few days of our own grand adventure, and when I looked back through the pages of our daily schedule, it felt like we had gone through an entire lifetime in just three short months, with events like leaving Belfast in the snow, sitting on the boat to Tunisia, riding through Sri Lanka in monsoon rain and marvelling at our first sight of Hong Kong bay or the skyscrapers of Shanghai like something we had done years ago, when we were young.

The next morning, I tore a page of my research notes out

of the ring binder in which I kept all the trip paperwork, and realised I was down to the last page out of the eighty-nine I had started with.

In the sun we rode to Chicago, with Richard leading the way as always. He had proven to be the kindest of souls, and that morning he did so again, stopping at a service station so we could buy transponders that would save us money on tolls all the way to New York.

'Hey, that Chrysler factory we passed back there was about the size of Kansas,' I said as we walked back to the bikes.

'Sure is,' he said. 'I built that when I worked in construction.'

'What, all by yourself?'

'Sure. Took me two days.'

In Chicago, we saw the first beggar of the trip since Tunisia and Sri Lanka: a young man in a grubby T-shirt sitting at traffic lights with a cardboard sign saying: Hungry. Need food.

'Got kicked out of college and everything,' he said as Gary gave him a handful of dollars.

He was not the last beggar we saw in the States, and it's hardly surprising: almost half of all Americans today describe themselves as living in poverty or barely scraping by, and 46.4 per cent pay no income tax.

Strangely, the country still manages to support more lawyers per capita than any other country in the world, and still churns out 35,000 new ones every year, 10,000 more than there are jobs for, and possibly 34,999 more than are actually needed.

When Clancy rolled up at the gates of the Henderson factory in Chicago, he was given a hero's welcome: they placed his battered Henderson in the front window and entertained him royally for two days solid, after which Allen left to visit friends in Chicago, and Clancy continued alone once more.

As for us, we were entertained royally for two hours solid at the Adventurers' Club of Chicago, founded in 1911 and the oldest in the USA. There was an older one in New York, but it closed, presumably because all the members had been eaten by tigers.

Inside, it was exactly as you imagined an adventurers' club should be. Either that, or they'd been really busy on eBay, for a stuffed polar bear and grizzly guarded the entrance, the heads of various other dead things stuck out of the walls with no obvious indication of where their nether regions had got to, various saddles, Zulu spears and shields leaned against the wainscoting, several shrunken heads gazed out blankly from glass cases, photographs and paintings of chaps in pith helmets peered sternly down from the few spaces in between mounted dead things, and the bookshelves were lined with volumes such as *How I Hopped on One Leg to the North Pole (And Back!)* by Hyram D Rickenbacker III.

At the main Henderson factory in Detroit, Clancy was feted even more than in Chicago, while the brand new machines rolling off the production line looked at, what he fondly imagined was mute admiration of, their older and wiser brother.

Detroit, of course, would go on to become of the home of the American automobile industry, with Henry Ford, Ransom Eli Olds, the Chevrolets and the Dodge brothers all basing their vast concerns there.

However, what they did on an equally grand scale was create vast segregated housing estates, and sack workers at the drop of a spanner when times got bad, at first in the depression of the thirties, and then during the oil crisis and Japanese competition in the seventies.

The inevitable results of such social and economic disenfranchisement were ghettos and riots, and the city which was once a 1957 Chevy, its new red and white paint and acres of chrome sparkling in the endless summer of post-war optimism, is now the rusted hulk of an Oldsmobile, with no hubcaps and four flat tyres.

When we arrived, the mayor was discussing plans to sell off

the contents of the art museum to help pay off the city's $18.5 billion debt.

The Henderson factory, an imposing building on Jefferson Street overlooking the river towards Ontario on the far bank, closed in 1931 and was subsequently demolished. Today, the site is a grassy park watched over by the grey stone Mariners' Church, although it wasn't there in Clancy's day.

Built in 1842, in 1955 it was moved 880 feet on rails to its present location in order to make way for the Civic Centre Plaza, since then joined by the towering Renaissance Centre which was supposed to herald the rebirth of the city.

From the number of homeless people sleeping in the park, the scheme has not entirely succeeded, and the large sign at the end of the street saying Tunnel to Canada may not be traffic information, but a recommendation.

At Niagara Falls, in Clancy's time a popular honeymoon destination described by Oscar Wilde as the second big disappointment of an American bride's married life – like he would know – we were standing admiring their thundering glory when I suddenly remembered the Pfizer factory we had passed the day before, and thought a great ad for their most well-known product would be a shot of a hand dropping a triangular blue pill in the river, then a shot of the falls shooting skywards above the words Viagra Falls.

I made a note to pen a memo to Mr Pfizer and secure my financial future, and we rode off in the company of a witty New Yorker called Daniel DiGiacomo on a well-travelled Suzuki V-Strom who'd also joined us after following Dr G's Horizons Unlimited blogs.

'You'll be German, then,' I said when we met at the entrance to the falls.

'Strangely enough, my mother was, but my dad was Italian, so we had the entire Axis coalition in one family,' he said.

Naturally, now that we were handing back the bikes in a

couple of days, I had become almost proficient at riding mine. I could do tight circles at walking pace, and come to a dead stop at junctions, look around me, read *War and Peace* and then move off again, all without putting my feet down. Another million years of this, and I might even be able to go around bends half as fast as Gary did while he was standing on the pegs and taking a photo.

'You are getting better,' he said when I mentioned it. 'I actually saw you leaning into a corner the other day.'

Even better, since the BMWs had been so reliable that Gary's duties as Head of Maintenance had involved nothing more than topping up the oil, he actually got a chance to use his mechanical skills later when Richard's clutch cable snapped and he had it replaced in about four minutes flat.

We rode east through the woods and cow meadows of New York State in the pale gold light of early summer, past clapboard mansions with rocking chairs on their shady verandahs, and past signs saying, Welcome to LeRoy: Birthplace of Jell-O! Vote Jimmy onto the Avon Town Board! Topsoil for sale – dirt cheap! and Scooters Family Restaurant: fish fry this Friday!

It seems that, as Americans moved west, they used up their entire supply of exclamation marks and were completely out by the Midwest, which is why Californians are so laid back. Like, whatever, dude.

On many lawns, the Stars and Stripes fluttered from flagpoles, and on some roofs, painted versions were accompanied by the words, God Bless America; an indication of Americans' quaint conviction that God is on their side.

Since that's a view which has been shared by the Nazis, Afghanis, Iraqis and Iranians, it must make life very difficult for God.

Once, cottonwood blossoms came fluttering down from the clear air, making us feel momentarily like extras in *It's a*

Wonderful Life.

By evening, we were settled into the Glen Motor Inn, a classic motel on a wooded slope overlooking the sparkling waters of Watkins Lake which has been there since Italian vintner Joseph Franzese and his new bride Helen started renting their spare bedroom out to travellers for 50 cents a night in 1937.

By 1947, they had twelve rooms; by the fifties it was forty rooms, a restaurant, gas station, tennis court and swimming pool; and from 1961 to 1980, it was where the drivers who raced in the US Grand Prix at nearby Watkins Glen stayed. On the walls are signed photographs of Jim Clark, Jack Brabham, John Surtees, Stirling Moss, Paul Newman, Graham Hill and Jackie Stewart, and neither the décor in our room, the background music nor the menu in the resident Italian restaurant had apparently changed since the days when they stayed here.

It was, in every way, perfect, and after a fine meal of beef medallions with capelli d'angelo washed down by a bottle of Montepulciano, I fell asleep that night thinking that my next book, if I ever write one, might be a tribute in words and pictures to the great old American motels which are slowly dying out at the hands of bland chains with their plastic this, disposable that and forgettable everything.

Clancy had one last mission before his triumphant return to New York, and that was a surprise visit to his parents in their large, rambling home in the wooded Berkshire Hills of Massachusetts, and thanks to Richard tracking down the location with some diligent research, the next day we rode out in search of it.

The weather, as it had been pretty much every day in the States, was perfect, and I rode in a T-shirt along the freeway savouring the perfect harmony between the hot sun and the cool wind on my arms, and as we turned onto the backroads for the last few miles to the Clancy home, the chill of plunging into the shade of trees, then the warm balm of emerging again into the light.

As I said right at the start of the journey, motorcycling provides the simplest of pleasures.

I was savouring, too, the visceral growl of the engine beneath me. On its own, it was just a collection of metal bits and bobs, but brought to life by the spark of ignition, it could take you to wherever your heart desired; in the same way that the spark of inspiration had made Clancy set out around the world, had made Dr G spend sixteen years digging up dusty magazine articles to write *Motorcycle Adventurer*, and had made me realise as I read it how wonderful it would be to recreate that same journey on its centenary.

And now, as we rode these last few miles to the home of Clancy's parents, I imagined how he must have felt as he too rode this old familiar road through the trees along the river and the railroad tracks.

How his senses must have been filled to the brim, with the same warm sun on his face and the smell of pine in his nose, as he waved to the astonished neighbours at the green mansion, then rode down the hill and turned right into his parents' drive past the leaning pine and the ancient oak.

How his heart must have swelled with pride and love as he pulled up on the Henderson, with his collar stiff and his tie knotted just so, to see his mother look out from the kitchen where she was preparing lunch, and his father come to the front door from the study where he had been working on a sermon, and to see the same pride and love reflected in their faces at the return of their prodigal son after his incredible adventure.

To see Carl Stearns Clancy, at just that moment a young man with his whole life in front of him, filled with boundless hope and optimism for a future in which, having conquered the world, he felt he could do anything.

We stopped near the same green mansion to check our way, only for a neighbour to tell us that the old Clancy house had become a boys' home, then burned down mysteriously ten years ago.

And when we got there, and turned right into the drive past

the leaning pine and the ancient oak, all that we found were the stone foundations of the old place in a grassy glade bright with wild poppies and buttercups.

As I stood at the end of the drive, where I imagined Clancy had climbed off his Henderson for a hug from his mother and a firm handshake from the old man, a small white butterfly rested briefly on my boot, then fluttered off into the woods, leaving only the whisper of the breeze in the leaves of the ancient oak and the call of a bluebird hoping for love.

After saying farewell to his parents at this very spot, Clancy rode into New York State and rolled in splendid happiness along the finest roads of the entire trip, and on the morning of 27 August 1913, a moving picture camera captured his triumphant return to Manhattan at the end of an eleven-month, 18,000-mile odyssey which had tested him to the limit countless times and taught him lessons he would remember for the rest of his long life.

'I have thoroughly enjoyed my trip and profited by every mile of it,' he told the *Bicycling World and Motorcycling Review* afterwards. 'I was accompanied throughout much of the journey … but I was also called upon to make some long and trying jumps alone.

'There is so much to be seen and discussed along even the most ordinary foreign route that the rider who travels alone soon finds that he is missing something. He needs a congenial partner.

'I do not know if I will ever make another round-the-world trip, but if I do it may be depended on that I will travel by motorcycle.'

Sadly, he never did, and when he took his boots off and hung them up, there is no evidence that he ever wore them again. And when he died in 1971, his housekeeper gave them to young Liam O'Connor, who then passed them on to me.

And so, having left Belfast on the coldest day of the year and carried them around the world a second time, we rode with them into New York City on the hottest day of the year, pulling up at Penn Station to see Lynda Clancy standing there with a broad smile on her face.

'I am so proud of you all,' she said as I handed her the replica around the world pennant that we had carried from Dublin. 'Our family had all been ministers, professors and the like, and Uncle Carl broke the mould by becoming an adventurer.

'You and Dr Frazier are not only men in the same mould, but probably know more about Uncle Carl than any of us, and you have honoured him by replicating his incredible journey with one just as incredible. Thank you.'

And so, at last, having carried the boots of Carl Stearns Clancy around the world, armed with his twin mottos that you should never believe what you hear, or take anything for granted, and with respect and pride at having followed in the tyre tracks of such a fine man, we handed them over at last to Dr Gregory Frazier.

It seemed like a lifetime ago that I had sat in the study on a dark and stormy night with them gleaming in the firelight, I thought as I looked at them for the last time, then I shook hands with everyone, climbed on my motorbike and rode into the unknown future.

Epilogue

What happened to Hendersons?

In 1917, Alan Bedell averaged 48mph for 1,154 miles at Ascot Park in California on a new Henderson Model G with three-speed gearbox, setting a new twenty-four-hour record, and then, on 13 June that year, broke the transcontinental record when he rode his 1917 Henderson the 3,296 miles from Los Angeles to New York in seven days, 16 hours and 15 minutes, a remarkable feat on roads which, as Clancy had noted, were primitive by today's standards.

Despite record-breaking and racing successes, the effects of the First World War on sales had damaged the company's financial position, and later in 1917 the Hendersons sold the firm to Ignaz Schwinn, the manufacturer of Schwinn bicycles and Excelsior motorbikes. Production was moved to Schwinn's factory in Chicago, and the motorbikes improved in leaps and bounds.

In 1922 the 28hp De Luxe reached 100mph in demonstrations to the San Diego Police, and a stung Harley Davidson decided to challenge Henderson to a contest that was held at in Chicago in April that year. The Harley won the first heat, but lost the other eleven, with the Henderson again exceeding 100mph.

Between 30 and 31 May that year, Wells Bennet and his Henderson Deluxe set a new twenty-four-hour endurance record at the Tacoma Speedway, Washington, clocking up 1,562.54 miles at an average of 65.1mph, a record that was not beaten until 1933, by a Peugeot with a team of four. The solo record was not bettered until 1937 when Fred Ham's 61 cubic inch Harley averaged 76mph.

It was a shining year for Hendersons, marred in the very last month when on 11 December 1922, William Henderson was killed in a motorbike accident.

On Black Tuesday, 29 October 1929, the Wall Street stock market crashed, but Henderson sales remained strong, with models such as the 1930 KL capable of pulling from 8mph to 116mph in top gear, making it an instant hit with several US police departments.

Then, in the summer of 1931 and with no warning, Schwinn called his department heads together and bluntly told them, 'Gentlemen, today we stop'.

His reasoning was that the Depression could easily continue for eight years, and even worsen, and despite a full order book, he had chosen to pare back his business commitments to making bicycles.

In 1993, Dan Hanlon secured the rights to the Excelsior and Henderson trademarks and founded the Excelsior-Henderson Motorcycle Company in Belle Plaine, Minnesota. The company designed and built nearly two thousand new motorcycles for the model years 1999–2000 before succumbing to the financial turmoil in the marketplace at the time.

What happened to Carl Stearns Clancy?
with thanks to Dr Gregory Frazier

Born in New Hampshire on 8 August 1890 to William P. Clancy, an Irish clergyman, and his wife Alice from Massachusetts, Carl Stearns Clancy was twenty-two when he set off with Storey to girdle the globe.

After the trip he planned to write a book about it but, according to Dr G, Storey wasn't keen on helping, so Clancy lost interest in the book and motorcycles in general.

He settled in Massachusetts then moved to California, was married in 1916 then moved to New York and established himself in the movies: writing, producing and directing dozens of Will Rogers films, divorcing his first wife then remarrying, and living in both New York and Los Angeles.

Although he never published a book on his round the world trip, he wrote one in 1927 called *The Viking Ship* and, in 1956, The *Saga of Leif Ericsson, Discoverer of America*.

Unable to make a successful transition from silent films to talkies, he moved to Virginia, where he wrote promotional material for the Water Board and scripted a ten-minute film on water conservation called *The Adventures of Junior Raindrop*.

After his second wife died, he retired and lived with his sister Agnes until his death in Alexandria, Virginia, in January 1971. He left behind no children, but a full and adventurous life, and a very fine pair of boots, which now rest in the National Motorcycle Museum of America in Anamosa, Iowa, beside the only original 1912 Henderson in the world.

Walter Rendell Storey was born in Philadelphia in 1881 to English parents, and was thirty-one, and working for the Board of Motion Pictures in New York, when he set out with Clancy. Dr Frazier's last record of him is his Second World War draft registration, when he was sixty, working for the *New York Times* and living with his wife Helen in New Jersey.

The fate of his boots remains unknown.

Acknowledgements

First and foremost to my wife Cate, for her endless tolerance in letting me disappear yet again for three months. Not many wives would be so understanding, and I appreciate it more than I can say.

To Adelaide Insurance Services director Sam Geddis and his trusty sidekick Nichola Pearce, for once again coughing up the dosh without which this trip would have remained a pipe dream.

In the previous Adelaide Adventure, around Oz, Sam showed his commitment to it by coming out with his wife Gloria to ride with us for the first three weeks, and this time around he showed the same involvement. First of all, he went to some trouble persuading his fellow directors that Adelaide should sponsor this trip, which they were reluctant to do given that the country is in the middle of a recession.

Then, when Triumph, the original providers of bikes, had to pull out because of a black hole in the sponsorship which they couldn't fill, it was Sam's suggestion to go to Jim Hill at BMW Motorrad Mallusk, a good friend of BMW's UK head of marketing, Tony Jakeman.

Then, of course, he got on the phone to Ian Paisley Jnr in a bid to sort out the Algerian visa problem, even if nothing came of it.

Although work commitments thwarted Sam's original plan of riding with us through Europe, he and Gloria came out to join us for a day in Barcelona, which was much appreciated.

To Tony Jakeman, the Head of Marketing at BMW Motorrad UK, for providing sterling support in bikes, equipment, backup and additional sponsorship, aided by Khal Harris of HPS Jardine. And to Lee Nicholls at BMW who, when Tony retired, became the new Head of Marketing, and who paid for the bike shipping, helped by top optician Geoff McConville.

To Dr Gregory Frazier for sending me copies of Clancy's original photos and for his endless patience in answering stupid questions from me, not realising that I have an unlimited supply of them. All of the quotes I use from Clancy are taken from his book *Motorcycle Adventurer*, which provides a marvellous account of Clancy's entire journey.

Along with Dr G, I want to thank our travelling companion in the USA, Richard Livermore, for his unfailing humour and kindness in turning every problem into a solution.

To Nicola Worthington at Virgin Atlantic, www.virgin-atlantic.com, Simon Large at Cathay Pacific, www.cathaypacific.com, and Shirantini Wijesuriya at Sri Lankan Airlines, www.srilankan.com, for providing the flights for the adventure either gratis or at discounted rates. Particular thanks to Nicola for rejigging the flights to make sure we got to stay in New York for the big post-trip press conference.

In Hong Kong, thanks also to Simon's trusty assistants Mickey Leung, Jady Ye and Veronica Ho; to Rupert McCowan and Wendy Chungsee of the Royal Geographical Society; and most of all to our man in HK, Peter Rolston, and to Martin Cubbon of the Swire Group, ably assisted by Mimi Lau, for their legendary hospitality. Our livers will never be the same again.

Thanks also to Martin Cubbon for covering the cost of the flights between Shanghai and Nagasaki.

In Shanghai, thanks go to Roger Owens (aka Junior), who showed us around then invited us home for a feast of sushi rustled up by his wife Daisy, and to Kent Kedl, who not only insisted on paying for all our admissions on his bespoke tour, but then bought dinner for us, Roger and Daisy.

Roger's company, the Drennan Group, also paid for our Cathay Pacific air fares from Tokyo to Los Angeles, for which many thanks.

To the endlessly helpful Roddy Warriman and his colleague Giles Ernsting at James Cargo for shipping the bikes without profit and for invaluable advice well above and beyond the call of duty.

To Professor Liam O'Connor of the University of Western Australia, who as a teenager growing up in Virginia, USA, was a neighbour of Clancy, and who passed on his boots to us. 'It was an idyllic period of my young life,' said Liam to me before he packed them up and posted them.

We moved into an interesting area around 1968, a secluded enclave of old houses on the banks of the Potomac River about ten miles out of Washington DC. The area was called Wellington Villa and I believe that the houses would have been summer homes in the 1920–30s for people living in Washington.

At the time we lived there, there were some interesting neighbours, many of them elderly. My sister and I used to enjoy visiting some of them and taking them small handmade gifts at Christmas time.

Mr Clancy, as I used to address him, for he was a kindly old gentleman, was a favourite of mine because of his past life and the interesting things he had. I used to fly my control line model aeroplanes in a vacant field below his house. His sister, Mrs Smith, lived next door to him with an elderly English female companion known only as Chips.

There was another lady, I suppose in her sixties at the time, who lived somewhere else but used to keep an eye out for Mr Clancy and do things for him. I don't know how they knew each other. Her name was Judy Heyne.

When Mr Clancy died in 1971, Judy took the responsibility for cleaning his house out and she gave me lots of things, including the boots he wore for the around-the-world ride. I had, even at that age, a strong interest in the past and in collecting old and interesting things.

We left the US to return to Australia in 1973 when I was sixteen, but I've kept everything from those days, including the boots, which I'm now passing on to you so they can recreate their journey of a hundred years ago then pass on to Greg Frazier for safekeeping.

Carl would have been thrilled at all of this interest in his adventure; he was such a reserved old gentleman. I did feel a sense of loss as I boxed up the boots this morning; they have been in the background of my life for so long. However, I couldn't really have hoped for a better fate for them.

To Geoff McConville, optician to the stars, for helping out with the dosh for the bike shipping.

To Kate Ferguson at Duffy Rafferty PR, for providing the Stena Line Belfast to Cairnryan and Harwich to Holland crossings.

To Rough Guides for all guidebooks.

To Peter Murtagh of the *Irish Times*, who was a witty, erudite and hilarious companion for the first two weeks of the trip.

Almost last and very much not least, to Gary Walker for his invaluable company, for looking after the bikes and taking the photographs, many of them outstanding. I never regretted the decision to ask him along although, since he turned out to be dyslexic, possibly delegating the task of organising visas to him, which involved filing in millions of forms in which he managed on several occasions to misspell his own name, may not have been my wisest move.

Still, in a stroke of genius which showed he wasn't as green as he was cabbage looking, Gary delegated everything to his wife

Janet, whose work on booking ferries and getting visas was well above and beyond the call of duty.

To Patsy Horton at Blackstaff Press for publishing yet another of my books. Will she never learn? Also at Blackstaff, thanks to Michelle Griffin for doing a brilliant job on the edit, as she had on the previous book about Oz.

And last but not least, to Carl Stearns Clancy, the inspiration behind this journey. Carl, I hope we have done you proud.

To see the photographs of the trip visit
www.adelaideinsurance.com